COST CONTAINMENT

COST CONTAINMENT

The Ultimate Advantage

Peter R. Richardson

THE FREE PRESS
A Division of Macmillan, Inc.
NEW YORK

Collier Macmillan Publishers
LONDON

The Free Press
A Division of Macmillan, Inc.
866 Third Avenue, New York, N.Y. 10022

Collier Macmillan Canada, Inc.

Printed in the United States of America

printing number
1   2   3   4   5   6   7   8   9   10

Library of Congress Cataloging-in-Publication Data

Richardson, Peter R.
   Cost containment.

   Bibliography: p.
   Includes index.
   1. Cost control.   I. Title.
HD47.3.R53   1988   658.1′552   88–2809
ISBN 0–02–926432–4

To Bill and Olga

Contents

Preface and Acknowledgments

Cost management is central to sustained corporate profitability. In spite of this fact, it is one of the least talked and written about issues facing management today. This situation has arisen in part because of management's perception of the task as routine and mundane and in part because very tough decisions lie at the heart of an effective strategy to manage costs.

In fact, meeting the cost challenge is one of the most critical tasks facing Canadian and U.S. executives during the next decade. Traditional approaches have proved inadequate in the face of intense international and domestic competition, and executive leadership and inspiration are called for if corporations are to find new ways to reduce costs. This leadership is embodied in symbolic, strategic, and operational actions necessary to inspire other corporate employees to involve themselves in cost reduction. The outcome of these activities will be corporations with a lean and keen profile.

Undoubtedly, executives face some tough initial decisions when they decide to face up to the cost challenge. Whole businesses may have to be divested, employment levels substantially reduced, and many perquisites of executive privilege sacrificed. Even for those corporations taking these actions, effective follow-up is necessary, however; otherwise the initial gains are soon dissipated. This book describes a strategic approach to cost reduction intended to build on these initial successes.

A variety of costs have to be managed if cost reduction is to be undertaken strategically. Traditional approaches that have focused on direct, operational costs are extremely limited in scope. The book demonstrates that an effective approach must encompass strategic as well as operational factors and must deal with intangible as well as tangible costs. Potential cost reductions exist throughout every corporation, and there are no areas that can be ignored.

The book is written for executives who must decide on how to manage cost reduction in their own corporations. Key formulation questions are addressed in the first part of the book. Why is a strategic approach necessary? What is a good cost management strategy? What are the principal sources of cost reduction? What information is needed to manage costs effectively?

The second part of the book, which is based largely on personal experience, deals with implementation and the creation of a lean and keen corporation. How should an initial, tough, quick-hit cost-reduction program be implemented? What actions are necessary to create a cost-conscious organization? How should a strategic approach be initiated and maintained? How can more employee involvement be obtained? What specific techniques and organizational processes are there for reducing costs? How should employees be rewarded for obtaining cost savings? These are some of the questions to be dealt with in the latter half.

Through the use of examples and cases, the book demonstrates that cost management can be one of the most exciting and fulfilling challenges facing all corporate employees. Some Canadian and U.S. corporations have been highly innovative in finding ways to meet the cost challenge, and many approaches that they have developed are described in the following chapters.

Acknowledgments

The book owes much to a variety of ideas formulated by people in industry and academia. Without the interest and support of Dr. William James, chairman and chief executive officer of Falconbridge Limited, many of the ideas and strategies described in the book would never have been implemented. Although never afraid to make personally the tough decisions necessary for effective cost reduction, Bill provides all his employees with opportunities to make their own contributions to meeting the challenge. He provides an outstanding example of executive leadership in this area. During the past ten years he has provided me with a unique opportunity to try out many cost-management ideas in a practical setting.

During this time, many people in industry have contributed to the elaboration of the cost-management strategy concept. In particular, Jim Corrigan, Jim Moore, Chuck Murray, Richard Osborne, Karen Stockdale, and Wigo Svensen deserve special recognition. These individuals were all outstanding champions of cost-management activities in their own organizations. I would also like to thank my fellow PIG (profit improvement group) members at Falconbridge with whom I have enjoyed working. I learned much from all these people.

I have also benefited from the creative contributions of a number of my academic colleagues. Wickham Skinner, professor emeritus at the Harvard Business School, has over the years encouraged and rewarded me with his interest in my work and was generous enough to read and comment on drafts of the manuscript. John R.M. Gordon, dean at the school of business at Queen's University, has taught and worked with me for many years, and his ideas have influenced my thinking in many parts of the book. Donald V. Nightingale, also at Queen's University and Professor Thomas Cawsey of Wilfred Laurier University have provided many comments and ideas on the behavioral aspects of the work. Eric Cousineau, now at Cornell, and Oyvind Hushovd, chief financial officer at Falconbridge Limited, provided insightful comments on Chapter 4.

Rose Marie Baird, Lilly Lloyd, and Annette Chiasson provided me with outstanding secretarial support in the preparation of the manuscript. Kerry McLorg, my research assistant, provided me with a mountain of background material and helped in many other ways. Olga Richardson ably and unselfishly organized my thoughts and much of the structure of the book and also spent many hours editing the manuscript. In part of this task she was assisted by Dr. Andrew Okulitch. I am also grateful to Robert Wallace, my editor, and Kathi Rosenbaum, editorial assistant, at the Free Press for their extensive comments and assistance.

Strategy Formulation

1.

The Cost Challenge

The Cost-Management Challenge

Cost management is the cornerstone of successful corporate performance. Ignored by executives for many years, cost reduction is now viewed as the central challenge facing Canadian and U.S. organizations.[1] Executives in manufacturing and service corporations are recognizing that future viability rests on reduced costs. Cutting costs improves income, provides increased margins for reinvestment in research and development and new products, and provides enhanced value for the consumer. Although external forces, such as price and demand, dominate other performance parameters, costs remain within management control.

In recent years, a fashionable argument has been that Canadian and U.S. firms can survive and grow if they differentiate their products and services from those offered by foreign competitors. The events of the last decade have proved that differentiation alone is not enough. For example, as depicted in Figure 1.1, few firms in the automobile industry, except perhaps Rolls Royce, Mercedes and Ferrari (all European, incidentally) can afford to ignore costs. Companies with low differentiation and relatively high costs, such as American Motors, Fiat, and British Leyland, are in permanent trouble. Canadian and U.S. firms have to meet cost competition head on.

3

Relative Product Differentiation

		Low	High
	High	American Motors British Leyland Fiat	Rolls Royce Mercedes Ferrari
Relative Cost Position	Low	Buick/Pontiac Chrysler Hyundai	Cadillac Volvo Toyota

Figure 1.1. Alternative Competitive Strategies: The Automobile Industry

Neither should Canadian and U.S. executives be mislead by apparent improvements in cost competitiveness brought about by currency devaluations. Temporary relief might be obtained by reducing the value of the dollar relative to its Japanese and European counterparts, but the resulting improvement in costs is unlikely to be lasting. Either domestic inflation or currency readjustments will erode the initial gains.

The cost challenge arises from many sources: intense international competition, declining margins as industries mature and the fight for market share intensifies, or in the case of government agencies, increased demand for funding in the face of a stagnant or declining revenue base. Meeting this challenge successfully requires tough-minded executive leadership of a very high quality.

Canadian and U.S. executives have traditionally viewed cost management as a purge or crisis activity, a view quite different from that of their Japanese counterparts. According to an automotive industry analyst Maryann N. Keller: "The Japanese regard cost control as something you wake up to every morning and do. Americans have always thought of it as a project. You cut costs 20 percent and say: 'Whew! that's over.' We can't afford to think like that anymore."[2] Executives have to start thinking of cost management as a strategic, continuous part of their corporate activities.

Executives who have recognized this threat to their organizations have already implemented tough programs aimed at reducing costs. As in the past, these responses are typically tactical responses to deteriorating financial performance. Cuts are made hastily on discretionary items such as research and development (R & D), market development, or plant maintenance that improve short-term results, but increase long-run costs. Across-the-board staff reductions can give immediate productivity improvements, but in the long-term they result in reduced service levels, employee burnout and lower morale unless appropriate management follow-up is taken.[3] A one-time improvement can be expected from these actions, but lasting benefits are unlikely to be obtained.

Executives now recognize that a strategic approach to cost management has to be implemented if short-term gains are to be made while also ensuring long-run improvements. Adopting this approach may require a revolution in behavior and attitudes among all employees in some corporations. Layers of middle management have to vanish, and ultimately cooperation rather than confrontation will come to characterize relationships with employees and unions.

Far from being negative activities, cost reductions in fact create business opportunities. Shared with consumers in the form of reduced prices, they can trigger market demand and generate massive volume expansions such as those experienced by the microcomputer and airline industries in recent years. They can revitalize stagnant markets for mature products such as automobiles.

Implementing a strategic approach to cost reduction is the subject of this book. Ten years of implementing and studying cost-reduction strategies in a variety of manufacturing and service corporations has convinced me that lean, keen organizations will dominate the economic landscape of Canada and the United States in the next decade. The growth of any such organization will be fueled both by market expansion and innovations made possible by virtue of its being a relatively low-cost supplier of goods and services.

In Darwinian terms, this outcome will be the result of a process in which the fittest survive the rigors of tough market competition which can be expected in this period. Government agencies will not be immune from this process, as they will face challenges from private-sector corporations determined to show that they can provide services such as health care, correctional services, and education at lower cost than the traditional public-service organizations.

Despite the prevailing pessimism about Canadian and U.S. industry, some corporations have already faced up to cost competition, and in the process have enjoyed financial success. Executives in these companies know well the tough decisions involved in becoming leaner, but paradoxically, they often describe the process as challenging and even exciting.

Business magazine articles and presentations at management conferences report how some companies have cut unit costs by more than 50 percent during the last five years. For example, to turn around Control Data Corporation, its new chairman cut employment by 25 percent in 1986, eliminated nearly half of the top-management jobs, and divested numerous unprofitable ventures. As a result, the corporation went from a loss of nearly $600 million in 1985 to a profit of approximately $75 million in 1987.[4]

What then follows in a few cases is a tale of innovation, communication, and widespread employee involvement in cost reduction, which can lead to a new approach for managing the business. In other companies, however, these one-time gains are not consolidated, and over time, costs creep back up, forcing a repetition of the process a few years later.

Executives and managers at all levels in public and private sector organizations need to know how to make their own corporation or operation a low-cost competitor. The purpose of this book is to set down a comprehensive strategic framework for implementing this process, and by using case histories, to provide practical insights into how to make this happen, and thereby arm executives to meet the emerging cost challenge.

The Challenge: International and Domestic

So far, the cost challenge has been most noticeable in manufacturing. Across the industrial landscape, Canadian and U.S. economic viability has been challenged by international competition. Basic industries, such as steel, automobiles, and electronics, in which the United States' dominant position was once taken for granted, have been hit hard. Consumer-product firms such as Black and Decker have found their dominant share of domestic markets seriously challenged by higher-quality European and Japanese manufacturers and cheaper products from developing nations, such as Brazil and Korea, which have low labor costs and relatively new plants.

Japanese firms have taken over the leadership in industries such as semiconductors and consumer electronics largely through the competitive advantages gained from low costs.[5] These advantages were not derived solely from lower cost labor, but also from process innovations and quality control which provided higher process yields than those obtained by their U.S. competitors. European firms have taken large shares of some consumer markets by offering well-designed, superior-quality products at competitive prices.

A variety of explanations have been offered for this dismal picture, and depending on the situation, many apply.[6] One view is that a strong dollar and correspondingly undervalued foreign currencies such as the yen, French franc, and deutsch mark have put Canadian and U.S. firms at a serious disadvantage. Yet in almost every industry said to be hurt in this manner, healthy, profitable firms can be found, side by side with those in trouble. Zenith and Hewlett Packard continue to be viable, profitable U.S. electronics manufacturers while others struggle.

The unwillingness of many Canadian and U.S. corporations to invest in new technology has been cited as another important factor contributing to reduced competitiveness in industries such as automobiles and steel. The failure of integrated U.S. steel producers to invest in new technology in the 1960s and 1970s when Japan and Korea were introducing significant process innovations is well documented. At the same time, however, nonintegrated producers such as Chapparrall Steel in Texas have used the new mini-mill technology to compete profitably.[7]

Relatively slow growth in Canadian and U.S. labor productivity is also viewed as a contributor to the lack of competitive vigor. Wage increases, combined with a lack of investment in new facilities, have put many U.S. manufacturers at a cost disadvantage. Wage rollbacks, plant closings, and a frantic rush to implement Japanese manufacturing techniques are now being used to make up for years of complacency.

The challenge is not coming solely from overseas. Cost-based competition is also fierce in many industries in which foreign competition is minimal. For example, cost competition in the domestic airline business has been ferocious since deregulation.[8] New companies, such as Texas Airlines and People Express, operating with lower overhead and labor costs than the older, established airlines have revolutionized competition and forced prices down. Similar situations exist in other industries, such as packaged goods and furniture.

Pressures to reduce costs have also been felt in the not-for-profit and government sectors as sluggish economic growth, budget deficits, and increasing demands for services force these organizations to re-evaluate their activities. The cost of government has come under increasing scrutiny, and agencies from defense to welfare are subjecting their own activities and those of their suppliers to detailed reviews. Traditional cost-management approaches are likely to result in sharply lower levels of service, as programs and field activities are cut, while the real problems, bloated bureaucracy and high overhead, are not tackled.

Limitations of Traditional Approaches

A variety of corporate responses to the need for cost reduction have been implemented in recent years. Typically, they fall into five broad categories, all of which have significant weaknesses from a strategic perspective:

1. Technocratic/capital-intensive solutions
2. Lean-mean cost-reduction strategies
3. Retreat to off-shore sourcing
4. Merger/rationalization strategies
5. Diversification

Technocratic/Capital-Intensive Solutions

The dominant approach to cost reduction in Canada and the United States in recent years has been capital and technology intensive. For many executives, frustrated with years of having to deal with a unionized work force, the ideal of an automated, robotized, nonunion plant is most attractive.

Consequently, many corporations have attempted to drive down costs by closing old plants and replacing them with new, automated facilities. General Motors' Saturn venture represents the pinnacle of this approach, blending radical new technologies with a large capital spending program to cut costs to levels that would be competitive with Japanese producers.[9] General Electric has also made substantial investments in advanced manufacturing technologies, hoping to use its electronic and automation control expertise as the basis for a major new business. Both these ventures have not lived up to their early promise, and their economic returns are likely to be disappointing.

These approaches are not appropriate for many corporations, where the potential financial returns do not justify the additional investment. Massive capital investment requires large subsequent profits, and if life cycles are shrinking, a fast payback is unlikely to be realized in mature industries characterized by continual cost cutting. Radical new technologies are risky and often take a long time to be made operational and productive, especially if a work force feels threatened by the change.

Computer-integrated manufacturing systems also have drawbacks and are not a universal panacea for manufacturing cost problems. They require sophisticated technical support, are hard to improve and modify incrementally, and often have limited flexibility. Many small firms lack the sophisticated skills necessary to implement and support the electronic and information systems needed to derive the full benefits out of this high-tech approach to cost reduction. One small foundry spent four years, $5 million, and countless hours of executive time attempting to implement a manufacturing control system that was ultimately abandoned after never having provided any significant output. Of course, technology does have an important role in cost cutting when appropriately employed, as discussed in Chapter 3.

Lean-Mean Strategies

Some corporations that have emphasized cost reduction as their principal strategic thrust have been characterized as being lean and mean. In these companies, cost management has been implemented through tough top-management policies and tight controls. Unlike past efforts, these cuts have not been focused solely on blue-collar employees. The increasing use of office automation technologies has led to massive layoffs of white-collar employees as corporations have attempted to reduce overhead costs through eliminating clerical and supervisory jobs.

Employee relations have generally been adversarial in such situations, particularly when management implemented tough negotiating postures for contract bargaining or resorted to lockouts to reinforce its bargaining position. Immigrant labor, hired at below prevailing wage rates has been employed to maintain low labor costs in industries such as agriculture and textiles. Layoffs and minimal job security are prevalent in such circumstances, as the work-force becomes the buffer against business down-turns.

The lean-mean organization runs well for short periods of time, especially when unemployment is high, and may even be appropriate in low-skill industries where turnover is not a problem. For most organizations, however, implementing a lean-mean regime has adverse long-run consequences. Good, creative employees leave, and morale declines. The remaining employees then become unwilling to give anything extra in the company's interest, without extra pay. Absenteeism and turnover costs climb, and real productivity gains are small. This approach also fails to take advantage of employees' skills and knowledge that have built up over many years of experience.

The Retreat to Off-Shore Sourcing

Faced with high domestic production costs, many Canadian and U.S. firms have moved sourcing or manufacturing to areas where labor costs are low. Japan, Korea, Singapore, and Taiwan have been the principal beneficiaries of this high-risk policy. However, as C.J. van der Klugt, vice-chairman of Phillips, a consumer electronics company, has noted: "First you move the industrial part to the Far East, then the development of the product goes there, because each dollar you pay to the overseas supplier is 10 cents you are giving him to develop new devices, new concepts, to compete against you.''[10] In addition, currency fluctuations may ultimately determine any cost advantage to this approach. For example, the revaluation of the Japanese yen and major European currencies against the U.S. dollar in 1986 and 1987 meant that many U.S. manufacturers with substantial off-shore sourcing arrangements failed to benefit significantly, because many of their costs were in these higher-valued currencies.

The long-run effects of this strategy are hard to gauge, but there is ample evidence to suggest that in domestic industries where this trend has been prevalent, foreign competitors have benefited. The obvious disadvantages of the move are:

1. The increased logistical complexity facing the Canadian or U.S. manufacturer
2. The move of all manufacturing learning experience off-shore, to a potential competitor
3. The likelihood that the firm will be setting up future new off-shore competition
4. The distinct possibility that the off-shore source is also supplying competitors at the same, or lower, cost.

In almost all industries, there are examples of firms that have rejected this policy, by maintaining domestic manufacturing capabilities, and continue to perform well financially.

Mergers and Industry Rationalization

Firms in trouble have tried getting together as a way to reduce costs, hoping to create one strong firm. Examples of mergers of this type are to be found in industries as diverse as steel, where LTV's Jones and Laughlin merged with Youngstown Steel, and in computers, where Burroughs merged with Sperry to create Unisys. Such mergers are particularly common where there is an apparently good "fit" of resources and product line. Products and plants can possibly be rationalized and overheads can be slashed, as Black and Decker hoped when it purchased General Electric's housewares division.

The success of these types of moves is far from assured. LTV's steel business still ended up seeking the protection of bankruptcy laws to reorganize. Black and Decker found that competitors cashed in on the transition period to erode G.E.'s dominant position in the housewares market. Too often, instead of building on strengths, these mergers compound weaknesses. There is no instant remedy when both firms lack a strong technological base or both possess high-cost, out-of-date manufacturing facilities. In addition, conflicts arise between the managements of the merged firms, often resulting in compromises and trade-offs which lead to lower benefits than expected.

Diversification: The Search for Greener Pastures

As an alternative to investments in cost reductions in their core businesses, many firms have attempted to diversify into new industries, usually through acquisition. In some cases, such as American Can, the move was so successful that the corporation ended up divesting itself completely of its original business. Such cases are relatively rare, however, because a complete revolution in management is usually required. More common are cases similar to the predicament of ARMCO. Its diversification forays into the re-insurance business resulted in disastrous financial losses, while at the same time the core steel business was starved of much-needed funds for modernization and cost reduction. In general, executives in mature industries should focus on strengthening their core business, and heed Peters and Waterman's advice by sticking to their knitting.[11]

Executive Involvement and Leadership

Chief executives who have recognized the importance of meeting the cost challenge have also realized that the cartoon character Pogo was right when he said "I has seen the enemy and he is us." In the past, the spending excesses of many corporate executives have created a poor climate for effective cost reduction within many corporations.

Given the strategic nature of the cost challenge, executive involvement and leadership are essential. The chief executive officer sets the tone for the entire organization through statements on corporate strategy and culture. Functional executives, division managers, and plant managers have to define appropriate cost-management strategies for their own areas of responsibility.

A variety of leadership roles has to be played by executives and managers in strategic cost management. These roles encompass: demonstrating commitment and involvement through making tough decisions and taking symbolic actions, establishing targets and objectives for the entire organization, communicating and creating an awareness of the need for effective cost management, and ensuring that an effective process is in place to reduce costs.

Setting the Pace

At the outset of an effective cost-management activity, senior management is likely to have to take the lead by making tough decisions that are necessary to trim fat from the organization and also through symbolic actions, such as cutting out executive frills and perquisites.

Top management cannot delegate the initial decisions to reduce staffing levels if the job is to be done effectively. Lower-level managers are unlikely to face up to the tough-minded actions necessary to reduce costs if top management does not first set an example. Senior executives are paid to make the tough decisions necessary to make initial cuts which may mean eliminating the positions of friends and associates in senior management ranks that are not compatible with a lean organization and a no-frills operation. Many find this task impossible to face and consequently end up being replaced by outsiders who do not have personal attachments inside the corporation.

Continuing top-management involvement in cost management is necessary from a purely strategic perspective. For significant cost reductions to occur over time, a variety of major strategic decisions are likely to be involved. These can be as diverse as an acquisition or merger designed to reduce costs through obtaining greater economies of scale or scope in manufacturing and distribution, the replacement of a manufacturing facility with an automated plant, or the restructuring of the corporate compensation system to give employees more incentive to tackle cost reduction.

Executives in corporations that successfully manage costs also establish quite clearly that rank carries minimal frills and privileges. At Cummins Engine, according to its president James Henderson, there are no reserved executive parking spaces, and an open door policy is maintained so that all employees feel part of the team.[12] At Gulfstream Aerospace Corporation, there is no executive dining room. Allen E. Paulson, the chairman and chief executive officer, takes his dirty dishes to the kitchen like other employees. Paulson's office is panelled with the same inexpensive wallboard found elsewhere in the operation.[13]

When Bill James took over as chairman at Falconbridge Limited, he moved into a small office on one of the main corridors of the company's Toronto headquarters and turned the former chairman's suite into accommodation for six employees. He also sold off the corporate jet, took charter flights wherever possible, shared a secretary, and after annual meetings entertained shareholders at Toronto's Shopsey's Delicatessen rather than one of the city's more fashionable eateries.

David J. Tappan, Jr. took over as chairman of debt-ridden Fluor Corporation in 1984. His first actions included selling the company's 727 jet and requesting that senior executives fly coach on business travel. He also sold off corporate artwork and cut salaries and executive perks which had built up during prior years of high profitability. To demonstrate that he was sharing in these tough actions, Tappan also reduced his own income from $773,000 in 1982 to $450,000 in 1986.[14]

Executive actions such as these make little direct contribution to the overall cost reduction, but they have a symbolic importance. They demonstrate that top management is serious about cutting out the frills and that none are sacred. Nothing undermines a cost-management effort more than a perception that executives are immune to the hard realities of economy.

Establishing Goals and Objectives

Senior executives and managers are the best placed and most informed individuals to set initial objectives and goals for cost-reduction activities. When corporations contain substantial organizational "fat," initial corporation-wide targets for cost reductions and work-force cutbacks can be set. As one executive commented, "It's better to cut too far initially, than forever go around afterwards wondering whether you cut enough: the worst thing is to do it once, and then go back in with a second round twelve months later."

Once the initial savings have been obtained, establishing realistic goals and objectives becomes more difficult for senior management. At this time, it is appropriate to delegate this task to lower-level managers, but continuing top-management support and encouragement are required. Ensuring that lower-level managers do not meet their cost-reduction targets by the traditional route of reducing long-term competitiveness requires constant monitoring of budgets and performance. Obtaining the involvement of all employees in meeting these challenges requires that top management continually communicate the activity's importance throughout the organization.

Creating a Lean and Keen Culture

Leadership from the top of the organization is also important if a lean and keen culture is to be established in which cost management is a continuing part of running the business. Effective cost reduction requires that values and beliefs are established that persistently drive managers to find more economical ways of doing business. A climate has to be established in which employees as well as managers can propose cost-reducing ideas without fearing that their own employment will be jeopardized.

Employees have to be continually informed of the financial and cost performance of the corporation. It is quite common for few employees below senior-management levels to know an organization's competitive position, financial results, or costs. Consequently, layoffs and cutbacks are unexpected, and the organization goes into a state of shock. Effective cost management requires that executives communicate costs continually to all employees, in good times as well as bad.

Developing an Effective Process

If executives want cost reduction to be a part of the organization's continuing activities, then a major aspect of their role is to make sure that an effective process is in place to enable cost savings to be identified and implemented from many different sources inside and outside the corporation.

In the past, executives have failed to develop such a process, and as a result have been forced to resort to periodic cost purges. Employees have found it impossible to contribute effectively to cost reduction, often being afraid that some cost-reduction ideas might result in the loss of employment for themselves or co-workers. Only now in some companies are executives making employees aware that the best form of employment security is to bring forward ideas that reduce labor requirements but in total create employment by making the organization a lower-cost competitor.

Collectively, the management team in an organization has to develop a cost-management strategy that fits its mission and capitalizes fully on the human, capital, and technical resources available to it. Initially this activity comes from the top down, but as the strategy becomes effective and gains acceptance, it is increasingly possible to involve employees throughout the organization in the process. When this situation occurs, the corporation is well on the way to meeting the cost challenge.

Changing the Image of Cost Reduction

Previously, in most corporations the chief executive officer and senior executives have viewed cost reduction as a prime responsibility for operating managers, not as one of their own major tasks. Making deals, acquisitions, financial strategies, and new products are far more glamorous tasks than cost management. In addition, executives who have risen through the ranks from either marketing or staff positions often have little experience in cost cutting.

Operating managers, who might be expected to be directly charged with the responsibility for cost reduction, frequently ignore the task if they are not challenged to take it up. New facilities or new products, often justified on the ostensible grounds of cost reduction, are much more enjoyable to implement, although the ultimate outcome might not be lowered costs.

Supervisors are often turned against cost management by their own experiences. Too frequently, cost management for them means having to explain variances in monthly reports which they spend many hours in tracking, only to find that an accounting error or a quarterly expense allocated in a single month is responsible for the deviation. Cost management too often results in clerical drudgery for supervisors and lacks any real challenge or positive motivation.

In addition, supervisors are often uninformed about overall costs until management determines there is a crisis. Then they have to watch while senior managers slash expenditures, such as preventative maintenance, safety, and inventories of supplies which might bring short-term relief, but which create endless headaches and requirements for futile explanations of performance shortfalls. Increased direct management control in these periods, such as personal signing of requisitions and rationing of essential supplies, also adds to the frustration.

Staff and operators frequently are the first to feel the effects of cost-reduction activities without ever understanding the reasons behind many of management's moves. When cost reduction is done in a hurry, management usually has little time to explain its actions or communicate effectively with the work force.

Apart from suggestion schemes, firms generally lack mechanisms to involve their employees in cost management. Rewards tend to be minimal or even negative if employees are perceived to be indirectly critical of management policies when they suggest changes they feel could reduce costs. In some corporations, employees are infuriated and demoralized as they see executives who have failed to manage costs effectively being rewarded with substantial golden parachutes upon departure. In such corporations, good employees feel that it may be better to be "de-hired" than to stay and face a lean, mean future with the company.

Too many executives fail to realize the profit potential of an effective, well-managed cost-reduction activity in good times as well as bad. Although at the outset tough measures may be necessary to reduce costs, it should subsequently be possible to develop a strategy that involves, challenges, and excites many employees. Several examples of corporations that have met this challenge are described later in the chapter.

The Competitive Advantage of the Low-Cost Producer

Cost management is strategic because of the major opportunities it makes available. Honda's low-cost production of motorcycles is a classic example of this situation.[15] Initially, being low cost greatly expanded the market for its motorcycles as basic transportation in developing countries, such as Japan and throughout the Far East. Then, using its high-volume production facilities as the basis for a higher-quality product, Honda proceeded to push the traditional European, Canadian, and U.S. producers into the high-priced segments of the market, and ultimately, in the case of the British, out of business altogether.

The Honda example illustrates two aspects of the opportunities available to low-cost producers: to stimulate market growth and to destroy the competition. In the first case, increasing the volume divisor without increasing overhead provides greater margins for investment in new technology and market development, in addition to profits. Unfortunately, this option is not available to all firms, especially those in mature industries, in which radical cost reductions to stimulate a major growth in demand may be extremely difficult to generate.

In the second case, a superior cost position can force competitors to close, leaving vacant markets to be penetrated. Opportunities can be sought beyond the boundaries of existing competition. For example, plastic producers are set to invade the traditional steel and aluminum beverage can markets with lower-cost containers. Aluminum is being substituted for base metals, such as copper, in automobile radiators and electrical conductors.

Cost reduction can also be an effective strategy for late entrants into an existing market. Although the Japanese were relatively late to enter the semiconductor chip business, they have been able to gain a dominant position through their ability to improve process yields, resulting in unit costs significantly below that of the competition. Zenith has been able to enter the personal computer market relatively late and use its low-cost manufacturing approach built up in radios, televisions, and other consumer electronic products to out-perform earlier entrants who lacked these skills.

Being low cost provides many business advantages even for corporations in declining industries. For example, mini-mills have been expanding in the U.S. steel industry in recent years, while the higher-cost integrated firms such as Bethlehem and ARMCO have been in decline. The failure of larger firms to control costs has not been at the operational level, but in costs associated with poor business and corporate strategy decisions, such as failure to invest in new process technologies.

The drive to be a low-cost producer also shapes major strategic decisions, such as acquisition and facility construction. As noted previously, costs can be lowered significantly by judicious mergers resulting in industry rationalization. For example, Alcan, the world's largest aluminium producer was able to dramatically improve the position of its U.K. subsidiary by merging it with its major competitor, British Aluminium. Through rationalizing facilities and work forces, the resulting business achieved higher levels of plant utilization while retaining a dominant share of the British market.

In addition to these growth opportunities, being the low-cost producer means that a corporation is better positioned to survive cyclical downturns in markets or the economy and is consequently well placed to take advantage of any upturn when it comes.

The stock-market upturn lasting through 1986 and into 1987 demonstrates another advantage of being lean and low cost. Stocks that performed exceptionally well were those of corporations that investors perceived to have addressed the initial cost challenge, as part of gaining significant profit improvements in the late 1980s. Companies that were slow to restructure and trim costs, such as AT&T, IBM, and General Motors, ended up with large write-offs that hurt the performance of their stock prices.[16]

Examples of Companies that Have Met the Challenge

Companies that successfully meet a cost challenge are often those once on the verge of bankruptcy. Three short cases follow, describing corporations that have deliberately adopted cost-management strategies. These illustrate the variety of choices available and the risks involved. Crown Cork and Seal was a pioneer of what has since come to be characterized as the lean and mean approach. People Express attempted to revolutionize the airline industry through a novel, people-oriented strategy. Falconbridge Limited followed up a tough turnaround with a melding of its limited human, technical, and capital resources into a focused cost-reduction strategy, subsequently emerging as a formidable competitor in the base-metal mining business.

Crown Cork and Seal: A Pioneer

John F. Connelly assumed the presidency of the ailing Crown Cork and Seal Corporation in 1958. The corporation was in danger of going bankrupt, and it was badly positioned in its attempts to implement a "me-too" full-line strategy against its formidable giant rivals, American Can and Continental Can. Over the next five years, Connelly forged a low-cost niche strategy which ensured that Crown remained the most profitable can manufacturer in the United States for the next twenty-five years.

Connelly's first move was to reduce debt by raising cash through liquidation of excess inventory and by cutting accounts receivable. At the same time he started to cut costs by tough measures aimed at driving out overheads. The number of vice-presidents was reduced by 11, cumbersome staff departments were pared down, and R & D was cut back and decentralized.

A major part of Crown's problems stemmed from the fact that most of its capacity was in large plants located near raw material suppliers and away from customers, resulting in high transportation costs and poor service. As soon as cash was available, Connelly started to decentralize plants to be nearer customer locations and to reduce the size of his work force. He also pruned from his product lines the very low margin packer cans which were not competitive with those of his larger competitors. From that time on, Crown's product line emphasized hard-to-hold applications. After three years, although total revenues had not grown, Crown possessed a much lower break-even point, plants near to customers, and a healthy balance sheet.

Connelly rounded out the strategy by upgrading equipment in Crown's plants to be the fastest and most modern in the industry. Because the cost of capital investment per can was low, capacity was matched to customers' peak seasonal demands. Plant managers were rewarded on profits, but were expected to keep costs low. Old equipment was shipped off-shore to Crown's new plants in developing nations.

From 1961 through 1965, Crown was the fastest-growing company in the container business, in spite of limiting itself largely to steel cans. In its chosen market niches, Crown's low-cost position made it unchallengable. As late as 1978, Crown's drawn-steel can lines were the fastest-growing segment of the canning industry. Net profits have rarely dropped below 5 percent of sales, even in the recession of the early 1980s, and return on shareholder's equity has remained high.

People Express: There and Back Again

The People Express story is about a new corporation that beat larger, established competitors by changing the rules of the game and lowering costs dramatically. Unfortunately, it then fell victim to its own success. People Express was the realization of the vision of its founder Donald Burr, who wanted to create an airline that would be a model for the rest of the industry, a great place to work, and very profitable. For a while he succeeded in all three.

Being a small corporation in an industry of giants, People Express had to conserve its capital for essential items: the purchase of aircraft. Burr was able to acquire a second-hand fleet of seventeen Boeing 737s from Lufthansa. These were the most fuel-efficient, lowest-cost-per-passenger-mile aircraft suitable for the routes People was flying. Maintenance was subcontracted to conserve capital and reduce overhead. Ground facilities were spartan, with none of the usual plush ticket counters, lounges, and offices associated with typical airlines. Burr's office even doubled as a conference room.

People Express's operating policies complemented its low-cost facilities: aircraft were kept in the air two hours per day longer than those of the competition; extra seats were installed to ensure maximum seat revenues; no meals were offered on board; baggage handling was minimized; no expensive overhead facilities or staffs were maintained; and computer systems were minimal.

People's human resource policies matched its strategy perfectly in its first few years. Employees were nonunionized, engaged in profit sharing, and many owned substantial amounts of stock. Work groups were self-managing, and job rotation was stressed. When they weren't able to fly planes, pilots performed ground staff roles. Involvement, participation, and commitment were stressed and encouraged.

The initial results were outstanding. People Express rapidly became known for its cheap fares, and its volume exploded. Unit costs quickly became the lowest in the industry, and after only eighteen months, the corporation was profitable. The business press hailed People Express as the new role model for U.S. industry, just as Burr had hoped.

Then People Express became a victim of its own growth, or maybe Burr's ambitions. To maintain growth (and the share price), the airline continued to expand rapidly, acquiring more and different planes, and more people. However, customers became frustrated with its poor reservation systems, and many travel agents refused to deal with the airline because of the time spent to obtain a booking. Employees began to suffer from burnout due to the extreme work loads imposed by the company, and the quality of service deteriorated. Competitors became more efficient and leaner and were able to match and even beat People's low prices.

In an attempt to expand its base, and perhaps avert disaster, People Express acquired Frontier Airline, a regional, unionized carrier, and attempted to turn it into another People Express. The merged corporation was a huge failure. Cash losses mounted, and in late 1986, People Express was acquired by Continental Airlines, the largest and lowest-cost U.S. airline at that time. Ironically, Burr and several of his executives had left Continental to found their dream corporation: People Express.

Falconbridge Limited: Back from the Brink

As the world's second largest nickel producer, Canada's Falconbridge Limited has always played also-ran to Inco, the traditional industry giant. Inco's large, high-grade ore reserves at its Canadian operations in Sudbury, Ontario and Thompson, Manitoba seemed to guarantee that it would remain the largest and lowest-cost producer.

In 1982, as the world economy slid into recession, the nickel price dropped from $3.40 per pound to $1.40. At the time, Falconbridge's operations were producing nickel for approximately $3.40 per pound, and the company tried to maintain its prices in order to avoid losses, but instead lost sales and built inventories. The mines in Sudbury were closed for six months in the summer of 1982, and a new chief executive, Bill James, was hired. The company ultimately ended up losing over $80 million that year.

James' first moves were exceptionally tough. He personally supervised reductions of approximately 40 percent in the corporation's work forces, and simultaneously demanded that previous production levels be met or exceeded. Employment at the corporation's Sudbury operations declined from 4,100 to 2,750, and corporate office staff was reduced from 240 to 120. Mine development and capital expenditures were slashed.

As a symbolic move, the corporate jet was sold, and its crew released. James moved out of the large traditional corner office of the chairman into a small office on one of the main corridors and shared a secretary with his vice-president of sales and marketing. In spite of the employment reductions, output in 1983 exceeded precutback levels, unit costs were down $1.00 to approximately $2.40 per pound, and only a small operating loss was recorded in the year as the nickel price recovered to over $2.00.

During 1983, James insisted that each major operation in the corporation institute a cost-management activity aimed at involving as many employees as possible on a voluntary basis. In addition, the company's central R & D facilities were closed and the employees relocated to operating sites. The mission of the technical groups in the corporation became implementation of new cost-reducing technologies, from any source, in the company's operations.

Full-time cost-management coordinators were appointed at each operation. Executives and managers regularly communicated financial and cost information on a company, operation, and departmental basis to all employees. A cost-management seminar, described as the "best short course in capitalism I've ever seen'' by one visiting executive, was made available to supervisors and operators. Ideas started to flow freely from the work force that, to their delight, were quickly adopted and implemented. Rewards of 15 percent of the first year's savings were offered to all nonstaff employees for these contributions. In the first year of its existence, the activity was estimated to have cut $10 million out of Sudbury's $200 million operating budget. In the two subsequent years, this amount rose to approximately $15 million annually as operating costs declined sharply. Similar results were obtained at other operations, and as a result, operating profits were recorded in 1985 and 1986.

The company's low-cost production base enabled it to compete success- fully in 1985 for a major contract to refine nickel matte from a Botswana mining company until the year 2000. In the process of obtaining this contract, Falconbridge virtually ensured that a competing refinery would close, thus reducing some of the overcapacity plaguing the nickel industry.

Complementing these operating-cost reductions, James and his chief financial officer completely refinanced the corporation in the period 1983– 1985. Long-term debt was reduced, and equity increased significantly. Pleased with James' aggressive cost-cutting approach, investors were eager to purchase new equity in the corporation.

James rounded out 1985 by acquiring Canada's premier copper/zinc producer, Kidd Creek Mines, from the debt-ridden Canada Development Corporation, thus diversifying Falconbridge's traditional metals base. This diversification also lessened the threat from Inco, which was finally starting to reduce its own costs substantially and intimating that it would start a price war for more market share in the nickel business.

By the end of 1986, operating costs at Sudbury were slightly under one-half of the 1982 levels. Although the average price of nickel during the year had fallen to below $2.00 because of severe price competition and continuing overcapacity, Falconbridge's cost-reduction strategy ap- pears to have ensured it survival in a tough business, as well as having provided a base for needed growth and diversification.

Need for a Strategic Perspective

Deployed effectively, cost management strategies can be powerful com- petitive weapons, often making the difference between failure and survival for businesses in mature or declining industries and between slow and fast growth for corporations in new markets.

In the past, the lack of a strategic perspective for managing costs has led to unsatisfactory results. Traditional cost management approaches have suffered from the shortcomings summarized in Table 1.1. Leaving

Table 1.1.   Shortcomings of Traditional Cost Management Approaches

- Responsibility lies solely with operating managers.
- Costs are only managed during crisis situations.
- The cost reduction focus is limited in scope.
- A partial approach is usually adopted: many important costs are ignored.
- Employees hold negative perceptions of the activity.
- Personal relationships and emotions stand in the way of objective action.
- One-time reductions are neither followed up nor maintained.
- The wrong costs are often cut first because they are the easiest to eliminate.

the task in the hands of operating managers has meant that a limited perspective has usually been applied. Significant opportunities to reduce corporate-level and overhead costs are often ignored, as are those associated with poor competitive positioning.

In contrast, effective cost management takes a total view of all the costs affecting the organization. In addition to the direct, measurable costs which are the focus of most traditional cost management approaches, other costs, many not so easily measured, have to be dealt with when a strategic perspective is taken. These range from costs associated with a weak strategic position, for example in the marketplace or in the geographic locations of plants, to those associated with operational problems, such as low quality or poor employee relations.

The strategic approach aims to balance the human, technological, and capital contributions to cost management. Trade-offs between possible contributions from each of these sources can be made. For example, considerable expenditures can be avoided if employees are challenged to find ways to cut costs without increasing capital investment.

This total-cost approach requires that all levels of management be involved in the activity. The cost of poor market positioning directly affects marketing and sales personnel, but the entire corporation should be involved if an effective solution is to be implemented. Corporations that identify poor employee relations as a high cost area are probably faced with the challenge of rebuilding the entire corporate culture for a lasting solution to be worked out. The lack of commitment or involvement on the part of key corporate executives can mean the difference between success and failure.

Meeting the Challenge

The purpose of this book is to provide executives and managers with a strategic framework for meeting the cost challenge. The contents draw from the author's own experiences in working with a number of firms to implement such strategies. This background has been expanded by the use of many examples of other firms that are devising new and innovative ways to meet the cost management challenge and by selected reference to articles and texts with pragmatic relevance.

The first part of the book is intended to create an awareness of the lasting nature of this cost challenge facing U.S. and Canadian organizations. This is not a problem a one-time solution will solve. As shown in Figure 1.2, an effective cost management strategy has to fit with corporate and business strategies so that all persons with a stake in the firm ultimately gain. This linkage is described in Chapter 2, along with the nature of cost management strategies. The principal sources of cost reduction are then explored in Chapter 3. Chapter 4 discusses the cost information needs of employees at all levels in the organization if they are to play an effective role in meeting the challenge.

The second part of the book describes the implementation of cost management in corporations that intend to be both lean and keen. The need for executive direction and an initial top-down cost reduction drive

Figure 1.2. A Strategic Framework for Cost Management

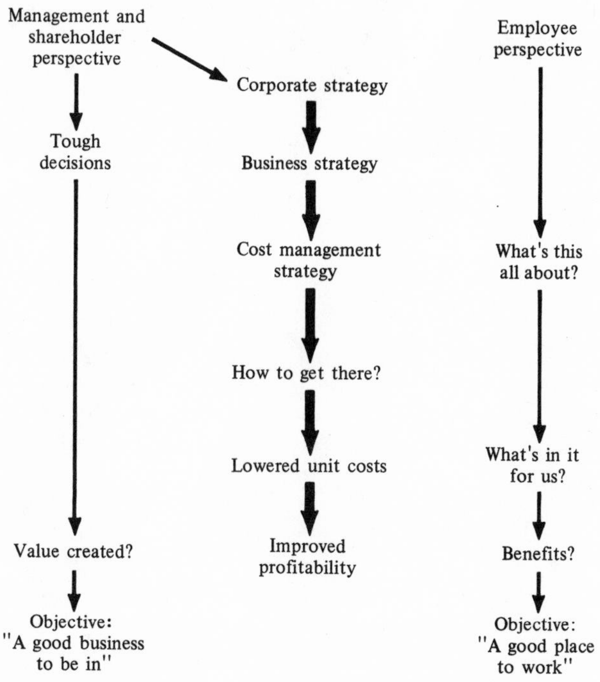

are described and illustrated with specific examples in Chapter 5. Then an action plan is laid out in Chapters 6 and 7 for establishing a long-run strategy and drawing in as many employees as possible, because there is little doubt that the culture and values needed for effective cost management must permeate the entire corporation.

Chapters 8 and 9 describe a variety of specific programs and actions involving people and technology that corporations have implemented as elements of their strategies to obtain tangible cost reductions on a continuing basis. Alternative ways of recognizing and rewarding their cost reduction accomplishments, which are essential to sustain any lasting employee interest, are then described in Chapter 10. Chapter 11 summarizes and integrates the major themes developed throughout the book.

2.

The Strategic Approach

Corporate Strategy and Competitiveness

Strategic thinking and action are recognized as essential parts of the management process in the modern corporation. Executives start to manage costs strategically only when they identify the significant costs in their corporation and focus resources on reducing them. Successful executives are those capable of recognizing the need for a radical restructuring of their business, and who possess the skills to carry it out. This chapter starts with a brief overview of the distinctions between corporate and business strategies and concludes with the development of a strategic framework for the management of costs.

Among larger enterprises, single-product corporations are now a minority, and a variety of different types of diversified corporations dominate the manufacturing and service sectors. It is not rare for a large corporation to have ten or twenty major business units. In more complex firms, such as the 3M Corporation and General Electric, creating intermediate groupings of divisions within business sectors is now common practice.

In this context of diversification, corporate strategy has come to be thought of as the selection of the businesses the corporation will engage in.[1] The implementation of corporate strategy focuses on acquisition and divestment, and the allocation of resources—especially financial and managerial—among businesses.

The dominant way of thinking about diversification focuses on the relationships between the businesses in the corporate portfolio. Related-product firms are those in which there is a common thread of markets, products, or technology among the different businesses. Shared approaches to doing business and a common culture may also link the different divisions. Examples of such corporations include Hewlett Packard, General Foods, and Bristol Myers. Unrelated-product conglomerates are those such as Textron, Allied Corporation, and Teledyne, in which there is no common technical or market thread.

The requirements for successful management in each type of corporation differ considerably, and the role of the corporate office varies according to the degree of diversification. As the scope of diversification increases and the number of business units proliferates, corporate management becomes increasingly distanced from running specific businesses and more involved in acquisition and divestment. In such circumstances, it can become divorced from the realities and rigors of competition and the need for cost management.

Within corporate strategy, individual business strategies define the scope of product-market activities and the basis for competition. In diversified corporations, it is usual for each business to develop its own strategic plan, which is a key input to the total corporate strategic plan. Business units operate with varying degrees of autonomy, often depending on the scope of corporate diversification and the culture of the firm. In some corporations, business unit managers are empowered to make major decisions on expansion and growth, as long as they meet their plans and budget projections. In other corporations, division executives may have the lattitude only to implement operational plans.

Until recently, business unit strategies were thought of as comprising functional strategies that focus on sales and marketing, manufacturing, R & D, and finance. A variety of frameworks have been developed around each of these concepts in recent years, and corporations have developed rigorous planning methodologies that enable the formulation of these in support of the overall business strategy and in the quest for competitive advantage.[2]

This approach focuses attention on and integrates resources within specific functional areas. For example, the use of manufacturing as a competitive weapon had been largely ignored in recent times in Canada and the United States until the opportunities inherent in this area were pointed out by writers such as Skinner, Abernathy and Hayes and Wheelwright.[3]

Unfortunately, in practice this functional approach does not integrate strategy across business units and for the corporation as a whole. Functional strategies tend to be developed in isolation and can become ends in themselves for the people involved. In these cases, severe dislocations can occur between marketing, production, and R & D, particularly with respect to innovation and cost control. For example, manufacturing may make quality trade-offs that facilitate production but have negative effects in the marketplace. R & D programs can become isolated from operations and end up failing to deliver commercializable technologies.

As a result, it has become increasingly apparent that strategies are needed that integrate corporate resources and activities both across businesses and across functions to highlight the critical competitive dimensions of differentiation and costs. A set of competitive strategies for technology and for cost management are becoming significant integrative driving forces in the corporate search for a competitive advantage. A third integrative strategy, for human resources, is also a necessary element in creating an appropriate culture and working environment in the corporation.[4]

The corporate strategy hierarchy that emerges is shown in Figure 2.1. Corporate and business strategies are broken down into functional strategies that focus resources and competitive strategies that are integrative. The scope and form of these strategies depend to a great extent on the nature of the global corporate strategy. Their formulation and implementation differ significantly in single-, related-, and unrelated-product corporations.

As one of the key competitive strategies, cost management deserves

Figure 2.1. The Corporate Strategy Hierarchy

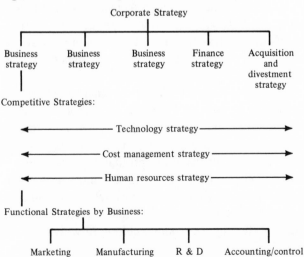

the attention of managers throughout the entire corporation. The opportunities created by a successful strategic cost management activity can add significant value to many businesses. The challenge is to determine the appropriate level in the corporation for managing each of the different costs. To resolve this issue, executives must take time to understand the impact of their own corporate strategy on the task of managing costs.

Where Costs Fit in Corporate Strategy

As previously noted, a variety of corporate strategy types exist, depending on the degree of diversification. These differences have important implications for both the way costs are managed and the nature of executive involvement in the process. Corporate executives in unrelated-product corporations are likely to involve themselves in different types of activities from their counterparts in single-product firms.

Single-product corporations are those with only one dominant business, such as Inco, the world's largest nickel producer, or Texas International, North America's largest airline. In these corporations, senior executives have to adopt an integrated perspective for the entire business and take actions aimed at gaining cost advantages from major strategy shifts within the business. For example, Texas Air Corporation undertook an aggressive acquisitions program which provided significant economies of scale. Inco improved its position by a variety of measures, including vertical integration, corporate investment in new technologies, and productivity improvement.

In related-product firms such as Hewlett Packard and Gillette, sharing experience across different business units can provide competitive advantages in new technology, production resources, joint marketing, and distribution. Multi-business firms may have economies of scope not available to single-product firms, arising from the breadth of their business activities.[5]

In these firms, responsibility for cost management has usually been delegated to division managers. Corporate executives have taken little active involvement in the activity, except when cost management has been perceived as a central strategic thrust and thus a shared corporate responsibility. Faced with declining profitability and limited degrees of freedom to respond to this situation in the short term, more top-level executives in these corporations are now taking a leading role in the process by personally making tough cost-reduction decisions they formerly abdicated and by creating a corporate culture in which cost management is a valued activity.

In unrelated-product corporations (often referred to as conglomerates), the only linkage between all the businesses in the portfolio is financial. In these firms, corporate management is generally preoccupied with acquisitions and divestments and plays a largely financial and legal role. Business strategies, of which cost management is seen as an integral part, are delegated to divisions which are managed and evaluated on the basis of return-on-investment (ROI).

Corporate management's role in controlling costs in these firms was formerly perceived as being limited to maintaining a small, lean head office and ensuring that division managers met their cash-flow projections. This process in itself tended to create the discipline and methodology required for effective cost management in the divisions, although an excessive concern for short-run profit performance in these companies can lead to higher costs in the long run.

Now, however, executives in unrelated-product corporations are realizing that they can have a far greater impact on costs than previously understood. Divestment is one way of reducing the costs incurred by poor strategic positioning, and many conglomerates have improved their profitability in recent years, without increasing revenues or investment, simply by selling businesses that fit better in other corporate portfolios.

These divestments can make a significant contribution to the reduction of overhead costs if the proceeds are used to pay off debt. High interest payments, often brought about by overly ambitious acquisition programs, have crippled the competitiveness of numerous corporations during the last decade by reducing the funds available for investment in new product and process technologies and the renewal of obsolete plants.

A Total Cost Approach

From an executive perspective, there are four categories of cost that need to be addressed by a management strategy. These are shown in Figure 2.2, together with examples of each. Strategic as well as operational costs need to be included if the approach is to have a total corporate impact. In addition, both intangible and tangible costs have to be considered for the approach to be truly comprehensive.

Changes in the costs on the right-hand side are likely to show up in measures of short-run business performance. Costs shown on the left-hand side of the quadrant tend to have more of a long-run nature, being associated with the management or mismanagement of assets and technology. Although cuts in expenditures which determine these costs can be made rapidly, the true impact of these changes on the business are likely to emerge only in the longer run.

	Strategic	Operational
Tangible	• Debt charges • New plants • Product development • Market development	• Labor • Materials • Energy • Supplies • Contract services
Intangible	• Poor product positioning • Technological obsolescence • Poor facility location	• Poor quality • Absenteeism • Turnover • Poor morale • Lost output • Late delivery

Figure 2.2.   Categories of Cost, from a Total Corporate Perspective

What Creates a Cost?

The process of how a cost is created and becomes permanent is of interest to all executives, especially in the case of overhead or opportunity costs which seem to make up an increasing proportion of the total for most businesses. Direct, variable costs associated with the basic manufacturing or service operations, such as materials, energy, and labor, make up a decreasing proportion. Labor, which used to be viewed as a variable cost, has now become fixed for most firms, concomitantly increasing breakeven levels and reducing flexibility.

Many overhead and opportunity costs are incurred because of a breakdown in the basic functioning of business activities. Like income tax, many corporate activities introduced as a temporary expedient become fixtures and an additional permanent cost burden. Generally speaking, when corporations attempt to control or manage problems, rather than solve them, they create additional indirect costs. These are difficult to recover from customers and make the corporation less competitive.

Activities that add value to the product or service must be distinguished from those that merely add to costs. For example, field service is a necessary part of the computer business, whereas "fix-it" teams to remedy poor quality construction work in the housing industry are an added cost of doing business. Well-directed technical development and engineering teams add value, whereas quality control inspectors generally create little value, but rather prevent high costs from being incurred through poor quality.

Writing twenty-five years ago, Peter Drucker perceived that unless management directed costs into revenue-producing activities, they would tend to allocate themselves *by drift* into "nothing-producing" activities.

In Drucker's view, the real cost of a product "is the proportion of the total cost of the business that corresponds to the ratio between the number of transactions (orders, production runs, service calls, and the like) needed to obtain the product's revenue and total number of similar transactions in the business."[6]

A variety of examples of these costs that create transactions but add little value can be cited. Executives create excess operating costs for their businesses when they:

Alienate employees to the point where they need substantial levels of supervisory policing and managing, leading to high supervisory-work force ratios

Tolerate high levels of absenteeism requiring substantial overmanning to ensure a full crew

Accept poor-quality output or ensure quality through instituting 100 percent final inspection of products.

Tolerate low-quality inputs and carry out 100 percent incoming material inspection

Create an administrative paperwork jungle requiring excessive clerical support staffs

Establish sophisticated and complex control systems requiring high levels of support and maintenance

Invest in "cheap" capital expansions that subsequently develop high maintenance requirements

Corporations with executives that do not accept these practices can today almost certainly out-compete most other firms. Mechanisms and programs designed to reduce transactions such as product simplification, just-in-time production systems, and reduction of change orders are characteristic activities found in these corporations.

The Need for a Comprehensive Approach

Traditional cost management efforts have concentrated on costs in the upper-right quartile of Figure 2.2, which are direct and easily measured costs. In a crisis situation, executives focus on reducing these, together with postponing or eliminating discretionary strategic expenditures, such as R & D, market and product development, and facilities investment. In the case of these latter costs, deferring expenditures often merely results in offsetting intangible strategic costs incurred in later periods.

Effective cost management, however, requires a comprehensive approach. High costs may result from a weak strategic profile, such as poor plant location, obsolete technology, or faulty product positioning.

Externally imposed costs can also have a strategic impact. For example, conforming to government regulations regarding safety, health, and the environment can increase the costs of Canadian or U.S. firms compared with those in other countries operating without such constraints.

In addition, intangible operating costs (also known as hidden or opportunity costs) can have a major impact on corporate performance. Examples of these include the costs of poor quality, failure to meet delivery, inadequate safety standards, and poor labor relations. Because they are hard to measure, these costs are usually not detailed in periodic reports and so never come to the attention of management. Actions to reduce intangible costs are key elements of successful cost-management strategies.

In many companies, the initial focus of effective cost-management efforts can be on these hard-to-measure but nevertheless critical cost elements. In one losing business, which may be typical of many in Canada and the United States today, costs associated with poor quality (internal scrap, customer returns, etc.) were estimated to be over 7 percent of total costs. A major drive lowered these costs to about 2 percent of total costs and was a major contributor to the firm's return to profitability.

A major challenge in many corporations is making sure that each cost type is recognized and managed at appropriate levels in the corporation. When senior executives do get involved in cost reduction, they tend to concern themselves with costs that should be managed at lower levels in the corporation, especially during purges and "quick-hit" programs implemented during periods of financial crisis.

Sound approaches take a holistic perspective and consider all four quadrants. Executives should be more concerned with managing strategic costs than with operational costs, which should be the prime concern of lower-level managers and other employees. In a well-functioning cost-management strategy, senior executives should concern themselves with such costs only when there is a need to demonstrate symbolically the actions that lower level managers should be taking.

For example, during a period of excessive inventory costs in the Cummins Engine Corporation, the chief operating officer took walks around the plant and identified misallocated components, not as a way of solving the problem, but as a means of demonstrating to his managers the kinds of action they should be taking themselves.

A total-cost approach also implies that executives include the entire spectrum of corporate activities within the scope of the activity. Porter has pointed out that cost studies tend to focus on manufacturing costs and fail to recognize the impact of other factors such as marketing, distribution, and overheads on the corporation's relative cost position.[7]

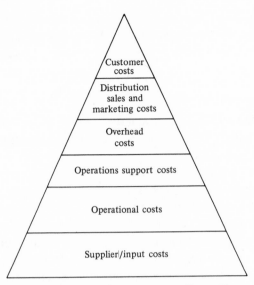

Figure 2.3. The Corporate-cost Pyramid

As shown in Figure 2.3, the total costs of a business can be viewed as a pyramid which may vary in size, depending on the cost structure. Costs to be included in the pyramid stretch all the way from suppliers to the ultimate customer, thus ensuring that any strategy includes everything that the corporation can influence. For example, Marks and Spencer, the British retailing giant, provides considerable help to its suppliers as part of its cost-reduction strategy because of their importance in providing value to Marks and Spencer's customers.

Many other corporations, such as IBM and Boeing, have gained major competitive advantages by instituting specific programs to help customers reduce the costs of using and maintaining their products. Aluminium producers, such as Alcan and Alcoa, have continued to increase their share of the beverage can market and created markets for heat exchangers by helping their customers to develop low-cost manufacturing processes. As these examples indicate, taking a total perspective on cost management is not merely a good defensive strategy, as many executives think, but can also be an important element in an offensive competitive strategy.

Obstacles to Thinking Strategically about Costs

The effectiveness of a cost-management strategy is largely determined by the beliefs and attitudes toward the subject held by the various players in the corporation. These attitudes in turn result in behavior that may adversely affect cost management, including overreliance on ROI as a criterion for evaluating cost-reducing proposals, inappropriate spending controls, and an unwillingness to spend money to generate savings.

Top-Management Attitudes

In many corporations attitudes at the top are the first and most critical issues to be tackled. Dysfunctinal views too often found in the executive suite include these four:

1. "Cost reduction is something for us to preach but it is the active concern of operating managers and accountants." Costs are not driven down by good intentions and fine words. Executives and managers must be prepared to approach cost reduction in a tough, action-oriented state of mind. A good place to start is with the frills and perquisites found in the executive suite itself, many of which add little value to the corporation. Cost management is viewed with considerable cynicism by most employees in corporations in which the top levels of the organization appear insulated from harsh economic reality. To gain credibility, executives must demonstrate by their own actions that the corporation means business and that nothing is sacred.

2. "Capital- or technology-intensive approaches are the most effective and least painful routes to cost reduction." Capital investment and new technologies are two legitimate sources for cost reduction, but by no means are they necessarily the best, nor the least painful. Massive capital spending and investments in high technology may improve labor productivity, but they might also lead to higher, rather than lower, cost levels overall. Also, the implementation of new technologies can be a very painful process, unless it is done well.

3. "Cost management necessarily means work-force reductions." This view leads to one of two associated beliefs: "Hand me the ax," or "Antagonizing the union is more costly than any potential savings, so forget it." Some executives become sold on cost reduction and wield the ax mercilessly. Encouraged by the initial success of cuts and work-force reductions driven from the top, they believe that more of the same is appropriate. Often the second round is less successful, as cuts become harder to identify from the top, and corporate muscle is chopped as well as fat. A third purge driven from the top down often actually increases costs, because more mistakes are made and lower-level managers become increasingly disaffected.

Instead of cutting the work force, restructuring work relationships and arrangements frequently offers significant cost-reducing opportunities through increased productivity. These are areas unions have traditionally considered to be immutable and unchangeable. In some corporations, such as Falconbridge, executives have proceeded with such innovations by dealing directly with the work force and initially bypassing the union. Depending on the situation, enduring a strike or lockout has been the price management has had to pay for proceeding in this manner, but some executives report that the catharsis of such a situation can subsequently lead to improved relationships all round.

In other companies, however, executives have been unwilling to either confront or work with the union and have taken other routes to reduce costs, and so missed opportunities to reduce payroll costs through reorganizing work, cross-skills utilization, and gaining greater employee involvement.

4. "Look after the nickels and dimes and everything else will be OK." Many "cost-conscious" executives and managers are obsessed with "nickel and dime" savings. Cost management is too frequently interpreted as controlling direct expenditures, often on minor items. Cutting out the free office coffee as a symbolic economy measure may appeal to management, but unless the organization is in dire straits, employees are likely to more than offset any savings by wasting time discussing the matter, going elsewhere for coffee, or simply getting angry at perceived executive stinginess.

Executives in the head office of one mining corporation that had been facing tough times for an extended period felt that some employees were leaving early. They decreed that the work day would last an extra half an hour and were surprised to find that instead of improving, productivity and service actually declined. The corporation's external auditors who had formerly praised the dedication of the firm's accounting staff now complained that morale and cooperation were poor. Many employees who had already been working two or three hours unpaid overtime had simply become upset with management's apparent insensitivity and started leaving work exactly on time.

Managers in these organizations measure the savings from these direct expenditure items but frequently ignore the high cost of wasted time and lower productivity that are the inevitable outcome of such policies. In a strategic cost-management activity, such savings are obtained. The difference is that here management provides the environment and opportunity for employees to come up with these cost-saving ideas, of which they subsequently assume ownership.

A variety of other factors also contribute to a less than satisfactory performance in this area.

ROI

One major reason why costs are often not managed strategically is because the wrong cost-reduction projects are selected. This error can come about for several reasons. Evaluation criteria such as ROI may favor projects with fast returns over those that take longer to earn back the investment but which promise to improve the strategic position of the business.

The dominance of ROI as a measure of performance and as a criterion for capital allocation has been a major factor governing Canadian and U.S. managerial behavior with respect to costs. Academics and practitioners alike have pointed out that this approach can be misleading, especially at times when ROI discount factors are high.

Many executives and managers fail to appreciate that ROI evaluates only the return on a specific project or venture; it indicates nothing about the proposal's total impact. Returns may appear small or be hard to determine on such major investments as a new process innovation, the adoption of statistical process control, or employee development and training. As a result they may be forgone in favor of others with more tangible returns. The purchase of new equipment or investment in a new plant may then be less than satisfactory because of the high costs associated with a failure to carry out tasks with less tangible value.

In fact, when a total cost perspective is adopted, corporations may even choose to implement projects with no apparent ROI, but which reduce customer costs (thus increasing value) and which may create additional future business opportunities.

Overly Tight Controls

In many firms, strict adherence to ROI evaluations results in tight-loose controls, as opposed to the loose-tight controls reported by Peters and Waterman to be characteristic of excellent corporations.[8] Tight-loose controls deter managers and supervisors from requesting funds for projects that may be important but for which tangible benefits may be hard to demonstrate, at least initially. Many important cost reductions are missed in this way.

Failing to "Spend to Save"

Another obstacle to effective cost management is the lack of recognition that spending money on soft items is important in generating future savings. Judicious investment in travel to visit other plants is one example of this type of saving. Cutting out travel in tough times sends out the wrong message to employees and deprives the corporation of possible ideas from outside sources such as customers, suppliers, and competitors which could lead to lower costs.

Seed money for exploring new ideas, increased plant maintenance levels, and funding for plant, crew, and departmental meetings out of work time are other examples of soft items that can lead indirectly to cost reductions, yet they are frequently among the first expenditures to be cut.

These misguided approaches are particularly debilitating in organizations in which supervisors and operators believe that large cost savings are possible, but they perceive managers to be concerned more about trivia. Particularly demoralizing are circumstances in which employees feel that the cost savings they have worked hard to achieve are offset by poor top-management decisions or simple waste. Large golden parachutes paid to departing executives who have performed poorly are one example of this type of irritant. Expensive executive trappings, such as chauffeured limousines and exclusive executive dining rooms, are others.

Driving Down the Long-Run Cost Curve

Strategic cost management aims to reduce unit costs continually in real terms over the long run. Driving down the long-run cost curve requires that corporations be proactive in accomplishing three key tasks:

1. Investing wisely in plant, equipment, and new technology
2. Building a shared employee culture in which cost reduction is viewed as an important, challenging, and rewarding activity
3. Being prepared to innovate in the business in ways that dramatically alter the shape of the cost curve

As a result, the curve will not be a smoothly declining line, but, as shown in Figure 2.4, will be interrupted by significant discontinuities as major innovations or investments in new facilities result in one-time gains. In between these discontinuities, progress will tend to be smoother and generally slower as the effects of scale, learning, and incremental innovations dominate. For short periods, the curve may actually turn upward due either to external forces, such as inflation, or deliberate management decisions that result in short-run cost increases.

The long-run cost curve should not be confused with the learning curve notion, popularized by the Boston Consulting Group, which suggests that the learning that takes place as the cumulative volume of production increases can be used to reduce costs. Learning is only one of several major contributors to cost reduction and does not necessarily determine the shape or rate of change of the overall cost curve.

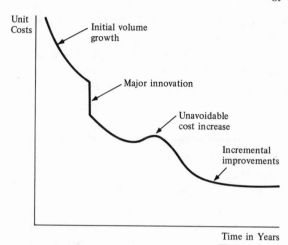

Figure 2.4.   The Long-run Cost Curve

Organizations frequently accrue the wrong type of learning and experi-ence with volume: inflexibility, bureaucracy, and inertia commonly leave large, well-established corporations open to competition from smaller, more innovative competitors who perceive new ways to reduce costs by challenging established business practice. For example, People Express was able to circumvent many years of experience and learning that estab-lished airlines possessed by changing the rules of the game. Apple Incorpo-rated generated a totally new curve in the computer industry when they successfully developed and marketed the personal computer.

Similar effects were noted in a comprehensive study of productivity change in the U.S. automobile industry carried out by William Abernathy.[9] He noted a trade-off between product innovation and unit cost in this industry, a condition which has caused severe problems for U.S. automobile manufacturers. Cost reduction as predicted by the learn-ing curve only occurred when designs were stable, and product innovation had been reduced to incremental or cosmetic changes. Radical product changes caused previous operational cost-reduction advantages to be lost. As a result, Detroit shunned new product designs that might increase manufacturing costs. In the late 1960s and early 1970s, major process innovations that might disrupt the tightly coupled production flow of U.S. producers were similarly ignored.

Unfortunately, as Abernathy goes on to point out, once an innovation is perfected by the major players in an industry, costs are reduced, the technology is standardized, and the innovator loses any competitive advan-tage. Predictably, the U.S. automobile industry went through terrible times in the late 1970s and early 1980s as foreign competitors, which had kept innovating and moving to new, lower cost curves, eroded the market share so essential to the profitability of the U.S. producers.

Thus, although the learning curve can have a significant impact on the total long-run cost curve for a business, it is only one part of a much more complex totality inolving scale, investment, and innovation effects. Strategic approaches that stress these sources of cost reduction contrast sharply with the traditionally reactive lean and mean approach, which emphasizes disinvestment, destruction of the existing employee culture, and, frequently, organizational trauma.

Most organizations need short-term gains, as well as long-term follow-through from cost-reduction activities. Once these short-term actions are completed, however, forward-thinking executives move quickly to put a long-term cost-management strategy in place. To drive down the long-run cost curve, this strategy has to be capable of taking advantage of a variety of sources of cost reduction, as is discussed at greater length in Chapter 3.

What Is Cost-Management Strategy?

One senior executive described his corporation's cost management strategy in the following way: "Our cost management strategy ensures that everyone associated with our corporation understands why we need to be the lowest cost competitor in our business, what we have to do to remain in that position, and how we will do it." Cost-management strategy supports overall corporate and business strategies by providing a consistent, comprehensive, and continuing focus on this critical competitive dimension. This focus is demonstrated in the specific ways corporations go about reducing their costs, together with the resources allocated to the task.

A strategy of this type need not necessarily aim at making the corporation the competitor with the lowest unit cost in its market, but it should ensure that a cost position can be maintained that is consistent with product positioning and a healthy profit margin. Volvo, for example, would be unlikely to strive toward being the lowest-cost automobile producer, but it would target its strategy at ensuring a cost structure that provided high profit margins within the price segments of the markets in which it competes.

Recognition of the need for cost containment through the implementation of an explicit strategy reduces the likelihood of executives and employees losing sight of costs, especially in times of high profits or

Table 2.1.   Characteristics of a Good Cost-Management Strategy

1. Fits with overall corporate and business strategies.
2. Establishes clear long- and short-run goals for cost reduction.
3. Balances human, capital, and technological inputs into cost reduction.
4. Identifies and aims at reducing the important costs, even if they are hard to measure.
5. Recognizes that there are high costs associated with capital when used as a cost-cutting source.
6. Generates a sense of excitement and challenge in participants.
7. Continually reduces costs in real terms.
8. Rewards the people who "make it happen."
9. Recognizes that information is a key resource and communication is essential.
10. Provides a distinct competitive advantage.

capacity expansion, and establishes a mission for a corporation or business through creating a shared set of cost objectives and goals and an understanding of how these will be achieved. The characteristics of an effective cost-management strategy are outlined in Table 2.1.

Formulation of the strategy initially requires top management to get together and work out what it wants from the strategy in both the short and long term. This process generally involves an initial one- or two-day meeting, during which specific cost challenges and areas of concern have to be identified. Once a shared understanding of the nature of the challenge and the characteristics of the organization's cost structure are established, the management team is faced with reaching two crucial decisions:

Determining the objectives and goals of the strategy
Agreeing on the method of implementing the strategy

The strategic art involved in this process is in determining what blend and balance of capital, and human and technological resources are required to achieve the targeted cost improvements. Realistically, it may not be possible to formulate decisions on all these issues at a first meeting, but small task forces can be created to define what is required and report back at a subsequent meeting. The resulting strategy will differ by industry and firm, as the following examples illustrate.

Strategy in an Insurance Business

A Canadian Life Insurance Company reduced its operating expense ratio by 30 percent in two years by focusing on the following costs:

Staffing levels, because employee costs were a high proportion of total costs

Customer service levels, because poor service could generate high opportunity costs in lost goodwill and business

Administration procedures, because improvements in these methods could result in substantial time and labor saving

Effective computer/MIS management, because data base management was a high cost, and poor information access had even higher opportunity costs

Improved computer hardware and software simplified procedures and reduced labor requirements. Employees were formed into teams and encouraged to develop and implement methods improvements. Management communicated progress and results continually. A profit-sharing program was introduced. Lower transaction costs and faster customer response resulting from improved methods and decreased bureaucracy were perceived by the company's management to have made a significant contribution to accelerated growth experienced in the second year of this activity. Planned reductions were made in staffing levels, with attrition, early retirement, and retraining being used to avoid large layoffs.

Strategy in a Consumer-Products Manufacturer

The labor-oriented strategy described above contrasts sharply with that of a major consumer products manufacturer for whom purchased components were extremely significant. In this company's cost-management strategy, the following objectives were emphasized:

Reducing the number of suppliers by 50 percent

Controlling supplier-related costs, unit component cost, quality, and delivery performance, because shortage of components or high defect rates caused costly disruptions to assembly schedules

Ensuring maximum component standardization across product lines

Automating and robotizing repetitive, high-precision operations

Redesigning products to maintain and improve customer acceptance while improving manufacturability

Augmenting product lines to increase volumes and reduce unit overheads

Reducing setup times so that switching products on assembly lines would not be a high-cost activity

Management in this corporation introduced a wide variety of initiatives to implement this production-oriented strategy, which it recognized would have taken years for the engineering and management staff to accomplish alone. Product family teams comprised of marketing employees, managers, engineers, and operators were established to plan improvements in design and manufacturing. Because labor costs were a small proportion of total cost, management felt it could offer a guarantee of job security to facilitate employee involvement in rationalizing and improving assembly operations.

The purchasing department was given the task of cutting-down the supplier base, but responsibility for day-to-day contacts on supplier performance was decentralized to the shop floor. Supervisors and operators were encouraged to visit supplier plants to work out quality and delivery problems. Engineering employees worked with smaller suppliers to help them improve their costs and processes. Management instituted annual supplier conferences at which the company's performance and requirements were communicated.

Implementing the Strategy

Comprehensive cost-management strategies consist of a blend of programs and projects with a variety of time horizons. For corporations in crisis, the time frame is short and decisions are likely to be centralized. Capital-intensive and systems responses, which generally take time to become effective, are unlikely to be stressed in such situations because funds are probably scarce. Staffing levels, overhead expenses, material inputs, and working capital are frequently the targets of short-term strategies to cut costs.

Executives in some firms seek to avoid tough actions in these areas by increasing volumes. This strategy may be the fastest way to bankruptcy, because increased volume levels may result in lower prices and slimmer margins where demand is flat, and more cash, not less, is required to support increased levels of business activity. If John Connelly had taken this approach at Crown Cork and Seal in 1958, the corporation may not have survived.

In organizations seeking to improve an already healthy competitive position, a mix of long- and short-term programs is appropriate. Cost-reduction strategies involving capital, human, and technical approaches can be developed, often cooperatively, with the work force. More-or-less formal procedures and processes can then be implemented to sustain the strategic initiative and to foster a corporate culture receptive to cost management.

Six essential elements of cost-management strategy implementation have to be defined from the outset, as shown in Table 2.2. Additional details on each of these elements, and descriptions of a variety of corporate approaches to them, are provided in Chapters 5 through 10.

As shown in Figure 2.5, formulation of the strategy places cost manage-

Table 2.2. Essential Elements of Strategy Implementation

1. Demonstration and communication of the need for a strategy to all employees and development of mechanisms for continuing periodic communication

2. Changes to either the formal or informal organization structure and hierarchy necessary to ensure effective sponsoring, championing, and implementation of initiatives

3. Provision of information systems that are capable of providing the essential data to employees at all levels in the corporation for managing costs under their control

4. Creation of specific activities to be undertaken as the nucleus of implementation and determining how these will change over time

5. Development of critical education activities that have to be undertaken to allow managers, supervisors, and employees to become effective participants in the strategy

6. Establishment of rewards and recognition that will be made available to employees who play an effective role in cost management

Figure 2.5. Strategic Framework for Cost Management

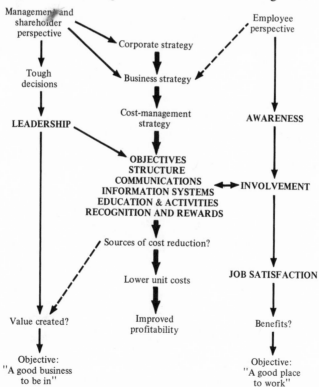

ment in the context of broader corporate and business strategies. The need for executive leadership and involvement at all levels in the organization has been described, and the major implementation levers have been identified. The next challenge is to understand the diverse sources of cost reduction that are available to all organizations and to link them into the strategic framework.

3.

Sources of Cost Reduction

Multiple Sources of Cost Reduction

There are a variety of different sources of cost improvement, and few corporations fully utilize all the options available to them. Although there are many different ways of obtaining cost reductions, the five primary ones are:

1. Investing capital in new plant and equipment.
2. Realizing economies of scale through increases in the volume of activities.
3. Developing or acquiring new product, process, and systems technologies.
4. Applying the benefits of organizational and individual learning from accumulated output and experience.
5. Simplifying the organization, its operations, products, and processes.

Although these sources can be individually identified, in practice they overlap each other, as shown in Figure 3.1, and cost reductions often embody more than one at the same time. For example, new processes can arise as a result of learning derived from accumulated experience,

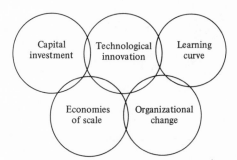

Figure 3.1. Overlapping Sources of
Cost Reduction

and the implementation of new technology is frequently associated with
capital investment.

Each of these five sources of cost reduction has both operational and
strategic aspects. The cumulative benefit of many incremental efficiency
improvements that reduce costs can be totally negated by one major
strategic inconsistency that reduces overall corporate effectiveness. For
example, the total cost impact of many small plant and equipment improvements might be negligible if either overall demand is slack and plants
are running at much less than capacity or if the products being manufactured are not competitive.

In addition to recognizing the potential contribution of each of these
sources, it is extremely important for management to judge at which
point in time, and in what circumstances, they are most appropriate.
For example, volume growth has been responsible for very large cost
reductions in electronic products in recent years, but as markets for
these products mature and become saturated, this source of cost reduction
has decreased in importance. Other sources such as process innovation
have become relatively more important.

Costs and the Product Life Cycle

Products, industries, and corporations can all be considered to move
through life cycles, similar to those for any living organism. The stages
of development encompass birth (or introduction), growth, maturity,
and decline. The nature of cost reduction changes considerably in each
of these stages. This section presents a conceptual framework centered
around these life cycles that can be used to focus on the relevance and
importance of each of the primary cost-reduction sources at different
times.

The life cycle for a typical product broken down into its four major

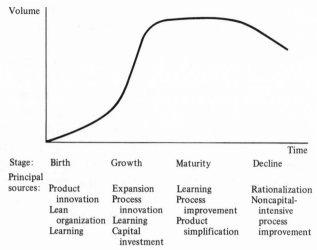

Stage:	Birth	Growth	Maturity	Decline
Principal sources:	Product innovation	Expansion Process	Learning Process	Rationalization Noncapital-
	Lean organization	innovation Learning	improvement Product	intensive process
	Learning	Capital investment	simplification	improvement

Figure 3.2. The Product Life Cycle: Major Sources of Cost Reduction

stages is shown in Figure 3.2. Each stage is characterized by the cost-reduction factors that have a major impact on unit costs during that period in the life cycle. Unless corporations choose deliberately to compete only in the very early stages, such as Hewlett-Packard has attempted to do, they must be prepared to face price competition at some point. This form of competition is unlikely to emerge until relatively late in the life cycle for those products where performance is the major purchase criteria, but it may be present at very early stages for products where price, and hence cost, are important determinants of buyer behavior and demand.

Introduction or Birth

In the introductory stage of the life cycle, unit costs generally do not drive competition, except when a product is developed and conceived as a low-cost substitute for some existing product. At this stage in the life cycle, novelty and innovation are the dominant product characteristics sought by purchasers, who are often willing to pay substantial premiums, for status or other reasons, to be early acquirers of the product. The introductory period for products such as VCRs, microcomputers, and microwave ovens was characterized by such consumer behavior.

Experimentation, obtaining market acceptance, and quality control are usually more important than cost control at this stage in the life cycle, and young, entrepreneurial firms organize around these tasks.

Production is likely to be derived from relatively general-purpose equipment, rather than dedicated production facilities. Learning is at its most powerful in this early period and is usually the major force driving costs down. Cost management is important at this time primarily as a means of reducing product costs in order to gain market entry.

The introduction of new products creates problems for many mature firms which are often organized around products and services that are at a later stage in their life cycle. The behavior, activities, and rewards associated with cost control of mature products may actually reduce the effectiveness of new product performance in this introductory period. Wickham Skinner, one of North America's leading manufacturing strategists, has argued strongly that this problem can be mitigated if plants have missions focused around specific types of products and processes (see pp. 65–66).[1]

Growth

As a new product gains increasing acceptance and new competitors are drawn into the market, high rates of volume growth occur. At this time, cost reductions start to play a larger role in business success. These reductions result mainly from the effects of greater volume and economies of scale working to increase the unit cost divisor. The benefits derived from learning-curve effects also continue to be important in this period, especially if the corporation is organized to capture the maximum value possible.

The growth period can be characterized as the race for volume and market share in an attempt to obtain a dominant product position. Texas Instruments (TI) used a pricing strategy linked to unit cost reductions derived from volume and learning-curve effects to reduce its unit costs faster than its competitors and secure dominant market shares for itself in several electronic products, such as calculators and watches, during the 1970s. By standardizing watch designs and developing a highly integrated and automated production process, TI was able to drive the cost of its digital watch down from $69.95 in its year of introduction to $9.95 three years later.[2]

The key capabilities required in meeting this challenge are an ability to design rapidly a product that can be manufactured easily on a high-volume, production-line basis and shipped through a broad distribution system. Process innovations, capital investment in high volume, and automated production facilities are the main driving forces behind cost reductions during this period.

When the rate of growth slows, however, as the market matures and becomes saturated, producers with dominant products and large market shares tend to be the survivors of the inevitable shakeout if these advantages translate into low unit costs. Competitors with smaller shares and higher unit costs, often still attempting to compete on product performance and features, tend to be driven from the business or into small, specialized niches.

Maturity and Decline

With the maturing of the market, the nature of the cost-management challenge also changes. The volume effects that drove unit costs down as output increased are no longer as powerful. From this point on, the divisor is likely to be a significant contributor to declining costs only when significant volume gains can be made by taking market shares from competitors. Gains must generally be derived from other sources.

In product maturity and decline, corporations have to focus on cost as their principal competitive thrust, and those companies with clearly defined cost-reduction strategies are likely to emerge as the long-run survivors. These strategies promote industry rationalization as stronger corporations seek to gain the maximum advantage from whatever volume gains are possible through acquisitions of weak competitors. Product lines can also be rationalized and simplified to eliminate marginal offerings. In addition, these strategies should create a corporate climate in which product costs can continue to be driven down in real terms through broad employee involvement and learning-curve effects.

As the product life cycle shifts from maturity to decline, corporations must become more cautious about additional investments. Decline is a period in which cash should be generated from aging products and processes and re-invested in those in the introduction or growth phases. Cost management in this period should focus on simplification, learning, and technical improvements requiring minimal cash to implement.

Product Life-Cycle Effects in Microcomputers

The effect of these changes on the nature of cost reduction, over time, is to create opportunities for different firms to dominate industries at different points in the product life cycle. For example, a multitude of small firms such as Osborne, Apple, and Commodore dominated the microcomputer business in its early years. Large, established computer manufacturers, including IBM and Burroughs, ignored this emerging market in its infancy.

As the market grew, however, a smaller number of large firms such as IBM, Hewlett Packard, and the now larger Apple and Commodore emerged as dominant volume producers. Apple maintained its position only after major organizational shakeups that caused the departure of its founders and the establishment of a new management regime. These corporations were able to track the growth curve by pushing increasing volumes of product into existing distribution systems. Smaller firms either left the industry or were limited to specialized niches. Even some larger companies such as TI were forced to abandon the business as they failed to achieve the volumes and margins necessary for survival.

A maturing microcomputer market has created opportunities for new entrants. Although established microcomputer producers such as Apple and IBM are much further down the industry experience curve, new entrants such as Toshiba and Zenith are competing on strengths and experience that have brought them success in related, mature electronic consumer markets, such as televisions and VCRs. These are lean firms with minimal overheads and low-cost manufacturing capabilities compared to their established competitors. When combined with product augmentation and feature enhancement, the resulting strategy has undercut the prices and eroded the market position of well-established competitors.

The Corporate Life Cycle

Corporations can be thought to move through life cycles much as products do, as shown in Figure 3.3. A few, such as the 3M Corporation and Hewlett Packard, seem to have found the secret to eternal youth and consistent profitability by keeping their products and the corporation relatively innovative and flexible. Unlike these two corporations, however, most corporations lose their flexibility and innovativeness as they grow in size and complexity. They become increasingly bureaucratic as a result, leading in turn to inertia and a lack of responsiveness.

Major corporations are initially founded around the idea of an innovation. Their whole reason for being centers around this fact, and their strategies and structures reflect the struggle for market acceptance and growth. Frequently, small new companies such as People Express can challenge larger, established corporations by changing the terms of competition and, on occasion, being lower cost, especially in industries such as airlines where the overhead costs of established competitors are high.

Lean, flexible structures coupled with innovative ways of structuring operations and work methods can give small, new non-union firms a significant cost advantage over larger, unionized corporations. Magna Corporation, a young Canadian enterprise, has grown to be one of the largest automotive parts suppliers in North America in the last ten years by employing such a strategy. A cornerstone of its growth strategy has

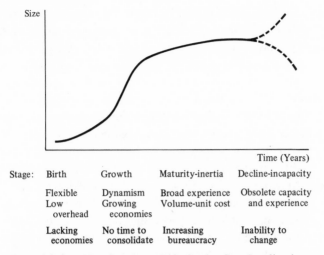

Stage:	Birth	Growth	Maturity-inertia	Decline-incapacity
	Flexible Low overhead	Dynamism Growing economies	Broad experience Volume-unit cost	Obsolete capacity and experience
	Lacking economies	No time to consolidate	Increasing bureaucracy	Inability to change

Figure 3.3. The Corporate Life Cycle: Cost Implications

been to build highly automated plants employing no more than 100 people per shift. Employees tend to be drawn from first-generation immigrant labor, among whom the work ethic remains strong. Rates of pay are lower than in many unionized plants, but profit sharing provides a considerable incentive. In 1985, automobiles manufactured in North America contained on average $100.00 (Cdn) worth of components manufactured by this relatively new corporation, up from only $20.00 (Cdn) five years earlier.

As corporations like Magna grow, the trappings of success and increased needs for coordination have tended in the past to lead to increased levels of management and supervision, more formal organization structures and job descriptions, and consequently, larger overheads. These structural changes are accompanied by dependence on and commitment to an existing range of products and services. The focus of organizational activities tends to switch from a predominant concern with innovation to maintenance of ongoing activities.

These changes are often accompanied by increased overheads and mounting inertia in the corporate ability to respond to change. Unless volume growth can compensate for these cost increases, margins shrink, leaving the corporation with fewer resources available to invest in innovation and new products. A vicious circle then develops in which the firm is forced to rely increasingly on cost competition as it fails to update and renew its product lines.

If cost management is undertaken in traditional ways by adding new cadres of staff to analyze, more supervisors to police, more capital investment to reduce labor needs, and more tightly integrated manufacturing and service systems, the ability of the corporation to respond to change is increasingly impaired, and ultimately a total incapacity to innovate may develop.

The ultimate result of these organizational changes is decline. The corporation becomes totally unable to respond to changing market demands and challenges posed by new competitors. Often, the organization becomes highly politicized as different management groups struggle with each other for control. Cost reduction is accorded a low place on the strategic agenda. Earnings may decline sharply in this period, leaving the corporation vulnerable to acquisition. At this time, the most effective medicine is the appointment of a new chief executive officer from outside with a mandate to restructure the organization and turn the business around.

An Industrial Renaissance?

The wave of business rationalizations and work force reductions that have engulfed many larger U.S. corporations in recent years are a visible attempt to break out of this cycle. Corporations are attempting to reverse several decades of such mismanagement through drastic surgery and in the short-term are meeting with considerable success. Layers of management and supervision are being eliminated, staff groups that increase overheads are being trimmed, product lines are being renewed, and manufacturing and service operations are undergoing dramatic changes.

The future management challenge, then, is both to implement a strategy encompassing the entire range of cost-reduction mechanisms available and to ensure that these measures are appropriate for the different stages of product and corporate life cycles. If such responses are successful, we may yet see an industrial renaissance in Canada and the United States.

Capital-Intensive Approaches

An approach to cost reduction that is currently enjoying considerable popularity with Canadian and U.S. executives is a capital-intensive solution intended to create the "factory of the future."[3] Many old, obsolete facilities are being closed and replaced with modern plants and technologies that are intended to be flexible and low cost, and which require lower inventories.

These new facilities typically have automated, robotic production equipment and require a minimum of labor input. Computer-integrated manufacturing, materials requirement planning systems, and just-in-time scheduling systems are characteristic of the information technology support systems that are implemented in conjunction with such developments.

These capital-intensive approaches can be major contributors to cost reduction, but they need to be implemented judiciously. If capital is available, a variety of investments can be made to improve manufacturing's competitive position, as shown in Figure 3.4.

Such capital-intensive cost-reduction strategies need absolutely the right conditions to be truly successful. These include sufficient financial resources to fund the program and adequate professional and technical capabilities both to maintain the facilities and support systems once they are up and running and to handle the enormous amounts of data necessary

Figure 3.4. Computer-integrated Manufacturing System

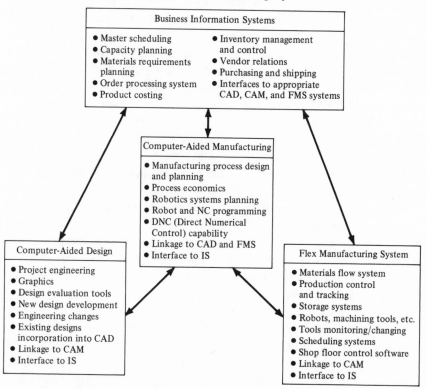

SOURCE: Leland Blank, ''Supporting Engineering Management,'' *Journal of Cost Management for the Manufacturing Industry,* Vol. 1, No. 1, Spring, 1987, p. 59. Copyright © 1986 Warren, Gorham and Lamont, Inc., 210 South St., Boston, MA 02111. All rights reserved.

for operations. A green-field location with a nonunion work force is also desirable.

The risks inherent in this strategy are large. Technology changes can render these investments obsolete quite rapidly, particularly in markets where the product life cycle is short. Either a fast capital recovery time is required or a guaranteed period of market and product longevity is necessary for a good return. Highly integrated systems make changes hard to implement and leave the operation vulnerable to product innovations from competitors with more flexible facilities.

Poor labor relations have an even higher cost in these plants than in more traditional operations, because strikes can result in high capital carrying charges. Employees, aware of this fact, may demand high wage settlements as the price for labor peace, resulting in higher-than-anticipated payroll costs.

This capital-intensive route was adopted by General Motors (GM) when in the early 1980s it embarked on the most massive and ambitious capital reinvestment program undertaken in the automotive industry in order to become competitive with the Japanese. The core concept was a brand-new division, the Saturn, which was to manufacture a totally new product line in automated plants with a nonunion work force.

GM also undertook large investments in new plants and new manufacturing equipment and in acquiring corporations that could provide it with expertise in needed new technologies, such as robotics, electronics, and artificial intelligence. The results seem to indicate that GM is not achieving its objectives with this program. The Saturn project has proved to be a disappointment, and the capital base of the corporation has expanded considerably without a corresponding increase in revenues and profits.[4]

This approach can result in a corporation being caught in a capital or cash trap and becoming what is colloquially known as a cash hog. Seeking cost reductions through capital investment requires that increasing returns be generated from the growing capital base. ROI calculations made on specific projects may show good yields but fail to reflect the broader business trends that push down returns across the business.

Thus, for example, new investments in modern smelters in the mining industry have not paid off in recent years, because low metal prices could not provide the margins necessary to earn a reasonable return on these investments. In fact, old, depreciated facilities have been able to outcompete modern plants in this business for the past few years, and some new plants have shut down while older operations remain open.

Very few corporations can rely solely on this capital-intensive route

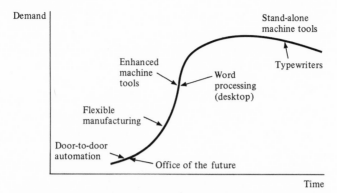

Figure 3.5. Stage of Life Cycle for Various Automated Operating Technologies

to achieve long-run cost reductions. Many smaller corporations simply do not have either the financial or human resources to implement the approach. Even if they could afford the capital costs involved, they probably could not finance the subsequent costs of systems maintenance and professional and technical services needed to support this investment.

As can be seen in Figure 3.5, some of these approaches are still early in their life cycles, and the risks of adoption are high. Nevertheless, corporations cannot afford to miss out on them in the long run. Firms are probably wiser to make educational investments in these capital-intensive new technologies than to gamble on a total commitment to advanced systems still in the developmental stage.

Partial solutions, implemented as part of a broader cost-management strategy, can be more satisfactory for firms with limited resources. Creating ''islands of automation'' with technologies such as enhanced machine tools and desktop work stations for low-risk applications in existing operations is likely to be a cost-effective approach in most businesses.

Exploiting Economies of Scale (and Avoiding Diseconomies)

Economies of scale have been around for a long time. When the gross national product (GNP) was growing at a fast rate and demand for most kinds of products was increasing, the easy way to reduce unit costs was to expand capacity. Fixed and overhead costs could then be allocated over a greater volume of production, and unless prices fell (which was unlikely in an expanding market), margins increased, and so did profits.

Potential economies of scale can be found in almost all aspects of corporate activity, including production, marketing, distribution and

R & D. They are also available to corporations in the form of discounts offered by suppliers to customers who purchase in large quantities and on similar types of transactions where volume dealing can result in price advantages.

Two principal types of economies of scale have been identified. Static economies are those that are derived from absolute size advantages. Dynamic economies are those derived from cumulative volume due to learning and experience.[5] These are discussed at greater length later in this chapter.

Although the concept of economies of scale has not lost its general validity, declining or negative growth rates in many mature markets mean that in most industries economies now have to be pursued much more judiciously than previously. Michael Porter, the author of *Competitive Advantage,* suggests that only those economies of scale that if maximized can provide advantages over the competition should be pursued.[6]

For example, it is unlikely to be in the best interests of a corporation in a mature industry with stagnant demand to decide to embark on a strategy of exploiting economies of scale by massive investments in large new plants unless new technology embodied in these plants can generate a new performance curve with much lower cost potential than that presently existing, allowing old plants to be closed. All that is likely to result is overcapacity and price wars, which occur from time to time in commodity industries such as basic chemicals and pulp and paper.

On the other hand, it is appropriate for a corporation in a new or emerging market to build capacity ahead of demand in an effort to preempt competitors by driving unit costs down rapidly through scale effects. The Japanese have exploited this strategy to great advantage in consumer electronic products such as VCRs and microwave ovens.

In the absence of sufficient demand growth to justify investment in large new facilities, many corporations seek to obtain economies by pursuing incremental plant expansions. These are particularly attractive when they can be obtained with only minimal capital investment. For example, one mining company was able to decrease its unit costs by 10 percent simply because its employees were able to eliminate a major operating bottleneck in the capacity of the system for transporting ore from underground. The alternative would have been an expensive investment in new facilities.

In many cases, however, incremental expansion is impossible without associated capital investment. On a marginal basis, the potential financial returns from such investments can appear extremely attractive, particularly in businesses with a high proportion of fixed costs. Even in slowly growing markets, the cost benefits of this strategy (often referred to euphemistically as de-bottlenecking) can be excellent.

In static or declining markets, however, the results can be far from satisfactory. Additional capacity being brought on stream can depress prices and make already slim margins vanish, especially if a number of industry players adopt this approach at the same time. In such situations, the incremental revenues derived from expansion may not be sufficient to offset the margin decline experienced across the firm's total production.

Returns from incremental expansions designed to obtain economies of scale are often less than anticipated for other reasons. Executives in industries in which this practice is prevalent speak of second-order effects resulting in unanticipated costs associated with increased scale that were not included in initial projections. These may include additional mainte-nance charges, because plants that have been continually de-bottlenecked can become high maintenance cost operations. Other unexpected costs are often incurred upstream or downstream from the expansion if feasibil-ity studies have failed to anticipate the total system effects of the increase in volume.

In the appropriate situation, seeking additional economies of scale can be an important element in cost reduction. As implied, however, they are not a universal panacea. There are diseconomies associated with scale, such as increasing bureaucracy and complexity, that can actually result in higher costs.

Diseconomies of bureaucracy result from an overly hierarchical and procedure-bound structure which large organizations often embody. Ex-cessive layers of management and staff can slow down decision making, lead to a loss in accountability, and result in a decline in the rate of innovation. Large staff groups are established to handle administrative procedures and create policies to guide routine decision making. Corporate bureaucracy can result in a significant decline in management effectiveness and lower profits, especially if competitors are more flexible and respon-sive to changes in technology and the market.

As the number of products and processes in a corporation increases, so does complexity, and there is a point at which the costs of integration and organization start to outweigh the advantages of scale. In these circumstances, coordinating roles and functions proliferate. Matrix organi-zation structures have been strongly advocated as solutions to this problem, but the results have been disappointing. Unless management skills of an extremely high order are available in this situation, high opportunity costs can be incurred from the confusion of roles, poor decision making, and most important, loss of focus.

Benefits from increasing size are further offset by opportunity costs associated with adverse human reactions. In manufacturing there is evidence that alienation, grievances, and other labor problems are greater in larger plants. In smaller plants, worker productivity and involvement in cost-reduction activities arising from the more personal culture can offset the simple scale advantage of much larger operations. Similarly, service operations that stress scale at the expense of personal customer service often incur high opportunity costs compared to smaller operations where direct costs may be higher, but where a good reputation increases customer traffic and often enables higher premiums to be charged.

Economies of scale in many plants and service operations are also limited by distribution costs and market size. For example, the location and size of cement plants is limited more by market size and the economic trucking radius around the plant than by physical constraints. The scale of many service operations, such as fast-food outlets and hotels, is limited by the size of the available consumer market. Multioperation service chains and franchising corporations usually have a range of operating capacities and designs tailored for different market sizes.

Although economies of scale can still be powerful sources of cost reduction, other factors can offset their advantages. Capacity expansions that are not fully utilized usually increase costs, rather than decrease them. Beyond a certain point, often much lower than managers realize, intangible diseconomies of scale set in that greatly reduce, or even totally offset, the physical benefits of scale.

Technological Innovation

Technological innovations can make significant contributions to a corporation's cost-reduction activities. Although some involve significant capital investment and must be viewed with the cautions presented earlier, technological innovations need not be capital intensive. These innovations can arise from multiple sources, and few corporations effectively organize to realize fully the cost benefits that can be derived from product, process, and material changes.

The overall framework for determining how technological innovation contributes to cost reduction is presented in Figure 3.6. Curve T-1 represents current technology embodied in existing plants and equipment. The lowest cost producers are those who can implement incremental process improvements that enable them to operate continually at the

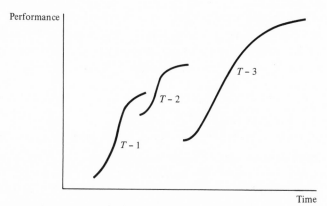

Figure 3.6. Technology Performance Curves: Cost
Management Implications

crest of the curve and keep the level of the peak slowly rising. The
best sources of these improvements come from employees and others
who have mastered the process and can innovate successfully.

Curve *T*-2 represents significant advances based on existing technology
that can only be embodied when strategic decisions are taken to build
new plants or invest in major retrofits involving considerable capital
outlay. These opportunities are only available to corporations that can
afford to reinvest in such facilities: many corporations cannot. The innovations that form the basis for this type of advance are likely to be created
by in-house process development groups, specialized consulting firms
and suppliers, or possibly competitors. Existing work forces and plant
engineering groups will be able to advise on incremental improvements
to this new technology during the design and startup phase, but they
are unlikely to be the source of such significant improvements.

A radical technology advance, often based on a totally new science,
forms the basis for curve *T*-3. This technology has the potential to render
obsolete all previously implemented technology when it is fully operational. Being based on a different science, a radical advance may arise
outside the existing industry and form the basis for future significant
competitive shifts. Very few firms in an industry are likely to be on
the leading edge of such technologies, and companies must base their
strategies for survival on being rapid adopters when the point in time
arrives that the new technology can be commercially applied.

The 3M Corporation provides an example of how these curves can
be reflected in the structure and strategy of the corporate technology
organization. At 3M, technological development is distributed among

three levels of research organizations. In the divisions, researchers develop products for current markets and modify existing technologies (T-1). Sector-level laboratories, which serve groups of related businesses, operate as scientific research departments with a focus on products and processes three to five years in the future (T-2). A corporate research center conducts primary research in leading-edge technologies such as new materials and biotechnology (T-3).

All three types of technology change described by this framework can make significant contributions to cost reduction. Corporations with operations that are extremely high on the T-1 curve can continue to compete successfully for considerable periods against firms that are lower down on more advanced T-2 and T-3 curves. For example, integrated steel companies with very efficient open-hearth furnaces have been able to compete against the potentially more cost-effective basic oxygen furnaces for many years. However, as more of the total capacity shifts to T-2 or T-3 and operations move toward the peak of these curves, the viability of the older technology becomes increasingly tenuous.

Executives are faced with tough choices in deciding what resources to devote to each of these types of cost-reducing innovations. Many corporations simply cannot afford the cost of exploring T-3 type technologies which may not be commercialized for decades. Corporations are turning increasingly to universities for this type of research. The decision to maintain central process development and engineering groups is of greater immediacy, especially if new plants or expansions are contemplated. The risks are that these groups will become substitutes or extensions for in-plant capabilities and will lose sight of their longer-run mission or that they will lose touch with existing technology completely and focus on the T-3 types of technology.

Radical Innovations

Radical product and process improvements can offer the potential for substantial cost reductions, but they can also be threatening to companies and employees. By its nature, radical innovation destroys and makes obsolete existing processes and skills. In effect, a radical innovation creates a new experience curve for a given technology, which can more than offset the accrued learning from years of experience acquired by established producers. In the extreme, this can lead to plant closures and mass layoffs in the work force.

Consequently, firms that are early adopters of radical new technologies often tend to be either new entrants to an industry or smaller firms with little to lose. Electronic watches were first manufactured by companies new to that industry. Traditional manufacturers such as the Swiss did not adopt this new technology early on and, as a result, endured a significant period of turmoil and loss of market share until they finally found a new niche in the marketplace.

Radical innovations occur relatively infrequently, and as noted, often necessitate considerable capital investment and corporate restructuring to accommodate them. In between these events, however, corporations have to ensure that a continuing stream of incremental investments are implemented to keep real unit costs declining. These innovations typically arise from quite different sources than radical innovations. In particular, users and customers are sources of product innovation, and operating employees can be the dominant resource for process innovation.

Incremental Innovations

For many corporations, the most immediate challenge is how to maintain a stream of incremental technological innovations that can keep an existing plant or operation at or near the top of the T-1 curve. Incremental product development and redesign contribute significantly to cost reduction and should be an important element in any cost-reduction strategy. For example, aluminum can producers have taken beer can markets away from steel and have protected themselves from substitution by plastics by reducing the thickness of can walls through a series of relatively small technological improvements.

The rapid pace of change in many technologies, such as computers, robotics, advanced materials, and materials handling, has made it hard for firms to keep up with innovations in their own industries, let alone those taking place elsewhere. Most corporations could significantly improve their own cost competitiveness simply by implementing some of these readily available technologies in their own operations. Unfortunately, few firms are organized in ways that allow this task to be accomplished easily.

The first step in exploiting these general advances in technical knowledge is organizing to take advantage of the extensive technical network of customers, suppliers, competitors, industry associations, consultants, and universities that any company has access to. Some corporations, including General Motors and General Electric, are actually acquiring firms such as EDS and RCA to bring these new technologies in-house. Many other firms are entering into joint ventures. In most cases, however, cost-reducing technologies can be bought off the shelf once their potential value is appreciated.

Exploiting the Learning Curve

The development of the learning-curve concept as a strategic and operational management tool has enabled the quantification of repetitive human activities. As people become more skilled in doing tasks, they naturally become more adept and faster. Corporations have for a long time taken advantage of this principal to speed up assembly lines in manufacturing plants, often to the chagrin of the work force. More recently, telephone companies and fast-food operations have applied the notion to the service sector.

In addition to working faster, employees generally learn to do jobs much more intelligently as their learning increases. They obtain new insights into the process, which are often not evident to managers and engineers who lack an intimate knowledge of the task. Canadian and U.S. corporations have largely failed to take advantage of this potential source of cost reduction, either because they fail to motivate the work force to bring forward new ideas or because some managers simply cannot bring themselves to believe that hourly paid workers can have significant cost-reducing ideas. By exploiting employee learning, costs can be reduced significantly, often with very low capital investment.

Learning-curve effects can contribute to cost reduction in a variety of ways. The basic notion behind this concept is that operating or production costs can be made to fall (they will not decline without management effort) in some mathematical relationship to cumulative volume. The principal factors that determine this relationship are:

1. Dynamic economies of scale from increased output
2. Product and process improvements based on knowledge derived from accumulated output
3. Improvement in external technical knowledge applied to the process

Studies have shown that, depending on the nature of the industry and the process, production costs can be made to decline by between 10 and 30 percent with each cumulative doubling of output.[7] Steeper declines will be experienced in those applications where more learning can be expected. The theory of the learning curve will not be discussed at great length here, but a variety of writings on the subject are available to readers who wish more information on the management implications of this effect.[8]

Failure to obtain the maximum benefits from this effect can clearly put a firm at a disadvantage compared to its competitors. However, the implication that the corporation with the highest cumulative volume of output in an industry will be the lowest cost producer is not necessarily valid. If it were, General Motors would be by far the world's lowest-cost car producer and USX the lowest-cost steel producer. In fact, both are relatively high-cost producers, because although they hold overall the largest market shares in their respective industries, they are leaders in very few specific market segments, which is where the learning curve is directly applicable.

Corporations need to be clear which characteristics of the learning curve are most relevant to their own strategy and seek to exploit them. For example, in industries where a high proportion of the costs are bought in, either in the form of components, services, or supplies, corporations need to establish good working relationships with suppliers and customers to exploit the learning occurring in their organizations. The automotive industry is now realizing that close relationships with sole-source suppliers can produce more significant cost benefits than their traditional arms-length, tough bargaining relationships with multiple suppliers.

Improvements from cumulative output are principally the results of employee "learning by doing." Canadian and U.S. corporations have been quite adept at utilizing techniques such as value analysis, a formal, engineering-based approach, to capturing some of these benefits. However, compared to Japanese firms such as Toyota, they have been extremely poor at developing cost-management strategies that facilitate learning-based cost reductions from the work force in general.

Texas Instruments did use the concept successfully to develop pricing strategies that gave it high shares in emerging electronic markets during the 1970s, but that notion did not carry the company successfully into the 1980s in the microcomputer market. Toyota, on the other hand, amassed $240 million in savings during 1984 from 900,00 ideas accruing from the experience of its 45,000 employees.

The future challenge is to provide a work environment in which employees feel motivated to pass on their learning in the form of tangible ideas and actions aimed at reducing costs. How to obtain these benefits is discussed at length in Chapters 7 and 8.

Simplification

Simplification is a powerful cost-reduction technique that can be applied to organizations, operations, products, and processes. High costs are often associated with complexity. In the case of organizations, convoluted structures and hierarchies can give rise to excessive administration, coordination, and paperwork costs. In operations, product and process complexity can lead to compromises on the key success variables. Failure to rationalize product families and obtain the maximum benefit of component standardization results in the cost of materials, inventories, and engineering being higher than necessary.

Organizational Simplification

The major victims, in percentage terms, of the current Canadian and U.S. preoccupation with down-sizing has not been blue collar workers, as has been the case in the past, but white collar, salaried employees. Middle-management ranks have been decimated in many corporations. Ford Motor Co. plans to cut its salaried work force by 20 percent, about 10,000 people, by 1990, and Union Carbide Corporation released 4,000 white collar workers in 1985 alone. Estimates suggest that up to half a million management jobs were eliminated in Fortune's list of the top 100 industrial corporations between 1980 and 1985: an average of 5,000 per corporation.[9]

These changes reflect a significant shift in the attitudes of top management toward corporate organization. Put simply, there is a growing awareness that much of the middle management and staff hierarchies have added little value to corporations in recent years. Instead, their salary and benefits have loaded up operations with high overhead costs which have hampered competitiveness. In addition, the paper chase that was created by these employees as they sought to justify their existence has created a significant impediment to innovation and organizational change.

Although this awareness is relatively recent, some corporations realized many years ago that bureaucracy fails to add value. For example, in 1956, the British retailing giant Marks and Spencer undertook a dramatic overhaul of its management procedures in an exercise known as Operation Simplification. Out of a total work force of 32,000, 10,000 jobs were eliminated, and profits moved up sharply.

More important than the direct savings, perhaps, are the indirect savings resulting from freeing up the organization from administrative excess. Decisions are often made faster. Executives are able to identify and deal with problems and concerns occurring at lower levels and in operations from which they were formerly insulated. By the same token, managers and supervisors can innovate and try new ideas without having to seek approval from endless committees and staff groups.

Several possible negative side effects, however, are associated with work-force reductions. An early study by Likert and Seashore identified that although short-term productivity gains and cost reductions were usually obtained from such actions, morale and productivity both suffered in the long run.[10] In lean operations there is also the likelihood of significant employee burnout as people struggle to cope with greater work loads. This problem is especially acute in situations where, even after extended periods of being lean and mean, there are few tangible signs of progress.[11] These negative effects can be mitigated by ensuring that any unnecessary activities are eliminated and by continuing communication with employees about the corporation and its competitive situation.

In recent years, a variety of organizational innovations such as quality circles, job enrichment, group technology, and quality of work life programs have been popular with Canadian and U.S. managers. Frequently, however, these innovations have not endured for reasons such as union resistance, management's unwillingness to share power, poor implementation, and supervisory resistance.

Another potential cause of failure which seems not to have gained wide consideration is that too often the programs have been seen as ends in themselves, particularly in organizations suffering from ''programitis.'' Organizational innovation has obtained a bad name in many corporations because of management's proclivity to leap from fad to fad at regular intervals, and never stick with an initiative long enough to make it work.

For example, many corporate executives have become disillusioned with the excellence notion because it does not seem to motivate their employees, who appear to be unwilling or unable to shake off the alligators and soar with the eagles. The sad fact is that in most corporations, survival, rather than excellence, is the bottom line for most employees.

Operational Simplification

Many corporations have been able to obtain a significant cost advantage over the competition by simplifying their operations, and at the same time focusing on a limited product range. This approach is at the core of McDonalds' strategy which revolutionized the fast-food business. A simple product line and process facilitate fast delivery, reduce waste (a significant cost in the restaurant business), and enable standardized operating procedures to be developed that minimize required skill levels.

Wickham Skinner has observed that conventional plants produce many products for a variety of customers in many markets. He has argued consistently that focused operations outperform those that have a broad array of processes and outputs. Skinner maintains that focused operations are able to tailor their equipment, systems, and work force to perform a specific manufacturing task for a limited set of customers and obtain lower direct and overhead costs than those in conventional, general-purpose plants.[12]

The reason for the proliferation of plants producing many products is not difficult to establish. Conventional accounting wisdom holds that unit costs can be lowered by increasing volume, and so managers seek to maximize capacity utilization by introducing new products. There is no problem if these products have the same characteristics and requirements as those for which the plant was originally designed. Too often, however, there are differences that require process changes, different quality levels, and different work-force skills. As more and more of these products are added, operating complexity increases, more sophisticated systems are required, and compromises are made on product quality and performance as employees lose track of the specific requirements of different customers and markets. Inevitably, costs rise and performance is reduced.

A major contribution to cost reduction can be made by heeding Skinner's advice and pursuing ways to simplify and focus operations. Executives need to examine operations with a view to ensuring that the hidden costs of multiple and possibly conflicting missions for these facilities do not outweigh the value created. In some cases, simply separating the various process streams and providing each operating crew with a focused mission can be sufficient, as illustrated by one of Skinner's articles (co-authored with Dean M. Ruwe). In this case, an ailing "rust-belt" plant was revitalized in part by building a concrete wall down the middle and creating two focused operations.[13] In other cases it may be necessary to prune some marginal products and operations.

Product Simplification

A third way in which simplification can be used in cost management is when it is applied to products. Simpler and cheaper products have a number of advantages for consumers, as well as producers. If simplification results in significant cost reductions, part of these can be passed on to consumers, which may lead to increased demand and sales, more than offsetting the price impact. Equally importantly, simpler products often reduce user costs, such as those of training and maintenance, and this benefit can be made into an important marketing advantage.

Product simplification has a variety of dimensions and can be undertaken in several different ways. A number of specific product simplification techniques have been developed and are discussed in Chapter 8, including value analysis and reverse engineering.

In its basic form, product simplification involves a search for ways to enable the product to perform the same function, but with fewer parts and less process time. For example, re-engineering the standard telephone reduced the number of components by over half and the unit cost by a similar amount for Canada's Northern Telecom Limited.

Substitution can also make an important contribution to simplification. In recent years, plastics have replaced metals such as steel and aluminum in a variety of products, including automobile bodies and beverage cans. Substituting complex machined shapes with castings can reduce manufacturing costs in many products.

Simplification through standardization has made significant strides since the introduction of computer-aided design (CAD). With this powerful computer tool now available to help in the design and modification of products, it is far easier for engineers to use standard components and materials across product families. Some manufacturing corporations have reduced the number of components and subassemblies by as much as 80 percent through increased use of standardization, dramatically lowering the costs of inventory, obsolescence, and lost production time.

An Integrative Framework

As shown in Figure 3.7, cost-management strategy has to be linked directly to corporate and business strategies for it to be fully effective. The five contributing elements of capital investment, economies of scale, technology, learning, and simplification outlined earlier in this chapter must be carefully balanced within the unique competitive position of each business or corporation, its strategy, and specific cost structure.

Executives and shareholders are looking for a good business to be in. This objective can be met if low unit costs result in improved profitability and investment opportunities. As was discussed previously, being the low-cost producer, even in declining or mature industries, can result in strategic advantages that lead to investment opportunities.

Employees are generally looking for a reasonable degree of employment security, which is usually to be found in firms with sound profit positions. Even in firms making substantial labor productivity gains, growth derived from being a low-cost producer can provide new employment opportunities for workers displaced from vanishing jobs. Corporations must be prepared to retrain displaced workers, though, and employees must be willing to accept employment security rather than job tenure for this approach to be truly successful. If work-force reductions are unavoidable, these can be handled in a variety of ways, such as early retirement and attrition, to minimize or even obviate the need for layoffs.

Involvement in cost reduction can be an important way of providing employees with job satisfaction in addition to a feeling that they are

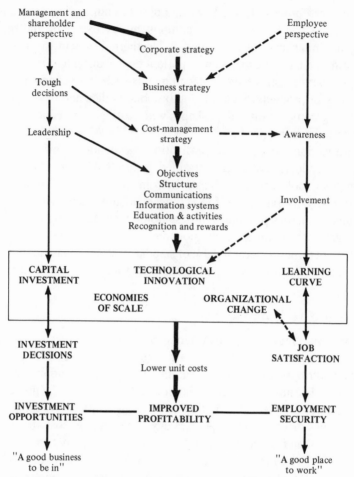

Figure 3.7. Strategic Framework for Cost Management

contributing to their own employment security. For this approach to work, however, a variety of actions are required from managers to make employees aware of the need for cost reduction and to involve them in specific activities that support the overall strategic thrust being adopted.

Without doubt, executives and managers who are effective at cost reduction need to be mentally tough, but this need not preclude working with employees to achieve the desired results. An outstanding example of this situation, which illustrates how an effective cost-management strategy can contribute to increasing corporate profitability and sustaining a competitive position, is provided by the current practices of the furniture manufacturing firm of Herman Miller Inc.

Herman Miller: A Cost-Conscious Producer of Prestige Products[14]

Herman Miller has for many years been one of North America's leading office furniture manufacturers. Several of its classic furniture designs are exhibited in the Museum of Modern Art in New York City. Each year the corporation devotes about 3 percent of its revenues to R & D, about twice the furniture industry's average. The company has practiced participative management for over 36 years, largely because of the religious beliefs of its controlling family owners, the De Pree family. They have used ideas borrowed from the Scanlon Plan, a gain-sharing program that rewards employees for cost savings.

In the fiscal year ending May 31, 1986, profits fell 7.6 percent to $37.8 million on sales of $531.6 million. This was the first decline in profitability in 16 years and followed a decade in which Miller's return to its shareholders had grown at an annual compounded rate of 48 percent. Initially, in response to this decline, some supervisors and managers tried to depart from the company's traditional participative style and be more authoritarian. This change is a typical response in many firms during hard times. In Miller, however, the participative approach was maintained as a key element in the corporation's drive to cut costs in its efforts to improve profitability.

Miller's overall strategy for profit improvement emphasized the various different sources of cost reduction identified earlier in this chapter. Incremental volume increases were sought by expanding markets in banking and insurance, industries in which Miller had not traditionally been strong. As a result, in a tough year, sales increased by 8.1 percent. Capital investments were made in cost-reducing new technologies, such as robotics and improved processes. Employee know-how and learning also contributed significantly to reduced costs.

As part of the corporation's overall strategy, monthly and yearly profit and cost targets were established. These were supported by all of its 3,400 employees, organized in a network of work teams, caucuses, and councils, which also served as a central part of the corporation's communication network. The aim of this structure was to enlist every employee in the effort to reduce costs, improve customer service, and ensure that each employee's views were heard.

Examples of the activities undertaken by the company's employees in their efforts to reduce costs included:

Instituting an improved sales-forecasting system developed by three production control employees with the potential to save several hundred thousand dollars annually because of reduced inventories.

Eliminating finishes to the unseen back of wooden work surfaces.
Cutting delivery times for the company's new Ethospace office system line from 22 weeks to 8 weeks.

Altogether, the corporation's employees suggested $12 million in cost reductions in a one-year period. Indirectly, employees helped minimize costs by keeping intangible employee costs extremely low. For example, absenteeism averaged 1.3 percent in that year. In return, as the company met its performance targets, employees received approximately $4.9 million in bonuses. The corporation's profit-sharing plans also resulted in $2.7 million of stock being shared by employees with more than one year of service.

Miller has traditionally been perceived by the investment community as an outstanding financial performer. These analysts forecast that the corporation's earnings would regain their momentum in fiscal year 1987/88. At the same time, Miller's employees still viewed the corporation as an outstanding place to work.

Clearly, Miller's approach to its business, with cost management as an integral part of its strategy, has allowed it to please shareholders, customers, and employees all at the same time, a rare occurrence in industry these days.

4.

Obtaining the Right Information

Obtaining the Right Management Information

Effective cost management requires that accurate, timely information be available throughout the organization for performance monitoring and decision making. This information has to be available at all levels in the corporation, not just at the top, especially when a cost-management strategy is based on broad involvement. Effective periodic reporting, accurate product and process costs, and special studies are key ingredients of a sound cost-management strategy. Putting these kinds of data in the hands of appropriate employees can provide great momentum to this activity.

Information has both historic and future dimensions. In cost management there is a need to ask: "How have we done?" This performance can then be compared to a variety of criteria, such as budget targets, costs in previous periods, or how the competition may be doing. This information is important for purposes of creating awareness, maintaining control, and stimulating new initiatives.

There is also a need to ask: "What do we have to do in the future?" Budgets and forecasts have to be developed that relate to specific cost targets derived from corporate and business plans, or simply what management feels is necessary to meet and beat the competition. These projections provide the yardsticks against which to measure the progress of cost reduction.

Executives who possess reliable information and breakdowns on product and manufacturing costs have a great advantage over their counterparts who do not. In medicine, a similar analogy would be the capability of surgeons before and after the development of X-ray techniques. In both arenas, operations can be planned with greater certainty and precision. For example, with such information, executives do not have to use across-the-board cost reductions to manage in tough times, but can focus on those areas where costs are out of line and the greatest impact can be made.

Accounting and computer personnel need to be made aware that effective cost management requires information that is reasonably accurate and timely, and not data that is precise and too late to be useful. In many corporations, the accounting department can provide top management with financial statements within three or four days of each month end, but it may take four or five weeks to provide monthly cost information to operating personnel, by which time it is not just history, but ancient history.

Computers could be a major tool in providing the information necessary for meeting the cost challenge, but too often computer-based management information systems are a corporate liability rather than an asset in this task. Systems have to be tailored to match organization needs. Overly complex systems in an organization in which employees have only rudimentary cost and accounting knowledge can be as ineffective as ones that are too primitive and simplistic.

Even when relevant cost information is made available, it is too frequently ignored or not used to its fullest potential. Many management reports are not used by their recipients. Sometimes this failure occurs because employees lack an understanding of how to use the data they receive. Departmental managers and supervisors rapidly lose interest in accounting systems when they have to deal with concepts such as fully absorbed overhead period costs and the like. When they have a difficult time understanding the information themselves, they are hardly likely to share it with the people who work for them.

The information challenge is to create an environment in which operating, computer, and accounting personnel can work together to define and create appropriate useful information systems that support the cost-reduction effort. The creation of a useful corporate cost management information system depends to a large extent on ensuring that the service functions obtain a clear understanding of the information imperatives that competition imposes on their activities. In this chapter, a broad framework for generating this understanding is provided, together with a discussion of what information is required for effective cost management to occur.

Why the Right Information Is Often Lacking

A variety of reasons, summarized in Table 4.1, lead to a failure to provide employees with the cost information that would allow them to manage costs effectively. Remedying these problems can, in principal, appear relatively easy, but in practice is often extremely hard to accomplish, especially if managers and accountants are primarily concerned with financial accounting. In many cost-management strategies, the weak link that takes longest to repair is the information system. Corporations turn employees on to the notion of managing costs, then frustrate them by failing to provide appropriate information.

Excessive Secrecy

In some corporations, especially those that are privately owned, management concerns over the secrecy of information are a major stumbling block. It is not unusual for fairly senior executives in some privately held corporations to be ignorant of costs and profits. Owners and senior executives often feel that if lower-level employees obtain this type of information, they will use it inappropriately, and the former fear even more that competitors will obtain these data and use them to their own advantage.

Although there are valid reasons for these concerns, most executives find that the value created by providing cost information to employees

Table 4.1. Barriers to Obtaining Useful Cost Information

Excessive management concern with secrecy

Accounting focus on financial rather than managerial information-reporting needs

Poorly developed architecture of accounting systems

Excessively ambitious accounting system development plans

Inadequate resources to both develop new systems and maintain existing systems

Failure to maintain accurate data bases, which erodes credibility of the system

Late, inaccurate, poorly formatted reporting

Managers using reports as a club with which to beat their subordinates

Overly complex, multiple, and conflicting reports

Poor cost-allocation practices

outweighs the downside risks. For example, cost and profit data provided to employees can make their demands more reasonable during wage and contract negotiations. Even during periods of high profitability, if employees are aware that considerable reinvestment is taking place, they are less likely to be intransigent in their demands. In addition, competitors generally gain little advantage from this type of cost information over and above what they can derive from other sources. The value to them is usually not worth the effort involved.

The Management Accounting Failure

A much more common problem for management in obtaining the right information is the failure of accounting and information systems to provide it. Two leading accountants in the United States, H. Thomas Johnson and Robert S. Kaplan, believe that financial accounting has triumphed over management accounting to the great detriment of U.S. industry.[1] Accounting is usually centralized at the corporate level, and given the apparent lack of interest of many corporate executives in cost management, it is not surprising that a traditional financial orientation predominates.

Johnson and Kaplan note, as have others, that U.S. executives are excessively concerned with quarterly and annual financial performance in their attempt to meet short-run profit and ROI goals. These concerns automatically relegate the management accounting system to a second-class status in the corporation.

The use of generally accepted accounting principles (GAAP) further distorts profit and cost-center reporting in various ways. For example, long-run investments in R & D, process improvement, training, and market development are reported as period costs. Managers who are being pushed by their executives to meet quarterly or yearly profit and cost budgets are prone to eliminate these investments when there is a need for quick performance improvements. Misreporting of some types of operating costs, such as capitalizing major maintenance expenditures, also distorts period costs, leading to flawed decision making.

This preoccupation with financial accounting can impair the budgeting process. Because it makes employees think about future costs, budgeting is an essential tool of cost management. For many accountants and senior financial executives, however, it is not the budget process that is important, but the cash projections that come from it. Most line managers have recognized this reality and adjusted their budgeting procedures to minimize their own workload and give the financial people what they want.

With the widespread use of computers, it has become relatively simple for managers to develop their budgets by simply projecting the preceeding twelve-month cost performance plus an appropriate allowance for inflation and any adjustments made necessary because of major changes or activities planned for the coming year. Accountants and senior executives are delighted because the budgets normally work out to be precise to 1 or 2 percent. They totally disregard the fact that management has failed to set challenging cost-reduction targets in its budgets.

Accounting System Shortcomings

A major reason why management often fails to obtain useful cost information is because the accounting system is flawed. A recent survey of cost accounting systems in Canadian and U.S. manufacturing revealed the following general shortcomings:

Cost-system objectives (e.g., pricing, cost control performance measurement, accounting records) are not clear.

Systems usually lack the necessary tailoring to be effective.

Cost management is addressed almost as an afterthought in the manufacturing environment.

Contemporary data-processing technology has not hit cost system design. Microcomputers, report writers, and data base systems are not being used widely, despite their availability and cost-effectiveness.[2]

In addition, accounting and computer personnel frequently select new computer hardware and accounting software with little input from management. Even if they are consulted in the early stages, managers very often find that their initial requests are changed considerably by the time the system is operational.

A major problem for corporations is reconciling the vision of an integrated, comprehensive accounting and control system with the corporation's ability to develop, deliver, and maintain it. Accounting and computer service professionals sell executives on the capabilities that new systems are supposed to be able to deliver, but given the level of resources available within the corporation, it may take five or six years to accomplish these feats, and in the meantime, information users must grin and bear the poor service.

During such periods, a major proportion of accounting and computer personnel are tied up in systems development, and service and support for existing systems may decline. Although parallel systems are often operated during such periods, in some cases it may be necessary to discontinue providing certain types of information until a new system is running, especially when hardware changes are involved. For example, in one corporation, any cost information on maintenance activities was unavailable for eighteen months while the system changed over.

The Poor Quality of Information

The architecture of computerized accounting systems developed in this manner may be such that obtaining management information by responsibility area, or in an appropriate breakdown, is virtually impossible. For example, many accounting systems do not provide accurate product costs. Accruals by product are either next to impossible to obtain or are distorted by allocated overheads that hide the true cost and profit picture. Total costs for manufacturing facilities may be developed, but an important breakout either by specific functions, such as maintenance, production, and engineering, may be impossible. Reliable cost reports for each first-line supervisor may also be unobtainable.

Even if such reports are available, they may not be useful. Monthly operating reports received five, six, or seven weeks late are virtually worthless as control documents, especially if they must be translated and condensed before they are meaningful. Their relevancy is further diminished if they are marred by poor cost allocations and the inappropriate reporting of period costs. Managers and supervisors often complain of the single large account that inevitably shows a substantial variance, primarily because it is a code to which everything that the accountants are not sure about is allocated. They also abhor the practice of reporting the cost of a three-month supply of materials in the month it is received.

These distortions are compounded if senior managers use monthly operating reports as instruments of supervisory torture. Managers often forward copies of these reports to subordinates with requests for explanations of variances and high-cost items. The result is more frustration and less cost management when, after a frantic search of source documents, 80 percent of the variances are shown to be simple accounting misallocations. Time is wasted, negative attitudes engendered, and little real cost management results. In these circumstances, it is not surprising that lower-level managers do not exert pressure to obtain improved cost information. If reports do not exist, or lack credibility, then criticism is more easily deflected, and accountability for performance shortcomings can be shrugged off.

At the other extreme of the information availability scale are the managers who are overwhelmed with a variety of contradictory reports. In one consumer-product corporation, managers received three product cost reports each month. Unfortunately, all three were generated from different data bases within the organization, and they varied considerably. One would show a particular product line to be in a loss situation, while another would show it to be comfortably profitable. The variability arose because of differing allocations and treatment of period costs, which most managers failed to understand, and so they largely ignored all three reports.

Even when well-designed and initially reliable accounting systems are implemented, problems can subsequently arise, especially if the capability to maintain the system is lacking. In particular, standards can rapidly become outdated and cause operating personnel to lose confidence in the output. For example, in some types of maintenance and operating systems, standard procedures printed out by the computer are difficult to update and modify and gradually fail to reflect learning and process improvements. As a result, the value of many cost improvements may be lost.

Poor Allocation Practices

As alluded to above, the method and practice of cost allocation is a major problem. Many corporations use direct labor or physical product volume as the basis for distributing overhead costs. In many corporations, however, direct labor is now a relatively small proportion of total costs, and allocations on this basis may be totally erroneous if other factors are more important in determining overhead distribution. Similarly, corporations that allocate costs such as sales, marketing, and distribution on the basis of physical product volumes may be seriously off base. Other factors, such as time actually spent by service departments, machine setups, and service requirements, probably exert greater influence on how these costs are really allocated.

If this situation exists, then as Peter Drucker pointed out twenty-five years ago, stable products with large volumes may be charged with more overhead than lower-volume products that take proportionately more than their fair share of overhead. Drucker argued that if some measure of the number of transactions associated with each product other than physical volume were used as the basis for cost allocations, a corporation would find that many smaller product lines are unprofitable, and it could take some appropriate action.[3]

Drucker's argument has since been supported by Miller and Vollman, who observed that factory overhead costs are driven by transactions involving the exchange of information. They argue that the best way to reduce product and process costs is to reduce the number of activities and transactions by simplifying and standardizing product designs and adopting techniques such as just-in-time inventory systems.[4]

Utilizing the Potential of Computers

Computers have an important role to play in providing timely, well-formated, correct cost information to all employees who need to use it. Used in this way, computers can be a major weapon in meeting the cost challenge. With currently available technology, it is quite conceivable that appropriate cost information can be made readily available to employees throughout the corporation.

For many corporate employees the following scenario may appear to be a daydream, but it is all technically feasible with existing technology. Senior executives and managers should be able to use terminals to call up cost information by division, plant, or product line and carry out budget comparisons and projections on the data at various levels of aggregation. Supervisors and hourly paid employees should be able to access screens that provide them with costs relating to their own work area, prices of materials and supplies, and possibly the costs and margins of the job they are currently working on.

As noted previously, however, many firms fail to realize this potential and end up managing costs by proxy. There are a variety of reasons for this situation, only one of which is the preoccupation with financial transactions which is commonly as applicable to management information systems (MIS) personnel as it is to accountants. The MIS department often perceives accounting to be their principal client and financial data their major output. Other problems arise from hardware, software, and liveware (people) decisions that determine the effectiveness of computer applications. Hardware constitutes a problem for many firms. As terminals and applications proliferate, the central processing unit becomes overloaded and accessability and response time deteriorate, causing line operators severe frustration. Supervisors and operating employees in many businesses still do not have access to terminals. Rigorous cost justifications required for the purchase of new peripheral equipment or of microcomputers keep them out of operations, because major reasons for such purchase are usually intangible, such as to allow supervisors to spend less time on clerical work or to permit employees to requisition materials without having to leave the work area to walk to a remote warehouse location.

Software development is also an area of major concern in providing cost data. A variety of typical problems that arise are shown in Table 4.2. These tend to vary, depending on whether the software is being purchased or being developed internally.

Table 4.2. Common Software System Development Problems

1. Users are not involved in systems specification and software purchase decision.
2. A system implementation plan and timetable are not developed and communicated.
3. Development lead times are unacceptably long because too many new systems are being worked on.
4. Information systems personnel fail to complete the development of applications.
5. The "fatal flaw" in purchased software systems is not recognized.
6. The previous system is removed before the new package is operational.
7. Systems development is used as an opportunity to measure and report on everything, resulting in a loss of materiality and relevance.
8. Accounting and computer personnel are overconcerned with precision in operational support systems.
9. The process for resolving system "glitches" that may involve several departments is not defined.

When carried out internally by a limited programming staff, deliveries of finished systems can become unacceptably long. Executives and managers frequently endure cost-reporting systems that are 75 percent complete for extremely long periods. Failure to articulate a comprehensive systems development plan, which includes applications requirements such as the automation of manual clerical functions and report generation, leads to partial completions. This tendency is compounded by the attitude of many information systems specialists who perceive their development task to be complete when the system is up and running on the computer.

Outside sourcing of software packages can be marred by failure at the time of purchase to recognize a fatal flaw: the single major program design feature that prevents the software from operating as required in the intended application. Some degree of customization has to be expected, and users are relatively dependant on the software vendor for major system improvements and upgrading. Greater user involvement in software selection can avoid some of these problems, as can trial runs on the vendor's system.

Many operating managers experience intense frustration with the systems development process when they see what they perceive to be excessive protocol and procedure debates taking place between, for example, accounting and systems personnel. In some cases relatively large amounts of time and effort are expended to ensure that irrelevant or immaterial amounts are fully allocated to the correct accounts. One manager spoke witheringly of three hours spent with two accountants and a programmer debating how to allocate $13.50 to seven different accounts. This is one more example of a problem that is only alleviated when a clear understanding of management accounting needs exists within these service departments.

The example also illustrates another snare to which accounting systems fall prey: that of data overkill. Paradoxically, this problem is often worse when users have been asked what they want and have responded with a "shopping list." Typical is the installation of a new accounting system that provides the opportunity to create a new chart of accounts. In one firm this change resulted in an increase from 35,000 accounts to 370,000. The average annual charge per account declined from $6,000 to $600. Computer run times exploded, and managers were swamped by a morass of trivial data. The worst of these excesses can be avoided if employees are made aware of the trade-offs and costs involved in providing information and so become more reasonable in their requests.

Finally, the effectiveness of computers in cost management is limited by the capabilities of people (liveware). There has been considerable discussion of the need to make computer systems user friendly, but in many companies there are still many barriers preventing employees from using data appropriately. Many employees still "fear" the computer and will not use terminals. Others lack any conception of what existing systems can do for them. In some firms, supervisors still manually accrue costs and track down orders even though their computer systems possess that capability. Executives still waste time making repeated telephone calls and writing paper memoranda in firms with excellent electronic mail capabilities. The best information systems are still limited by the capabilities of the people who use them. Greater employee skills in using cost information has to parallel the development of improved information.

Uses for a Cost Information System

In their landmark book on management accounting, Johnson and Kaplan identify four uses for a cost information system:[5]

1. Allocate costs for periodic financial statements
2. Facilitate process control
3. Compute product costs
4. Support special studies

To these uses might also be added the support of the budgeting and resource-allocation processes.

As noted earlier, Johnson and Kaplan are concerned that the overwhelming Canadian and U.S. preoccupation with the first of these uses relegates the others to a residual status. To alleviate this problem, they recommend that while companies should drive for a common data base for cost information, they should maintain three separate systems for financial, process, and product costing.[6]

Although this solution makes a great deal of sense in principal, it seems unlikely that executives who are currently seeking ways to reduce overhead are readily going to sanction the probable cost increases involved with this approach without first looking for cheaper alternatives. In addition, given the apparent preoccupation of information systems and accounting personnel with quantity of data, it seems likely that if this approach were adopted, many firms would simply drown in an ocean of paper.

Figure 4.1 shows show the cost pyramid defined in Chapter 2 can be broken out to meet the cost information needs of employees in the firm. As noted earlier, this information has both historic and future time frames. Operating executives are principally interested in the three types of cost breakout shown: by process stage, by activity or function, and by resource input.

For example, an integrated mining company would break its process down into the major stages of exploration and development, mining, concentrating, smelting, refining, and distribution. Of course, finer divi-

Figure 4.1. Alternative Ways to Break Out Costs

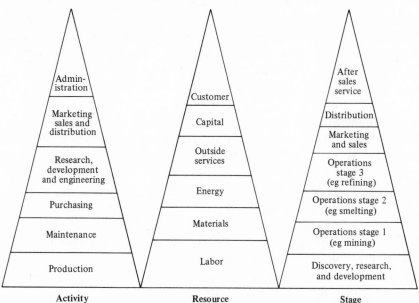

Activity	Resource	Stage

sions within each of these are also possible. This information is important for both control and competitive reasons. The executives in the mining corporation will also want to break out total costs for each by principal activity or function, such as production, maintenance, purchasing, R & D, administration so long as a reasonable allocation process is used for overhead costs.

In this example, if a work order system is used, then maintenance costs can be directly allocated to each user department. This information is useful for budgeting, control, and cost-reduction purposes. If, on the other hand, maintenance is charged out on the basis of some reasonable allocation basis, such as machine hours or direct labor costs, then it is highly likely that the information is not useful for cost management, although it may be of interest to accountants. In the former case, operating department managers have an incentive to reduce their maintenance charges either by good operation or by having their own operators carry out some minor maintenance. In the latter case, the department manager only reduces his maintenance charge by reducing the number of machine hours or direct labor hours worked in his area.

The third dimension to the break out is by major resource input: labor, materials, energy, and the like. This information is useful to managers for identifying the appropriate focus of cost-reducing activities, either across the corporation or in specific departments. Because some areas will be labor intensive, while in others, labor costs will be insignificant, the thrust of cost-reduction activities will be different in each.

These data also should be used to generate costs by product (or in a job-shop environment, by individual order) and, in some cases, individual markets, as well as for the entire business. This process is difficult in some firms, but it is important for well-informed strategic marketing and sales decisions, as the following example demonstrates.

Japan appeared to be the most profitable market for one multinational corporation, which produced a commodity product in a variety of forms and packages. The corporation's net margin (after production and overhead, but before marketing and finance costs) on sales to Japan was 10 percent larger than on that for the United States, and the corporation was thinking of expanding sales to the Far East. At this point, a second net-net analysis was carried out, this time taking into account the inventory tieup caused by extended delivery times to Japan, a 180-day receivable period (versus 45 in the United States), higher unit marketing costs in the smaller Japanese market, and larger distributor commissions. Based on this analysis, sales to Japan were calculated to be 5 percent less profitable than those in the domestic market.

Cost information is required at varying levels of aggregation. Senior maintenance executives routinely require data on the total maintenance costs for plant and equipment. Maintenance foremen, engineers, and operators want to be able to access the cost histories of specific operating units on a daily basis to facilitate replacement decisions. Division general managers receive profitability and cost reports by line of business, while brand managers require that data for their own product.

Most corporations with computers accrue the bulk of this information on a transaction basis and can provide lengthy summary printouts at periodic intervals. Their computer systems are then architectured in such a way that one or more different accruals can be made on these data for reporting purposes. Thus, for example, it is usually possible to break out functional and activity charges by stage in the process.

The problem in many systems is that it is impossible, or extremely costly in machine and programming time, to develop reports that blend data from different files and create additional reports that provide different cost breakouts. In the sales example mentioned above, all the required marketing and financial data were in the computer data base, but it was virtually impossible for the programmers to structure the different files in such a way that a periodic net-net marketing cost report could be issued. Fourth generation computer languages hold promise for easing this situation, but at a cost.

Who Needs What Information?

In the absence of clear statements about cost-management information requirements, accountants and information systems personnel tend to overwhelm managers with data. Much of this problem can be avoided if the purpose of cost information is clearly defined and if a management accounting function or role is created to champion the process of obtaining and managing the required data bases.

The first challenge is to identify both the cost data needed by different users and the purposes for which they are required. The second challenge is to turn them into useful information. Until accurate cost allocations are available, executives might consider reverting to a direct cost accounting method for management control purposes, rather than continue to introduce distortions in management behavior and decision making by continuing to allocate erroneous, fully absorbed overhead costs. The principle of charging managers for all the services used in their areas of responsibility is fine, as long as the charges are reasonably accurate and do not produce poor decisions. Cost allocations and distributions should be determined realistically and GAAP principals applied only where appropriate.

Using such an approach, managers have to clearly distinguish between information for control, which is received, reviewed, and acted upon periodically, and that for decision making, which should be available for access on an as-needed basis. Most senior executives in corporations need relatively short reports that summarize performance on a regular basis and need to access detail only on an exception basis. In addition, cost-management systems should be able to generate special one-off reports that focus management attention on specific problems or opportunities that might not be regularly caught in routine reporting methodologies. For example, it should be possible to generate reports that estimate all costs associated with safety or the costs of absenteeism to a corporation or business.

As noted earlier, there are a number of interesting concepts being developed at the leading edge of MIS technology that may affect the nature and form of cost information received by managers in future years. Realistically, however, most firms are not anywhere near adopting these approaches in the immediate future. A more pressing task for the majority is simply to obtain reliable information on costs that can be used to help improve a given firm's competitive position.

To this end, executives must first define clearly what cost-management information is needed by different groups of employees, then determine whether their information system has the capability to deliver either immediately or at some point in the future. As pointed out in Chapter 2, different costs should be managed at appropriate levels in the corporation. Clearly, then, cost information requirements will vary accordingly.

One way to assess what types of information different employee groups require is to create a general information needs matrix for the organization. In some cases, where a single information system exists, this document can be prepared for the entire corporation, as shown in Table 4.3. Although the listing of information needs shown in this example is not exhaustive, it illustrates the type of cost information needed at various levels in a typical multidivision corporation. The task of providing information is more complex if there is a network of loosely linked corporate, division, and plant information systems and associated departments. In such cases, a hierarchical approach is necessary.

Cost Information Needs of Corporate Executives

Corporate executives have an overriding responsibility to determine appropriate cost structures for the entire corporation and its major busi-

Table 4.3.   Major Cost Information Requirements: One Aspect of a Total MIS

GROUP	INFORMATION	USE AND FREQUENCY
Corporate executives	Costs of business units and major corporate departments (break-even levels)	Assess performance and viability (quarterly, yearly)
	Major corporate overhead costs (debt, head office, R & D, etc.)	Direct cost management (quarterly and yearly)
	Tangible and intangible strategic costs	Major programs and initiatives (as required)
	Cost of personal expenses	Control (monthly)
Division executives (single businesses)	Overall corporate costs	Information (quarterly, yearly)
	Division capital and operating costs	Control (quarterly and yearly, possibly monthly)
	Major projects	Control (monthly)
	Costs by product line	Product line decisions (quarterly, yearly)
	Cost by major department and functional area	Control (quarterly and yearly, possibly monthly)
	Strategic division costs	Major initiatives (as required)
	Intangible operational costs	Cost-reduction drives (as required)
Department managers, first-line supervisors	Overall corporate and division costs.	Information (quarterly and yearly)
	Department operating costs.	Control (monthly and quarterly)
	Intangible operating costs	Action (six monthly—proxy variables interim)
	Major high-cost areas and purchases	Focus activities (monthly or as required)
Operating employees and staff	Overall corporate and division costs	Information (quarterly and yearly)
	Department costs	Performance feedback (monthly, quarterly)
	Major high-cost areas	Focus ideas (on-going from supervision)
	Material costs	Control (each time a purchase or withdrawal is made)
	Intangible operating costs	Create awareness (as required)

nesses and to ensure that progress is made toward these targets. In multidivision corporations, senior executives cannot routinely receive detailed cost information by business and product line without incurring a massive case of information overload. Accordingly, executives need information that allows them to monitor routinely three basic dimensions: the cost competitiveness of businesses, cost management in the divisions, and major corporate overhead costs (see Figure 2.3).

The cost competitiveness of major business units is a major element in new investment and divestment decisions. Information on cost competitiveness should have both a future and an historic dimension, because executives are concerned more with how competitive a business unit can be several years down the road under various alternative scenarios than with its past performance in this respect.

Corporate executives should also be willing to ask for special studies to be carried out on costs that are not usually reported or aggregated, especially on intangible strategic costs, such as those associated with poor facility location or product positioning. This information can then be used as input to strategy development and provide impetus for major new cost-reducing programs.

Corporate executives also have to involve themselves in divisional budget reviews to ensure that long-run costs are moving downward at an appropriate rate. There is considerable debate over how frequently such reviews should occur. In some lean and mean corporations or those in a cash bind, these reviews take place monthly, which could cause an excessive focus on short-run performance. In other corporations, senior executives never review costs with division managers as long as profits are satisfactory. This practice sometimes results in unpleasant surprises. A more appropriate review period lies between the two extremes, for example, quarterly or half-yearly.

There are a number of corporate costs and expenditures with a significant bearing on profitability that have to be reported on, budgeted for, and managed. These include the costs of the head office, financing charges, and of other corporate-level activities, including market development, R & D, and human resources. Although these last three items are treated as period costs by the accounting system, there is a growing body of opinion that they should be treated in the same way as capital, that is, as investments for the future.

Finally, executives should receive and be accountable for their own costs on a monthly basis. This report should not just cover out-of-pocket expenses, but be a full-cost report on each executive. The results can be startling. This exercise is good not only for self-discipline, but it also symbolizes for other employees the commitment of senior executives to cost management.

Cost Information for Division Executives

Division executives and chief executive officers in single-business corporations have the most diverse set of information needs within the corporation. Strategic as well as operational cost data have to be routinely reported for decision-making and control purposes. To be able to respond to inquiries from corporate executives and also to ensure that subordinates are managing costs, these executives must be able to digest large amounts of information.

Routine needs include periodic reports on operating and capital costs compared to prior periods and budget projections. Well-organized executives have either accounting personnel or a trained executive assistant identify major variances and items of concern. In divisions with major expansion programs underway, periodic reporting on major project costs is also an important element of reporting strategic costs.

Divisional costs have to be broken down by major departmental and functional areas so that division executives can intelligently follow up with their subordinates, either in cost review sessions held quarterly (if held more frequently they tend to focus overly on specifics and fail to identify major patterns and emerging trends), or in one-on-one sessions with appropriate managers.

Costs also have to be broken down by product at this level in the corporation, because major marketing and sales decisions usually are made by division heads. As noted previously, full costs are desirable, but only if executives can be confident that overhead cost allocations are reliable, for simplistic procedures in this area can lead to poor decisions on adding or dropping products.

Division executives have similar needs to those at the corporate level for special, one-off studies on strategic and intangible costs that are not routinely reported. Division executives also need special studies carried out on intangible operational costs. For example, if a division executive becomes concerned over a poor safety record and high compensation and insurance costs, a thorough investigation, followed by widespread dissemination of the findings, is appropriate.

Along with other employees throughout the corporation, division executives should periodically receive information on total corporate costs and those of other divisions. This information provides a sense of how well cost-reduction activities are working and can provide a bench mark against which to assess the performance of the executive's own division.

Keeping Departmental Managers, Supervisors, and Staff Informed

These employees need to be kept informed periodically about corporate and divisional costs and profits. On a routine basis, however, they are much more interested in the operating costs related to their own department or area of responsibility. Monthly reports on departmental operating costs are appropriate for control and for providing feedback to operating employees. This information has to be received rapidly; otherwise it is useless for the purpose it is intended to fulfill.

Some supervisors and department heads claim that they would like this information weekly. Those who do, however, fail to realize the omissions and distortions usually present when cost accruals are made over such a short time frame, and few operations truly need costs to be so closely controlled.

Normally, a variety of the proxy nonfinancial indicators that are used as the basis for preparing budgets can be used to provide an indication of short-term performance. Production rates, overtime hours worked, absenteeism, defect rate, material usage, and machine utilization are some of these which can be used in a daily, or even hourly, monitoring function. Relying on these as indicators over longer time periods, such as months, is inappropriate, because managers and supervisors begin to lose touch with prices and total dollar costs.

These employees also need to be provided periodically with special reports on intangible costs associated with operating practice. Supervisors can be galvanized into action when they receive reports showing the cost of absenteeism, poor safety, or defective quality costs in their department. Frequently, these are larger than many of the direct costs they control, and they are easier to reduce. For instance, a manufacturing supervisor with 20 employees was experiencing an absenteeism rate of 14 percent. This translated into costs of $114,000 per year, almost half the annual costs of supplies used by her department. Armed with this information, the supervisor could see that it was far more useful for her to decrease absenteeism costs than material costs, which she had been struggling to reduce by 10 percent.

In a similar way, department managers and supervisors appreciate regular reports that identify high-cost areas within their control. For instance, in one chemical plant, supervisors started receiving quarterly summaries on the twenty pieces of equipment with the highest maintenance costs. Using this information, they subsequently put together a program that reduced these costs by 25 percent during the following year.

Providing Cost Information to Operating Employees

Apart from periodic information on corporate, divisional, and departmental cost performance, operating employees have their own needs for specific information to help them be effective in reducing costs. In organizations in which self-managing work groups are changing the traditional role and responsibilities of these employees, their information needs are similar to those of supervisors in traditionally managed operations. In both types of organizations, employees require specific cost information. Typical queries illustrating this need include:

How much does an accident cost this company?
How much does reworking a faulty product cost?
How much can I save the company if I find a better way to do a particular job?
How much does this warehoused part cost?
What are the high-cost areas in my department?

Providing information that anticipates these types of queries can focus the attention of employees on useful cost-reduction priorities. Senior executives have to be willing to pass cost information down to operating employees much more than they have in the past, keeping in mind that these employees have even less incentive than managers and supervisors to dig the information out of thick, badly formated reports.

Creating an Effective Cost-Management Information System

A first step in developing an effective cost information system is to ensure that executives provide clear directives to both accounting and information systems groups, stating that cost information for management purposes is to be accorded a high priority. Otherwise, these professionals will continue to neglect operating systems in favor of financial reporting.

In many corporations this task should have sufficient priority and importance to warrant forming a steering committee or task force to ensure that effective cost information systems are either in place or rapidly developed. This group should be made up of corporate and division executives, together with those who head up information systems and accounting. Apart from sponsoring the development of an effective system to facilitate cost management, this move makes employees, particularly those in accounting and information systems, aware that information is one of the cornerstones of this strategy.

A Role for Management Accounting

The rapid rise of management accounting as a professional field of expertise in its own right demonstrates a further way in which corporations are attempting to incorporate sound cost information in decision making and performance evaluation.[7] In most corporations, this activity has been little more than a by-product of the financial accounting function for many years, but recently, specific executive appointments at a senior corporate level have increased the power of this function.

Management accountants can be cost-information champions and may help break down the barriers between operating departments, accounting, and information systems. Personnel in this area can catalyze the formation of multidisciplinary task forces to define information needs and champion implementation. They can also specify time frames, determine the necessary degree of accuracy and precision of cost information, and indicate where the use of GAAP is appropriate and in what situations it tends to distort management decision making.

Management accountants can also provide leadership in resolving the allocation problems that affect product costing systems. By understanding more exactly the forces that determine the distribution of overhead costs, they can champion the fight for more realistic, long-run product cost data. This task can largely be accomplished by interviewing and surveying personnel who provide support functions such as marketing, field service, and distribution to determine appropriate time and resource allocations for different products.

Applications Teams

Rather than decentralize accounting and information systems personnel to individual departments (many corporations already have departments at both corporate and divisional levels), a move which could lead to duplication and wasted effort, some corporations have created applications teams in which personnel from accounting and information systems have specific user clients in operations. Over time, these relationships tend to build a good understanding of user needs and constraints in the service departments. Indeed, informal cross-functional teams that spring up as a result of such moves often contribute important cost-saving and revenue-generating ideas derived from their multidisciplinary skills and knowledge.

Putting Information to Work

In addition to ensuring the development of good cost information systems, management has to ensure that the maximum value is obtained from them. This task requires that employees understand the cost information they receive, that they share information, and that they do not use it in isolation. Considerable employee training and development may be necessary for this desirable state of affairs to come about. In addition, the establishment of clear communication channels for cost information may be necessary. These are discussed at length in Chapter 6.

Accounting personnel can contribute to this task through one or two simple actions that both create a desire among users to obtain reports and facilitate their use. In some corporations, the accounting department analyzes performance and issues a report identifying the five best and five worst performing units or departments in a particular time period. Managers are usually eager to see this report. In addition, the use of reports is facilitated if accountants can provide short footnotes drawing attention to any significant variances, or if they highlight issues of management concern and provide accompanying explanations.

Implementation and Action

5.

The Lean and Keen Corporation

The Basis for Strategic Cost Management

Experienced cost-cutters, like good surgeons, learn to know when to use an ax and when to take the scalpel or laser. Similarly, executives who are successful at cost reduction recognize that the initial moves in corporations that are quite fat have to be made from the top and that broad cuts are unlikely to work as well as selective incisions. Like good surgeons, however, they recognize that in an emergency, precision is likely to be traded off against the need for survival. Both also appreciate that blunt instruments are not going to do a satisfactory job.

In corporations unused to cost reduction as a way of life, the initial experience is something like a heart attack. The pain is awful, and the treatment may be as bad, but it is so good still to be alive. Afterward, the memory of the pain lingers on, and in many cases, corporations remain lean for some time after a cost-reduction purge. Gradually, however, the memory fades, and unless some sound cost-reduction disciplines have been instituted as part of a cost-management strategy, the fat slowly returns.

Cost reduction has to be ongoing if the benefits of the initial treatment are to be retained. Following the initial campaign, senior executives are unlikely to be able to identify potential reductions easily and could well make serious mistakes if they continue to act autocratically. Opportunities must be identified and implemented at lower levels in the corporation if the right costs are to be cut, and a sound cost-management strategy is the best way to ensure that the needed methodologies and disciplines are in place.

Certain beliefs and attitudes are essential to an effective cost-management strategy. The most important of these is to remember that cost management is an element of business strategy, not just an assemblage of concrete cost reductions. Thinking strategically about costs necessitates placing the deliberations in the broader context of the total corporation or business. In addition, the first costs that must be considered are the strategic costs: those of being in the wrong businesses or markets, having plants in the wrong locations, having obsolete technology, and the like.

The next critical element is to move beyond analysis and into the do-it or action orientation that Peters and Waterman identified as characteristic of excellent corporations in their book *In Search of Excellence.*[1] The first sign that a cost-management strategy is starting to work is that many ideas and suggestions that have been around the corporation for years finally start to be implemented.

Complementing this action orientation is the essential belief on the part of management that many employees can contribute to cost management. An individual who has performed a task for five, ten, or twenty years probably has many ideas about how to do it more quickly and cheaply. Usually, however, employees are not allowed to experiment and innovate because managers and supervisors believe that the hourly paid have nothing worthwhile to contribute. When they are finally given the chance to perform, the results usually surpass prior expectations.

Positive and open attitudes to change and innovation also characterize the culture of organizations with effective cost-management strategies. Managers and supervisors are not tied to past processes and ways of working. Ideas and suggestions are treated with respect, no matter where they originate. The "not invented here syndrome" often prevalent in technical groups has to be expunged. The work force has to feel and understand that cost-reducing ideas will not threaten job security, but will ultimately enhance it.

Organizations are finding that these attitudes toward cost management are not that hard to develop, especially if the corporation has been through tough times and there is a general awareness that survival and growth in the future depend on continued cost reductions. Paradoxically, the hardest situations in which to implement an effective strategy are those in which the corporation has not had too much difficulty in recent periods and where there is no general awareness of the need for a new approach.

As a result, the Chryslers and Fords of the world are starting to outperform the General Motors.

Initial Corporate Strategic Thrusts

The first cost-reduction challenge facing corporate executives is that of strategically realigning the corporation and its major businesses so that the full value of operating cost reductions can be realized. For many executives, this can be a painful and traumatic process, especially as it may necessitate the abandonment of traditional business practices and possibly the divestiture of businesses that no longer fit that corporate strategy.

The reluctance of executives to tackle these tasks is apparent from business articles dealing with "merger mania." The Wall Street financial whiz kids and corporate raiders driving this phenomenon justify their actions by saying that they are carrying out the task of restructuring and slimming down U.S. corporations, a job senior corporate executives have been incapable of doing. Some experts even suggest that those manufacturing and service industries, such as mining and finance, that have had a disproportionate share of mergers and acquisitions have led the way in productivity and cost improvement.[2]

There is no doubt that although strategic cost-reduction activities usually take longer to implement than operational initiatives, they can potentially have far greater impact and should occur in parallel to other moves. For example, debt reduction can be an important cost-reduction measure in highly leveraged corporations in which interest costs may be the difference between losses, merely breaking even, or a respectable profit.

This restructuring need not take long. For example, financiers such as Sir James Goldsmith and Lord Henson have made substantial profits by acquiring ill-fitting U.S. corporations such as Diamond International and Smith-Corona Marchand. Following these acquisitions they rapidly reduced corporate debt and costs by selling off poorly performing units and retaining a coherent, low-cost core of businesses.

These two cases add weight to the accumulating evidence that major strategic change or turnaround often requires new top executives with an objectivity lacking in those who put the corporation together. Most "turnaround artists" give themselves a year before they begin to lose their effectiveness by getting too close to the businesses and the people running them. Strategic restructuring is particularly difficult in diversified corporations because senior corporate executives lack insight into the key success factors in specific business units.

Corporate restructuring options are significantly different, depending

Table 5.1. Restructuring Options for Strategic Cost Reduction

Type of Corporation	Action
Unrelated-product corporations	Divestment of low-performing and ill-fitting divisions Creation of related sector groupings
Related-product corporations	Sharing of functions and resources where technologies or markets are common to different divisions Joint procurement Selective divestment Creation of sector groupings
Single-product corporations and divisions of diversified corporations	Reduced vertical integration Simplifying product lines Reducing corporate-office costs Reducing break-even levels Mergers aimed at industry rationalization

on the degree of relatedness between business units. A list of options available to different classes of corporations is shown in Table 5.1.

Unrelated-Product Corporations

In unrelated-product corporations, businesses can be dealt with individually. High-cost or noncore divisions can be sold off to other corporations in which there is a better degree of strategic fit and which possess capabilities to turn the misfit into a useful performer. There are many examples of this kind of move: Allied Corporation's sale of its Warner and Swasey machine tool division to Cross and Trecker, the largest U.S. corporation in that business; Coca Cola's sale of its Wine Spectrum business to Seagrams; and the Canada Development Corporation's sale of Kidd Creek Mines, a major copper-zinc-silver producer, to Falconbridge Limited, the world's second largest nickel corporation.

Single-Product Corporations and Business Units

In single-product firms such as Chrysler and Cummins Engine Inc. and in individual business units within diversified corporations, strategic cost-reduction options should focus on the degree of vertical integration, the breadth of product lines, and the cost of corporate overheads. In such corporations, a major thrust, especially in industries characterized by cyclical demand, is to reduce break-even to ensure profitable operations even in business downturns.

The turnaround engineered by John J. Nevin at Firestone Tire and Rubber Company is an example of this kind of cost-reduction approach.

When Nevin took over as president of the company in 1979, plants were outdated, wage and salary costs excessive, and a large debt was eroding cash flow. Nevin closed seven out of seventeen plants in the United States and Canada, reduced the number of employees from 105,000 down to 80,000, narrowed the product line, and sold off a money-losing subsidiary to raise cash. Plant capacity utilization increased from just over 50 percent to 90 percent, and a nine-month loss of $98 million for the period to July 31, 1980 was turned into a net profit of $121 million for the same period a year later.[3]

Reducing vertical integration by shedding high-cost raw materials supply or distribution operations is another way to lower break-even volumes. Some integrated steel companies such as Chicago's Inland Steel Industries are considering purchasing coke from specialized suppliers rather than producing it in their own relatively high-cost operations.[4] Automobile companies such as Chrysler and American Motors have been divesting themselves of component manufacturing operations for a number of years to cut costs and reduce break-even levels.

Many smaller single-product firms have unnecessarily high costs as a result of trying to replicate the full-line strategies of larger competitors. In the past, such noted corporations as Crown Cork and Seal, J.I. Case, and American Motors have flirted with bankruptcy in this way. In each of these cases, the solution was to reduce unit costs by abandoning the full-line strategy and dropping the manufacture of uneconomic products which filled out the line but lost money. Some of these products were subsequently purchased from other manufacturers. All three firms ultimately increased profits by becoming low-cost producers in niche markets.

In the past, single-product firms have commonly carried large corporate staffs for planning, engineering, administration, and sales and marketing, which have contributed to high overhead (and which operating staffs have generally viewed as unresponsive and expensive). In unrelated-product corporations, most overhead costs are also at the individual business unit level, because corporate headquarters in these firms usually contain minimal executive, accounting, and legal staffs. Strategic cost-management efforts can reduce these costs by determining which functions can be decentralized and which can be contracted out to consultants and other suppliers.

Related-Product Corporations

Although strategic cost reductions perhaps offer the greatest opportunity in related-product corporations, they are hardest to obtain in these firms. On the one hand, rationalization through divestment is more difficult than in unrelated conglomerates because of the market and technical relatedness that exists between different business units. On the other hand, cost reductions from resource sharing appear hard to obtain in practice because of insufficient integration, the desire of divisional executives for autonomy, and loyalty to divisional as opposed to corporate profit centers.

Opportunities for cost advantages exist in related-product companies all the way from shared purchasing functions to production facilities, marketing, sales, and distribution. Many of these corporations, however, fail to use a shared technology base as a lever to obtain first-mover and other competitive advantages in new product markets.

Since 1982, American Express (Amex) has been seeking these benefits through its One Enterprise drive, sponsored by its chairman, James D. Robinson. In the five years between 1982 and 1987, Amex examined about 260 ideas for collaborations between businesses and has implemented about 70 percent of them. These include cost-reducing activities such as the sharing of office space and data-processing capabilities and using people from one division to sell the product of another. Even though executives were evaluated and rewarded on their contribution to One Enterprise, internal politics are reported to have significantly slowed up the implementation of some projects. By 1986, largely as a result of only one or two big winners, 10 percent of Amex's net income was estimated to be the result of such synergies.[5]

As was mostly the case at Amex, the cost advantages of sharing may be small and possibly offset by cost trade-offs. These are discussed at length by Porter.[6] For example, when related-product corporations examine the potential savings from corporate procurement of major common items such as fuel and basic materials, divisions can often show that their purchases are at comparable rates and that the intangible benefits of decentralization, such as the service and responsiveness of suppliers, compensates for any small cost disadvantage.

The challenge for corporate management in related-product corporations is to determine where major direct or opportunity costs can be saved through divisional sharing of resources and activities. These savings are likely to arise from economies of scale or scope, such as distribution and shared experience. When such economies are identified, corporate executives must actively promote their attainment at the divisional level.

Getting in Fighting Shape: The Cost Audit

Corporations generally need to get lean quickly when the need for a serious cost reduction is first recognized. This initial process is usually aimed at achieving quick gains to improve short-term earnings or avert a cash crisis leading to bankruptcy. Measures commonly include reducing staffing levels, cutting discretionary spending, and generating cash by liquidating short-term assets such as inventories and receivables.

These actions do not need a broad base of support to be implemented effectively. In fact, the more people involved in this process, the longer it is likely to take and the more diluted it is likely to become as parochial interests are defended.

During this period of getting in fighting shape, many corporations deserve the title lean and mean. It is a time for hard, objective appraisals of all corporate activities that have a significant cost impact. One of the first steps for senior management to take in getting lean is to carry out a cost audit of its corporation. During this process, senior executives should participate in rigorously reviewing not only costs and cost structures, but also the approach to cost management taken in the corporation. The dual objectives of this exercise are to identify the major areas of short-run cost-reduction opportunities and to determine what initial actions are needed to create a cost-aware culture.

Sophisticated cost audit techniques are likely to be inappropriate for this activity. Most corporations simply do not have the accounting information available to carry out such an analysis rapidly. For many companies, just obtaining reliable information by product line will be a challenge. According to one executive, sensible approximation is what is necessary in this phase of cost reduction. Data should be simple and focus on major cost areas, to avoid a deluge of detail. The important point for executives to bear in mind at this time is that the audit should focus on the total corporation and should be comprehensive in its cost perspective. Implemented well, it forces executives to take a hard, objective look at the question: How are we doing?

The scope of the cost audit needs to encompass several dimensions. Trends in absolute and unit product and process costs need to be identified and interpreted. These data often reveal the shortcomings of productivity analysis. Wage and benefit payment increases over periods of several years often more than offset productivity gains, and manufacturing productivity gains can be eliminated by increased overhead costs, especially in those corporations that have gone heavily into computer-aided manufacturing.

Estimates of costs against those of competitors are also essential. Executives in some Canadian and U.S. corporations that have been reducing costs in recent years have been uncomfortably surprised to find that their foreign competitors have been reducing them at an even faster rate. Obvious examples are the steel, semiconductor, and automobile industries. In spite of General Motors' $50 billion capital investment program of the early 1980s, the cost advantage of Japanese manufacturers actually increased by $200.00 per unit in the period.

Costs can be evaluated and structured in the cost audit in a variety of ways, as discussed in the previous chapter. Simple ratios, such as those shown in Table 5.2, have been found to be extremely useful to executives in creating a snapshot picture of their business. In multibusiness corporations, such measures need to be derived for the corporation as a whole and for individual business units.

Major leverage areas for cost-reduction activities can be made using the different breakouts of the cost pyramid described in Chapter 4. If, for example, this type of analysis revealed that labor was a small fraction of total costs (i.e., 5 to 10 percent), as in some assembly operations, then management might well decide that even drastic work force cuts would affect the total direct-cost picture very little and that intangible opportunity costs would more than erase the direct savings. If labor and salary costs are shown to be 50 or 60 percent of total costs, then

Table 5.2.   Useful Cost-Reduction Ratios

RELEVANT QUESTION	USEFUL RATIO
How competitive are we?	Costs per unit of output
Are our costs competitive on a cash basis?	Expenditures per unit of output
Are we spending enough on the future?	Future costs (R & D, market development, etc.) : total costs
What's our break-even point?	Total fixed cost : (price–variable cost) per unit
How much of our costs are directly related to value-producing activities?	Direct : undistributed indirect costs
How big a cost burden do corporate activities impose?	Corporate costs (head office, debt, etc.) : total costs
What is our basic cost structure?	Purchase costs : payroll : capital costs
What importance do we place on managing supplier costs?	Purchase costs : total costs
How labor intensive is the corporation?	Payroll (including fringes) : total costs
What value added does each employee generate?	Total sales revenues–purchased inputs : total payroll costs
What proportion of costs are spent getting products to our customers?	Total marketing, sales, distribution, and after-sales cost : total costs
How important are opportunity or intangible costs?	Estimates of intangible costs (lost time, output etc.) : total costs

clearly a major cost-reduction effort cannot succeed without reducing these levels, and a more intensive analysis to identify specific saving opportunities is warranted.

A useful framework for considering wage, salary, and fringe benefit costs is shown in Figure 5.1. Core employees are those directly involved in producing and delivering products or services and other key technical and sales personnel. Core support employees are those who facilitate operations directly, such as maintenance, supervision, and computer staffs. These two categories contain direct, value-producing employees. Peripheral employees are all other categories, including clerical staff, managers, and service employees. Unless properly managed and directed, these peripheral employees can be value absorbing and cost increasing. In some corporations the residual value created by core employees is more than absorbed by the overhead. In such cases, the ratios must be improved between the core and peripheral employee groups before cost-effective operations can result.

Another way executives should examine the cost pyramid is to determine how costs are added to products and services all the way from manufacturing to sales and marketing, distribution, after-sales service, and on to the customer. Corporate and business-unit overheads not attribut-

Figure 5.1. A Framework for Analyzing Payroll Costs

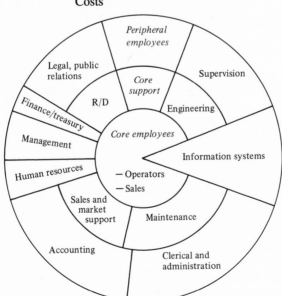

able to any specific function should be aggregated separately. Frequently, the pyramid is found to be unstable, with a small value-creating base carrying too much overhead. In this case, major areas of overhead can become the target for closer inspection.

The techniques described previously focus on breaking direct, easily measured costs into their major components. As noted earlier, however, intangible or opportunity costs may offer major opportunities for harder-to-measure reductions which may have an equal or larger impact on corporate and business profits, although they will not show up in monthly cost statements.

Some of these costs can be estimated with a fair degree of accuracy. For example, costs associated with rework, warranty claims, and excess inspection due to poor methods can be obtained quite easily. Other quality costs, such as lost customer goodwill, are more difficult to determine. Similar calculations can be made to estimate the relative magnitude and importance of poor labor relations; absenteeism; lost operating time; poor safety; and inadequate recruitment, training and development policies.

Substantial cost savings can be rapidly derived from these areas of soft costs. For example, one Canadian mining company in which labor accounted for 44 percent of total operating costs, estimated that absenteeism levels running at 11 percent in its work force of 2,250 was costing approximately $10 million annually in overtime and extra employees. A variety of initiatives implemented throughout the operations brought absenteeism down to 6 percent within six months, saving approximately $4.5 million for a minimal investment. Although part of a broader cost-management strategy, this move alone was estimated to have reduced unit costs by 2 percent.

Accompanying this cost audit should be an assessment of current cost-management processes in the corporation. This activity is intended to examine critically the mechanisms, procedures, and attitudes that support an effective cost-management strategy.

This evaluation should attempt to ascertain the extent to which employees view cost management as an important corporate activity and to discover if perceptions differ according to type of employee. Objectives and goals for cost reduction are important, and executives need to know whether they exist throughout the business, whether they are understood, and what is being done to achieve them. Going through this process can be extremely revealing for executives, because it usually identifies many weaknesses in an organization's cost-management approach.

For example, one chief executive new to a major corporation on the verge of bankruptcy was astounded that even competitors knew his costs better than any employee in the corporation below the level of vice-president. Employees spoke openly of being treated like mushrooms: kept in the dark and fed on manure. One of his first actions was to tour the corporation, speaking to groups of employees about the situation and clearly showing the cost problem. This created a much more receptive environment for the tough actions that followed, and this particular executive ensured that his vice-presidents regularly communicated cost performance to all employees from then on.

Implementing the Quick Hit

The need for fast results exists in any corporation implementing a cost-reduction strategy. Executives in corporations that are in trouble need fast cuts to stay afloat, while those that are taking preemptive action need to obtain some initial early successes to show that the approach can work. In either case, top management needs to demonstrate leadership by initiating a quick-hit program based on the findings of activities such as the audit described in the previous section.

There is little sense in taking this kind of action unless significant short-term changes to the cost structure are contemplated, because of the organization trauma which is likely to ensue. In this respect, the advantage of the top-down approach to getting in fighting shape is that it sends out a message throughout the entire corporation that a watershed has been reached, that the corporation is going to operate with a different mental set and culture in the future.

The purpose of the quick hit is to focus on major cost areas and get significant reductions fast. In corporations with high wage and salary bills, this approach generally necessitates uncompromising actions aimed at either reducing employee numbers significantly, cutting employee costs (through wage and salary takebacks and reduced benefits), or both.

This approach is consistent with the requirements for building a lasting cost-management strategy. A successful long-run cost-reduction activity needs to be broadly based throughout the corporation, and continuing work-force layoffs attributed to cost management ultimately destroy the base of support. Organizations and work forces can adapt to continuing attrition through early retirement and employee turnover, but the trauma and uncertainty associated with "black fridays" or "bloody mondays" are ultimately self-defeating.

If payroll costs are relatively small, the quick hit usually involves a radical organizational shakeup and an intensive short-run program aimed at major savings in materials, overhead, and similar costs. If no major work-force layoffs are contemplated, management has much to gain by driving hard to gain involvement from all levels of the corporation in cutting costs.

Although force of circumstance frequently determines when the quick hit will take place ("We'll be out of business in a month unless we act fast"), there are better and worse times to carry it out. If significant employee cutbacks are contemplated, the period prior to Christmas is psychologically poor and makes management look like a group of uncaring capitalist scrooges. Better times seem to be spring and early fall, because job markets are typically stronger in these periods. Sometimes layoffs can be timed to coincide with summer shutdowns so that a cooling-off period can occur before employees return to work.

Before actually moving to action, executives need to take the results of the cost audit and establish clear objectives and targets for this push. For corporations in a loss situation, they may focus around break-even and a fast return to profitability. For those that are profitable, the objectives may focus on achieving a target rate of return, generating cash, or increasing margins. In both cases, management should have a clear concept of the cost structure it is aiming to achieve.

Start at the Top

For symbolic reasons, it is important that the quick hit start right at the top of the corporation, even though this area may not be the most important or the highest priority. Senior executives should find ways in which they can visibly reduce their own costs to the corporation.

Some of the options include cutting back on the executive frills, such as dining rooms, chauffeured limousines, private aircraft, club memberships, and first-class travel. Equally tangible but less visible are executive pay and benefit cuts, either on a permanent or temporary basis. Regular salary increases can be replaced by pay-for-performance bonuses which do not inflate salary levels.

One of the first places to look for cost-reducing opportunities is in corporate and divisional headquarters. In many related- and single-product companies, overlapping structures and responsibilities can create significant duplication. Many decentralized related-product corporations have several corporate and subsidiary headquarter units, which in total may create a significant overhead burden for operations to carry. Reducing this superstructure can lead to significant cost savings.

More draconian options include reducing the number of senior executives through early retirement, and in the case of poor performers, termination. Connelly "lost the services" of 11 vice-presidents in the first year of his tenure at Crown Cork and Seal Corporation. In Canada, the Urban Transit Development Corporation had the number of its vice-presidents reduced from 33 to 7 when Lavalin Corporation acquired it from the Ontario Provincial government.

Reducing Staff and Overhead Costs

As manufacturing and operations become a smaller part of the total cost picture, corporations are finding that major savings can be made quite rapidly by reducing staff and overhead costs. As shown in Table 5.3, there are a variety of ways in which staff and overhead costs can be quickly reduced, although the initial savings may be offset by one-time payments associated with severance and early retirement.

To identify which staff positions can be eliminated, executives should be asking how roles add value to the corporation. An objective assessment may identify layers of supervision that really are not needed, staff and executive assistants who create little value, and many clerical or administrative jobs that were created for activities that are no longer required.

Although executives can personally identify specific staff-reducing opportunities in the top echelons of the corporation, identifying positions to eliminate at lower levels may be more difficult, especially if a good performance evaluation system is lacking, as is the case in many corporations. In such situations, executives have to rely on the judgment of lower-level managers who may have their own games to play, who may, for instance, protect friends and long-service employees at the expense of high-performing newer employees. Managerial and supervisory positions may be justified while key technical and marketing jobs are sacrificed.

Some of the worst effects of such behavior can be mitigated by making lower-level managers justify their decisions and demanding that they

Table 5.3. Opportunities for Fast Savings from Overhead Staff Reductions

- Release staff employees consistently identified as poor performers in performance evaluations
- Increase supervisory span of control
- Eliminate layers of supervision and management
- Cut out staff functions: do not replace; contract out
- Push corporate office functions down into divisions
- Identify one-on-one reporting relationships and eliminate positions
- Consolidate executive and managerial roles
- Identify jobs that are basically clerical and objectively assess value

review the resulting organization changes with senior managers before irrevocable decisions are made. Significant discrepancies, such as the bulk of the cutbacks being borne by one department, can be identified in this way.

Executive followup of this type avoided a potentially serious situation in one corporation going through the process of staff reductions. A review of total cutbacks amounting to 20 percent of the personnel in this technology-intensive corporation revealed that 40 percent of the reductions were being proposed in the research, engineering, and quality-control staffs, while reductions in purchasing, accounting, and administration were around 10 percent. A newly recruited engineering graduate was being released while a long-service employee who looked after the operation's automobile fleet and coordinated the employee suggestion program was being retained. A second look, this time with senior executive involvement, resulted in a considerably different profile of terminations.

With organization down-sizing becoming a major corporate activity, considerable outside assistance can be obtained from specialist firms. Out-placement consultants are available who can advise on severance packages and take over dealing with employees from the moment they are informed of the decision until they find alternative employment. Other consulting firms can assist corporations in organizing the quick-hit activity, work with executives and managers during the process, and provide objective advice on which areas, functions, and roles can be cut.

Many corporations use sweetened early retirement packages to assist with this process of slimming down overhead. Adding two or three years to length of service and a similar amount to an employee's age for pension calculations is now a common incentive. IBM even offered a 5 and 5 formula of this type. In many jurisdictions there are now legal requirements that these packages be offered to all eligible employees. As a result, corporations are finding that they are losing key employees they would like to retain because they still have valuable contributions to make. It is not unusual for these people to be subsequently retained as consultants.

Faced with the dilemma of losing key employees, some executives are now starting to preempt those they wish to retain by approaching them and indicating that future benefits for staying will be greater than those obtained by leaving. If it proves impossible to dissuade staff employees from this course of action, a deal can often be struck to retain them for a year or so to develop younger replacements for their positions.

Debt reduction is another area of opportunity for reducing corporate overhead. Corporations needing to implement cost reductions quickly are frequently short of cash, and reducing bank borrowing to avert bankruptcy may be the single most important short-term priority. In this situation, increasing sales volumes are unlikely to solve immediate cash needs and can even worsen them by creating a demand for increased levels of working capital. Instead, the quickest way to reduce debt costs— and let the bank manager sleep more easily—is to liquidate current assets tied up in receivables and inventories.

Even corporations not in this precarious position can benefit by mobilizing a crash debt-reduction program. In 1978, Hewlett Packard executives were concerned at the growing level of corporate debt. By instituting a tough working-capital regime and tighter cash-management approaches, they virtually eliminated borrowing within two years without affecting the company's growth.

Reducing Work-Force Costs

Where work-force costs are significant, the quick-hit approach usually focuses on down-sizing or wage rollbacks as major opportunities for savings. In an operation in which labor-related costs account for 50 percent of the total, a 20 percent reduction in labor costs with no loss of production volume reduces total costs by 10 percent, which may make the difference between a financial loss and profitable operations.

Paradoxically, employers without unions are usually more reluctant to initiate layoffs for fear of losing cooperation and creating a climate in which an organizing drive could flourish. Many corporations in this situation have a no-layoff policy and choose to carry the short-term costs associated with excess employees using attrition, early retirement, and other methods to gradually bring numbers down. Although this approach may be considered as enlightened, in consistently profitable firms, employees can come to perceive a country-club type of atmosphere in which major productivity shortfalls go unaddressed.

Executives are usually less inhibited about taking tough action in unionized operations. In the quick-hit phase, corporations may be experiencing slim profit margins, and management may be more willing to deal firmly with opposition, such as a strike, than when margins are good and profits high. A significant work-force cutback, coupled with wage rollbacks, may even be accepted with little opposition if other corporations in the industry have already shut down or implemented tougher measures.

A key decision facing managers at this time is whether to adopt a focused or an across-the-board approach to cutbacks. If sufficient information is available, actions should concentrate on eliminating high-cost products, plants, and departments. Management should expect that proportionate overhead costs can be eliminated with the closure of plants: if such savings are not achieved, unit costs at other plants will subsequently rise as they are forced to absorb additional overheads. This focused approach has the benefit of shielding high-performing operations from the negative consequences associated with layoffs and production cutbacks.

On many occasions, however, management will have neither the information nor the time to be selective, and across-the-board cuts must be mandated to get wage and salary costs back into line. In this case, cuts in some operations may not be deep enough, and in others, too severe. Consequently, a second round of readjustment is often necessary six months to one year later. If these later reductions are not too large, attrition and further early-retirement incentives may take care of the problem.

Layoffs cause considerable job and skills dislocation, because of union bumping rights. Costs can increase and productivity may suffer as high seniority employees without the requisite skills transfer in. Some companies have mitigated the worst effects of this situation, and simultaneously dealt with the seniority issue, by holding a job auction for employees eligible to bump across operations. In addition, crash retraining programs can be used to provide transferred employees with the necessary skills.

If the timing is appropriate, management may use contract negotiations as a period in which they seek to force through significant reductions in labor costs. A mixed package of demands can be made to facilitate this restructuring, including wage rollbacks, reduced benefits, decreased statutory holidays, and elimination of productivity restrictions in the collective agreement.

In some circumstances, it may be worthwhile for management to endure a long strike as part of the quick-hit strategy to force acceptance of stringent measures, as was the case at Kennecott in 1984–1985. When the striking workers returned, it was at greatly reduced pay levels, which contributed substantially to significantly lower production costs per pound of copper, Kennecott's major product.

Frank A. Lorenzo used the protection of the bankruptcy laws to break Continental Airlines' union contracts in 1983, enduring a major labor dispute in the process. Since that time, the airline has operated with wage rates that are sometimes as low as half the industry averages.[7] The catharsis of bitter negotiations or a long strike can sometimes lead management, the union, and the work force to seek better relations to avoid similar situations in the future.

Over the years, a variety of cooperative mechanisms have evolved to assist the work force to cope with readjustment and finding new employment. Sweetened early-retirement incentives are now well accepted as one way of reducing the number of actual layoffs. Some corporations actively assist workers in finding new employment by working with other firms in nearby communities to find job openings. Joint union-management committees can be established, and government support and services are available to assist in this process.

Another mechanism to cut labor costs but avoid layoffs, especially when the need for work-force reductions is seen to be temporary, can be work sharing and reduced work weeks. In this scheme, employees work only three or four days per week for the duration of a business downturn. Corporations have met with mixed results from this approach, however. Productivity can suffer, and employees with seniority become upset over their loss in income. Junior employees who avoid layoffs are generally supportive of the approach, though. The best results appear to be obtained in operations in which there is a strong paternalistic or family culture.

Supplier, Distribution, and Other Purchased Costs

A typical ongoing approach to cost reduction in areas of purchased costs is to have purchasing and engineering specialists carry out detailed analyses and implement programs aimed at obtaining lower costs and better deliveries. Frequently, however, these people are so loaded with routine work and so lacking in resources that results take far too long for a corporation needing a quick hit. This situation is especially serious for a corporation with a significant proportion of its costs in these problematic areas.

The fastest results can be obtained through negotiations with existing suppliers on price reductions. Much of the success of this approach rests on the purchasing clout of the corporation. Better results can be anticipated with key suppliers and those who make a large proportion of their sales to the corporation.

A top-down approach that some corporations have used successfully in getting results in days or weeks is to call a meeting of their ten or twenty largest suppliers and enlist their help in meeting the cost-reduction challenge. Presentations on the competitive and financial situation of the company made by senior executives can impress on suppliers the need for cost reductions. Specific examples of how costs are increased by supplier failures such as poor quality and late delivery can force home the message, especially if executives are willing to then follow up by cutting off the worst performers.

In addition to first-order quick-hit activities, corporations need to engage in ongoing measures that make possible further cost reductions. These include searching for alternative, lower-cost sources of supply and redesigning products and processes so that cheaper materials and techniques can be substituted without compromising customer utility and value. By focusing these activities on areas of high potential for cost reduction, rapid implementation is achieved.

A bottom-up approach which has been found effective, particularly in corporations in which staff and employee layoffs associated with the quick hit are minimal, is to establish and empower product and process task forces. Their job is to identify and implement major cost savings on purchased goods and services within a short time period, such as three months. These teams, especially when organized by product, are usually given a scope covering purchased materials, supplies, and services, including distribution. They may also have the authority to cut through red tape, such as capital approval processes, to get results. Task forces are discussed in detail in Chapter 8.

Although direct cost savings may be the primary focus of these task forces, a total cost perspective should be encouraged. For example, opportunities to lower unit costs through either increasing volume or yields or reducing scrap should be sought, especially if any of them can be achieved at minimal expense. In addition, task forces may be given the mandate to address issues such as absenteeism and poor training, or special groups can be set up to reduce costs related to these areas if they are significant.

The time frame for such task forces can be as short as one month, but allowing four to six weeks for analysis is usual, with implementation of results starting from the following day, if possible. Most of the cost-saving ideas can be implemented within six to twelve weeks, with 90 percent of the cost benefit being realized after three months. Most of these savings normally accrue from 20 percent of the projects and ideas proposed, so it is important that precedence be given to those ideas with the largest potential value.

Ensuring Results

Following the decision to proceed with a quick hit, the CEO and other senior executives have to find time to take part in a communication blitz aimed at creating a shared awareness and understanding throughout the organization of the need for such an approach. Generally speaking, an informal grapevine will have already initiated rumors of possible action, and it is important that top management communicate directly the actual situation. All possible channels should be used to push this message across: personal talks, newsletters, bulletin boards, and staff meetings being the most appropriate. For shift workers, video-taped presentations can also be effective.

Once the quick hit is underway, constant monitoring of progress is necessary. The senior executive group should hold weekly meetings to review progress and to consider each individual's actions and accountabilities, a process that in time creates peer pressure to obtain results. In addition, when tough action is being taken on down sizing, these meetings can provide mutual support and reinforcement during a stressful period.

Senior executives should parallel these reviews with similar meetings with their own staffs and any task forces to which they may have been assigned. Executives must be prepared to slaughter sacred cows and cut red tape when cost-reduction projects get hung up on these obstacles. A lot of time is likely to be spent counseling and advising junior employees. This is a time when cost management by walking around is especially appropriate, because employees do not wish to appear weak by voicing their concerns in such periods.

In short, during the quick hit senior executives can demonstrate leadership through personal example (and sacrifice) and direct involvement. Although employees dislike such tough periods, executives can earn great respect from the work force by not delegating the hard decisions and by being open and honest with employees about the reality of the situation. If the quick hit is effective, subsequent opportunities can capitalize on the successful cost reductions achieved and can contribute to an effective, continuing strategy.

A Few Cautions

The way in which the quick hit is implemented is particularly important. This approach can be especially demoralizing and the cause of much cynicism if it mirrors the following example. An operating executive in a U.S. electrical manufacturing corporation noted that in his organization, executives would leave their luxurious downtown New York offices, be chauffeured to the airport, fly in the corporate jet to a rural plant location, mandate budget cuts and work-force reductions, leave the local management to communicate the news and wield the ax, and then be flown home in time for an executive dinner at a downtown restaurant. In such circumstances, which are not unusual, it is clear that any cost reduction will lack real support and continuity. In organizations in which cost reduction is taken seriously, on the other hand, senior executives share in the tough times as well.

In a short-term program of this type, executives must accept that mistakes will be made, part of the price for fast results. There are some tempting targets for fast cost reductions which management should be very cautious about during the quick hit, but which poor managers, or even good lower-level managers under budgetary pressure, perceive to be an easy way to obtain demonstrable results. These costs include apparently discretionary spending items such as travel, R & D, rewards for outstanding performance, and other items that seem candidates for deferment to better times, such as maintenance, personnel training and development, and market-development expenditures. Unless there is obvious abuse of these items, cost reductions here can lead to high opportunity costs.

Senior executives who try to implement a quick hit by mandating a 10 percent across-the-board budget reduction exercise are occasionally horrified by subsequent customer complaints of sales and marketing people unable to visit their operations to discuss problems; of gaps in communication between geographically separate operations, costing millions of dollars; and of vital operating time being lost because of shortages of parts or missed maintenance schedules.

Another caution mentioned by executives with considerable experience in down sizing is that attrition or early retirement is preferable to layoffs if at all possible (unless there are significant cost advantages to be gained from major work-force reductions). Although a layoff undoubtedly sends out clear signals to the work force about the financial state of the company, negative side effects can offset any direct savings. For example, high-performing employees may become uncertain about their future and leave; grievances and absenteeism often rise; morale and productivity can drop; and employees may stop bringing forth ideas for cost reduction.

Staying Lean

After the kind of tough period usually associated with the quick hit, executives probably feel emotionally drained and want nothing more than to withdraw into themselves for a time. Such a move is a mistake. Meetings and discussions with employees are not likely to be spiritually uplifting, but they are important to resolving doubts and uncertainties and communicating cost management. Most important, this period is an important bridge to the future: executives must let employees know that the quick hit was not merely the culmination of a dismal period, but rather, the beginning of a more effective way of reducing costs and meeting the competitive challenge.

The initial period after a quick hit provides a unique opportunity to demonstrate to employees that the nature of cost management is going to change and that management is serious about continuing the effort. If layoffs and employee cutbacks have been minimal, executives can use dinners and similar low-cost social occasions both to recognize the efforts of employees who may have worked unusually hard during the quick hit and also to communicate the results and the ongoing need for the drive.

In organizations that have gone through a sharp down sizing in employment, executives should try to reassure the remaining employees about the future. As one industrial psychologist in Canada noted: ''After a major layoff, many employees spend two or three hours a day worrying if they are next.'' At such times, grievances, back injuries, and absenteeism may rise sharply, although in the immediate period after this type of quick hit, productivity usually remains high or even increases, because people fear being considered superfluous. If appropriate, statements can be made such as: ''We foresee no further layoffs at this time.'' Although employment guarantees probably cannot be made, the implicit message is: ''We're the survivors—let's try and keep it that way.''

Executives may wish to make special efforts at this time to ensure that key employees, such as scientists, engineers, and other specialists, feel that their employment is not in jeopardy. These individuals are usually not in the inner circle of management decision making and may feel extremely insecure after major cutbacks. Their skills are highly mobile, and their loyalties are often more to their discipline and profession than to the company. It is not uncommon for the main occupation of these individuals at such times to be résumé writing.

Dealing fairly with employees who must be released is extremely important within the organization. Open hostility to management can break out if popular former employees are perceived to be treated harshly. For example, in one corporation several employees were released just days short of qualifying for important benefits, such as a share bonus for long service. Another employee was terminated just before his daughter was to be considered for a major company university scholarship. In both cases, lower-level managers were following company policy to the letter, but the CEO gained considerable respect by personally intervening and allowing the awards to proceed when he learned of the circumstances.

Becoming Keen

Cost management has always been the plain sister of product innovation, acquisitions, and other growth-related management tasks. The activity has borne the image of being negative, boring, and unchallenging, except among some engineers and a few corporations, such as Emerson Electric, which have seen cost containment as one of their competitive edges (not surprisingly, perhaps; many people perceive engineers and Emerson to be boring also).

Corporations cannot get keen about cost reduction until their employees are involved, excited, and rewarded for meeting the challenge put up by cost management. If employees aren't keen, then when times are tough, management has to be mean. Since most executives are not naturally inclined this way, in most corporations the lean and mean approach has little likelihood of surviving beyond one or two quick hits. The reputation of being mean gained during this period will be hard to shake off, unless a different approach is subsequently demonstrated.

The quick hit usually reinforces the negative image of cost management, even if it is done well. Some employees inevitably suffer, mistakes are made, and unproductive busy work increases for a time. However, it does involve employees either passively or actively, and it can play an important watershed role in changing attitudes toward the importance of cost reduction throughout the corporation.

A major challenge facing executives in the first two or three years of a cost-management initiative is to imbue positive attitudes and beliefs about it. If they demonstrate that they are keen to continue and, like the chairman of Amex in his One Enterprise program, put in place mechanisms and rewards that encourage appropriate employee behavior and actions, a lean and keen corporation can emerge.

In multibusiness or multiplant corporations, a strong incentive to change exists when the CEO, recognizing that cost reduction directed from the top is often imprecise, states that as long as each area implements an effective process to keep costs coming down, it can remain in charge of its own destiny. The challenge is then laid down: develop your own strategy, and carry it out. The reward for success, at a minimum, is autonomy, and possibly other recognition and financial rewards. An implied threat is also there: fail, and we will come and do it for you.

Having laid down a challenge, top management cannot then abdicate responsibility for cost management to lower levels, as in the past. A long-term strategy that builds on the gains of a quick hit startup must continually involve top management. A corporate umbrella is needed for activities that division, plant, and other managers initiate in various parts of the corporation. Without this executive commitment, many lower-level managers will lack the confidence to try new approaches, and unless the corporate culture as a whole is generally supportive of new cost-reduction initiatives, these initiatives are unlikely to have great longevity. In integrated businesses, some corporate coordinating functions are necessary to ensure that cost-reduction activities in one part of the firm do not simply raise cost elsewhere.

Even if this leadership is provided, some managers may be reluctant to take personal risks and experiment with new ways of managing costs. The old approach may be perceived as far safer, and many managers may not have the skills or knowledge necessary for a strategic cost approach. They may also feel that top management now wants to make all the major decisions.

Senior executives must take the lead in personally encouraging and sponsoring initiatives, developing cost-management skills and attitudes in junior executives and managers, and creating a shared understanding of how cost-management strategy will be implemented in the corporation.

Actions such as these may not make for a keen corporation initially, but they are important first steps in gaining managerial awareness, understanding, and commitment to a new approach. This process may require several years to take hold across a large corporation, but the early successes of managers who start to implement well-thought-out cost initiatives ultimately create a climate in which more risk-averse managers can safely follow along.

6.

Creating a Cost Conscious Organization

Changes Necessary for Effective Cost Management

Implementation of an effective cost-management strategy usually requires changes in organizational structure, processes, and culture. Because innovation and organizational change are principal contributors to cost reduction, a successful cost-management strategy should become an umbrella for these activities. In addition to organizational change, executives have to find numerous ways personally to sponsor cost-reducing initiatives and to provide champions in all parts of the corporation with the opportunity to implement their ideas.

Organizational Changes

As discussed earlier, no-frills management is first embodied as a state of mind. Executives who are operating in this mode look at everything with an eye toward value creation. Does the executive assistant really create value for the corporation? Can the function be performed more cheaply in another way? Does the activity need to be performed at all? In an effective cost-management strategy, as many employees as possible are imbued with these attitudes.

To permit this type of questioning to take place, and for employees to be able to implement their ideas and proposals, management has to be concerned both with minimizing internal political forces that resist change and with simplifying the organization to facilitate implementation.

Excessive layers of management and supervision are barriers that must be stripped away before good communication can take place and involvement obtained. In addition, high costs resulting from poor working relationships caused by the inappropriate centralization of activities such as maintenance, development, or engineering have to be eliminated through reorganization.

Traditional staff and supervisory roles often inhibit changes, rather than facilitate them. For supervisors, innovation and change add considerable stress and uncertainty in an environment often fraught with conflict, crises, and cover-up behavior. Staff groups are frequently more concerned with process than results and see change as disrupting systems and procedures. Computer and information systems personnel often display this type of behavior, which executives find difficult to control because of the apparent logic of the systems view.

Once management has started to eliminate these barriers, they have to encourage employees to actively champion change. In Falconbridge Limited, the slogan "do it" became the driving force of the cost-management activity in their Sudbury mining and metallurgical operations. Under this banner, individuals and groups of employees were able to implement thousands of ideas to reduce costs.

A Strategic Change

The organizational implications of adopting an explicit cost-management strategy are so substantial that startup needs to be viewed as a period of major strategic change for the corporation. For most organizations, the appointment of a full-time director or coordinator to champion the activity is warranted.

The early period of strategy implementation requires a significant amount of vision and demonstration activity. These attributes of leadership are the cornerstones on which the culture of the cost-conscious corporation rests. In addition, corporate executives have to ensure that the eight key requirements of successful strategy initiation outlined in Table 6.1 are met.

In the early stages, senior management must establish cost-management objectives and goals, although as commitment grows, this process can be pushed down the organization. At the start, however, executives have to identify long-run strategic aims for the strategy, as well as short-term goals and milestones.

Defining the scope and nature of the cost-management strategy deter-

**Table 6.1. Eight Key Executive Roles for Strategy
                  Initiation**

1. Establish clear objectives and goals for the activity.

2. Define the scope and nature of the strategy.

3. Provide appropriate training for employees.

4. Ensure an effective strategy implementation process.

5. Appoint an effective champion.

6. Eliminate barriers and sacred cows.

7. Manage expectations and motivations of employees.

8. Ensure short-run successes, and reward them.

mines the rules of the game for employees and lets them know what is expected of them. This process typically involves some education and development, especially if the organization is lean and new demands are placed on employees to go beyond their traditional roles and become more involved in cost reduction.

Well-developed plans need to be established for implementing the strategy and making the changes associated with it. The stages of startup and the sequence in which employees are to be involved in the activity need to be given careful thought. Tough measures, such as plant closing and layoffs, should be taken before extensive direct involvement is sought. Similarly, until a core of supervisors and operating managers believe in and support the activity, there is little use in promoting extensive work-force participation.

An effective implementation process helps ensure that cost management is not derailed either by opposition from disaffected groups of employees or by a loss of momentum. Barriers to implementation, such as those posed by geographic and organizational boundaries, can be anticipated and eliminated before they cause major problems, as can traditional ways of managing and taking action that have become sacred cows.

Throughout this whole process, it is important for executives to manage carefully the expectations of corporate employees with respect to cost management. This task requires allaying unnecessary fears about employment and job security and ensuring that once the strategy has been communicated, the rather simplistic notion will be avoided that things can be magically and immediately different. Short-run successes will build commitment to the strategy among the work force.

Values in the Cost-Effective Culture

Executives in cost-effective corporations appreciate the concept of value. They do not confuse being a low-cost competitor with being cheap and offering shoddy products or poor service. Lean and keen corporations such as Marks and Spencer and Toyota learned this fact long ago and built corporate strategies that focused on customer needs while remaining low cost.

Jan Carlzon, president and CEO of the SAS group of companies, in which award-winning Scandinavian Airlines is the major operation, has said: "For SAS the turning point came in 1980. We better accommodated our products to customer needs. Low per seat costs are futile if they result in products no one wants to pay for. Instead we strive for the highest possible revenue per flight at the lowest possible cost."[1] In other words, managers in truly cost-effective companies recognize that when direct cost reduction is driven to the extreme, value for the customer is lost, resulting in unacceptably high opportunity costs.

Executives in cost-effective cultures also believe that all employees have the potential to make significant contributions to cost reduction, especially if their activities are focused on appropriate targets and opportunities. There is little likelihood that assembly-line workers will develop revolutionary automated processes to eliminate their own jobs, but they may have significant incremental contributions for improving productivity, process control, or manufacturability if they are asked and motivated. On the other hand, few process engineers possess the insights or skills that come from years of carrying out specific tasks, but they are likely to be able to create significant cost reductions through reverse engineering and product redesign. To be good cost competitors, corporations must prize values that let them tap these and other sources of cost reduction.

As noted in Chapter 5, corporations that really tackle costs firmly usually pass through a lean and mean stage. In this period, economic values are stressed over human concerns. Job security is minimal, stress is high, and involvement is likely to be low as employees avoid personal risk.

In some businesses, this approach can be successful over extended periods of time, especially if a strong, tough, centralized ethic is in place. The approach has also been effective in "sweat-shop" industries and businesses located either in areas of high unemployment where little alternative work is available or where immigrant labor makes up a substantial part of the work force. In the long run, however, most Canadian and U.S. workers, especially younger people, will not tolerate these conditions, and substantial opportunity costs may be associated with a lean and mean culture, such as high turnover, absenteeism, and poor employee relations.

This situation appears to have been the price Frank Lorenzo had to pay at Continental Airlines after several years of operating a no-frills, low-wage airline. Complaints of fatigue and stress, low morale, and high turnover among key employee groups and concerns over the declining quality of maintenance employees all started to emerge in 1987, four years after Lorenzo adopted a lean-mean approach.[2]

Most Canadian and U.S. businesses that have built successful cost-management strategies have implemented them around the lean and keen philosophy described in Chapter 5. Employees who are aware of competitive and economic realities can be involved in cost reduction in this culture, while at the same time recognizing that without growth, employment levels will inevitably decline over time. Many employees are willing to accept this fact, as long as they perceive the corporation to be making every effort to plan for down sizing through attrition, early-retirement, and retraining options wherever possible.

Some corporations that have been successful at reducing costs have evolved a rich corporate philosophy that guides the cost-reduction approach and underpins a cost-conscious organization culture. Table 6.2 lists the major elements of the cost-management philosophy at Falconbridge Limited's Sudbury operations.

The values reflected in this statement demonstrate a commitment to productivity through a balance of people, technology, and capital. It stresses the importance of implementation and broad involvement and emphasizes letting employees get on with innovation. As already noted, the overall call to action in this operation, reflected in posters and anything associated with cost management, is *do it*. Bill James, the CEO of the corporation, reinforces this approach with statements such as: "If you aren't making a few mistakes, you really can't be trying very hard to do new things."

As with any other type of culture, those that are lean and keen develop

Table 6.2. Cost-Management Philosophy at Falconbridge Limited

- Broad cost awareness is critical to low-cost operations.
- Cost management is challenging and important.
- Every employee has a responsibility for managing costs.
- Implementation is through line management—supervisors and managers must be aware, educated, and involved.
- Employees doing a job know best how to reduce the costs associated with it— ask, and involve.
- An idea by itself is nothing—DO IT—get the job done.
- All employee involvement is voluntary.
- Effective cost management is the best way to avoid possible future layoffs.
- Seek cost reductions that are not capital intensive.

their own set of myths, legends, heroes, and heroines, as well as villains and villainesses. Once the culture becomes established, stories start to circulate about the work groups that meet at each other's houses on Saturday afternoons to identify their next cost-reduction idea; how the CEO was seen on a charter flight while traveling on business; or how employees came up with a particular cost-reduction idea that earned them $50,000 and saved the company $400,000 annually. These stories are important, because they reinforce the ideals of the strategy and provide recognition for those who play a leading role.

Getting Going

If the initial period of putting a long-run cost management strategy into place is handled as a major strategic change project, three separate streams of activity need to be integrated, as shown in Figure 6.1. These include:

Executive actions that create awareness and symbolize commitment to the cost-management strategy

Development of an effective process to put the strategy in place

Substantive cost-reduction activities that show fairly quick results.

An outline of a timetable for these activities is shown in Table 6.3. Initially, the top management group must meet to discuss and agree on the need for a strategic approach. Given the requirement that these startup meetings be relatively frank and open, an outside facilitator with a strong

Figure 6.1. Strategic Change Activities Driving Cost Management Startup

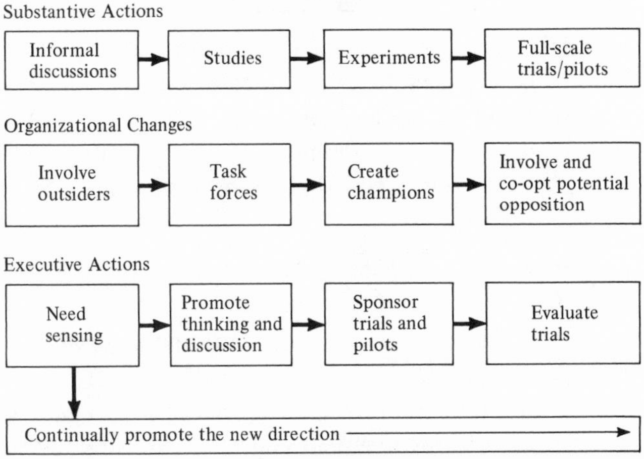

SOURCE: Peter R. Richardson, "The Challenge of Strategic Change," *Canadian Business Review,* Autumn, 1986, p. 30.

Table 6.3. Example of a Startup Timetable—First Four Months

First month, weeks one and two:
* Hold initial management meeting to review cost-reduction performance, discuss strategy concept, and gain commitment.
* Establish task forces.
* Appoint coordinator/director.
* Make presentations to employees on need for cost-management strategy.

First month, weeks three and four:
* Complete task-force reports.
* Outline objectives, goals, and major policies.
* Make executive visits to other corporations that have taken similar initiatives.

Second month:
* Give executive presentations on outline of strategy to all employees.
* Make initial coordinator assessments of training and development needs and promotion requirements.
* Implement initial changes identified by task forces to improve effectiveness of cost-reduction mechanisms.
* Start to identify initial major cost-reduction opportunities.

Third month:
* Commence initial cost-reduction training and development activities with managers and supervisors.
* Promote first- and second-line supervisory involvement.
* Start to identify specific implementation bottlenecks.
* Commence planning sessions with managers at each operation and major department.

Fourth Month:
* Deliver first round of quarterly cost-management presentations to all employees.
* Establish specific cost-reduction objectives for all major businesses, operations, and major departments.
* Review at the executive level how the strategy-implementation process is proceeding.
* Communicate operational cost-reduction plans to employees and initiate local cost-reduction projects.

grasp of strategic cost management can play a useful role in ensuring that the concept is well developed and explained and that concerns and personal fears are brought up and addressed effectively.

This first top-management meeting, which may last one or two days, should conclude with the establishment of task forces to assess key items such as:

Initial objectives for the cost-reduction strategy in both the short run and long term

The communications network necessary to support strategy implementation

The informal structure and championing necessary to gain appropriate levels of employee involvement and make the strategy work

A review of the effectiveness of any major cost reduction activities currently in place

The ability of information systems to provide the required data to support the cost management strategy

An initial recommendation on the nature and form of reward and recognition for cost reduction initiatives

These task forces should report back at a subsequent meeting held as soon as possible after the first session. In this second meeting, agreement should be reached on these six key components of the strategy and any changes that are needed.

At the same time as these initial meetings are taking place, senior management has to create an awareness of the need for a strategic initiative throughout the organization. This task can be accomplished through presentations, crew meetings, and written vehicles, as described later in this chapter.

Once this awareness begins to grow and the initial objectives, goals, and policies are determined (as described in the next section), executives can undertake a second round of presentations in which the outline of the strategy is described and an opportunity for detailed employee questions and comments provided. By this time, a coordinator or director to champion strategy implementation who can organize and run these sessions may have already been selected.

A variety of initiatives can subsequently be started to enhance cost-management capabilities throughout the organization. Planning sessions with managers and supervisors can be held to determine how the strategy will develop and be implemented in individual operations and departments. Active involvement of first- and second-line supervisors in the cost-management strategy can be promoted. Business or functional managers can help identify training and development needs specific to cost management and assist in putting the appropriate programs into place. Of course, implementation bottlenecks should be identified and dealt with immediately.

With these building blocks in place, some initial substantive actions can be taken. Top management can carry out business-wide and cross-functional reviews of major cost areas using inputs from a variety of employee groups. From these reviews, major short-term cost-saving opportunities can be identified and assigned to groups of employees for action.

Establishing Goals and Objectives

Many corporations that are developing a comprehensive cost-management strategy already have a budgeting process in which expected costs for major expense areas have been forecast for one or possibly several years ahead. As noted in Chapter 4, these budgets are unlikely either to have been developed in a way that makes them suitable for use as goals and objectives for cost reduction or to be widely enough known and simple enough for this use.

If traditional budgeting procedures cannot be relied on to develop challenging goals and objectives for a cost-management process, then a significant aspect of the early strategy formulation activities of top management is to determine what targets are appropriate. Initially, these have to be determined by senior executives, as only they are likely to have a clear sense of both what the corporation must achieve and what is possible. In such circumstances, department and division managers should be told straight out by their superiors what they should aim for, then be allowed to go and do it.

Ideally, though, managers and supervisors should become involved in setting cost-reduction targets for their own areas of responsibility because of the commitment this approach builds toward attaining them. As the strategy develops and lower level managers and supervisors develop an appreciation of the importance of tough goals and objectives for their own areas, the responsibility can and should be delegated.

Cost-reduction objectives should have both long- and short-run components and should be stated in simple terms that can be understood by the entire work force. An insurance business which adopted this approach defined its long-run objective in terms of reducing its expense ratio (the ratio of corporate expenses to the value of business written) to the level of the leading firms in the industry within three years while continuing to meet its growth and profit objectives. Goals were then established for each year in line with the long-run target.

A major copper smelter in North America defined its long-run objective in terms of bringing its costs down to levels at which it could compete with Japanese custom smelters for supplies of custom concentrates from abroad. This target amounted to a 30 percent decrease in real terms over five years. Because it had a sophisticated strategic-planning activity, this firm was able to further subdivide this target into the principal sources of savings: capital investment based, technology driven, and employee generated.

In contrast, faced with an existing loss situation, a Canadian foundry elected not to set long-run goals initially but established a total cost-reduction target of 10 percent for the first year, while maintaining sales volume and prices. Meeting this target enabled the firm to move back into a profitable situation, which was management's most urgent priority. Longer-run objectives were subsequently established when it was clear that the firm would survive.

As these examples show, a variety of bases can be used to underlie objectives. Meeting competitive costs, remaining in the lowest quartile of firms in an industry, or achieving absolute cost reductions, either on a per unit or total basis are all examples of long-term aims. Goals, which are used as milestones to demonstrate to all employees whether the organization is on track, should be specific and quantitative. Once established, these targets have to be broadly communicated, and managers and supervisors need to be encouraged to discuss with the people who report to them the implications these goals present for their own areas.

At the outset, it may be unwise to break objectives down beyond the level of individual businesses, because very often specific targets set for individual departments or functions limit results and tend to inhibit cross-functional searches for cost reduction. Open-ended goals for each area within an overall target for the enterprise can produce results that far surpass executive expectations.

Communicating the Cost-Reduction Mission

Continuing communications on all aspects of costs are an essential part of cost-management strategy. The first challenge facing many executives is to be open with their employees about costs and profits. Fears that information given to employees will find its way to competitors, customers, and suppliers are usually exaggerated.

At the start of a strategic cost-management initiative, executives have to undertake a communications blitz, usually through a series of presentations and meetings. Simply publishing the strategy in company magazines or newsletters or posting information circulars on bulletin boards is insufficient. These initial presentations should tie the strategy into the organization's competitive position, financial performance, and overall strategy. For many employees, this information will be new knowledge, and a followup presentation at a later date is often necessary to reinforce the message.

Once the strategy is established the need for communication is by no means over. In fact, a belief in frequent and more substantive communication is one of the new corporate values that cost-reduction activities bring in their wake. The core of the continuing communications activity should be regular monthly or quarterly cost presentations made to small groups of employees. These sessions should be held during working hours, preferably at the start or end of the day. Presentations of this type made off company time may be enthusiastically received at first, but attendance soon dwindles to a core of committed employees while others, who really need to be communicated with, do not attend.

In these cost presentations, which should be made at first by senior managers but later by supervisors, information can be presented on the performance of the corporation, the specific operation in which the employee works, and the employees' own work area. Time is needed at the end of these meetings for questions and discussion. Initially these may be minimal, because employees feel uncomfortable asking questions of executives, but as such meetings become routine, employee confidence grows and extensive discussion may ensue.

Employees may start out being skeptical of the information provided, perceiving it to be management's way of justifying their actions. However, after two or three sessions, attitudes generally begin to change, and employees start to rely on and use the information presented in these meetings.

The burden on senior management can be eased if their subordinates can be induced to make these presentations. Lower-level managers and supervisors, however, may be reluctant to perform this task, and a major education effort can be necessary to break down the information iron curtain existing between them and the work force. Many supervisors can run a crew meeting but lack the necessary confidence and style to make a good presentation using visual aids effectively. Short courses on communication skills may be required first.

These communication efforts can create a considerable workload for managers and supervisors at particular times of the year. Preparation time can be minimized if a standard package of slides and supporting documentation is made available to everyone involved.

In large corporations in which it is impossible for the chief executive to make personal presentations to all employees regularly, important strategic developments and corporate performance can be communicated through preparation and delivery of a videotaped message. This can be shown at crew meetings and similar occasions, but it requires that managers and supervisors in attendance be briefed so that they can handle questions. Before they are widely shown, however, these presentations should be reviewed to make sure that the right message comes through. Some executives make an extremely poor showing on such recordings, especially if the presentation appears to have been "staged." In such cases, showing the videotape may be worse than doing nothing.

Personal communication efforts can be supplemented by a variety of additional information discussing costs and economic performance. Some of these options are listed in Table 6.4. Annual shareholder reports are informative, but often difficult for employees to understand. Some corporations now produce a special annual report for employees. Cost-management articles in company magazines can be effective, especially if they

Table 6.4. Supplementary Communication Vehicles for Cost Management

1. Corporate and plant employee magazines
2. Annual shareholder or employee reports
3. Bulletin board notices
4. Electronic notice board over plant/office entrances
5. Quarterly senior management bull sessions with employees
6. Posters on cost management
7. Crew meetings held to discuss costs on a periodic basis
8. Periodic letters from senior executives to all employees

are accompanied by pictures and stories on individuals who have implemented specific cost reductions.

One small foundry discovered that a programmable electronic notice board fixed above its plant entrance was an effective way of communicating important cost information to its employees on a daily, weekly, and monthly basis. A variety of cost information could be programmed in, such as month-end results or information on major orders currently in process. In addition, the notice board soon became an accepted way to recognize outstanding performance by posting the names of employees who had received awards for cost savings.

Some executives have taken to writing periodic letters to all employees at their homes informing them of major corporate developments and also reinforcing the cost-management message. This instrument has the advantage of reaching the employee's family and may provide the employee's spouse with information on the corporation which might not otherwise be received.

Although these communications may not stimulate cost-reducing activities directly, they are useful in changing employees' attitudes and beliefs toward their work and the corporation. One corporation that started providing this type of information regularly to its emplyees noticed that both union representatives and employees were much more reasonable during subsequent contract negotiations. Executives directly attributed this change to the mood of economic reality the communications sessions had imparted to the work force.

Freeing up the Organization

After the initial gains from becoming leaner and improving productivity are achieved, working smarter becomes a much more important force for cost reduction than working harder. Consequently, one of the important first steps in implementing an effective cost-management strategy is to start freeing up the organization for innovation.

Barriers and inefficiencies that act against cost reduction are introduced in complex organizations. Matrix structures and large staff organizations can create unnecessary jobs and excessive paperwork which can then become self-serving and stifle decision making and action. More important, organizations can become so large that complexity itself becomes a significant part of the overall cost structure without creating any additional real value.

The principal dimensions of organizational complexity that have to be managed are:

Excessive layers of management and supervision which inhibit communication and lead to inertia.

Loss of accountability for basic control over costs and productivity at lower levels, resulting in poor morale and reduced effectiveness.

Staff groups that become detached from reality and cease to be a service, but instead end up creating unnecessary procedures and delays which can result in loss of value.

Matrix structures which lead to ''groupitis'' and lack of accountability.

Overlapping jurisdictions and responsibilities between divisions and departments, leading to confusion and high costs due to duplication or, on occasion, necessary actions not being implemented.

High costs can be associated with each of these aspects of complexity.

In addition, many different barriers and obstacles to the implementation of cost-reducing innovations arise from diverse organizational sources. A group of mining engineers took only five minutes to list twenty-four major obstacles to innovation in their corporation. Some of the most common are listed in Table 6.5. Many of these obstacles can be laid squarely at the feet of managers and supervisors who are unwilling to give up some degree of operating control to lower-level employees.

Powerful barriers can be erected aginst innovation if workers perceive managers and supervisors to be unresponsive or, worse still, hostile to their inputs. In many corporations, employees feel that it is best to keep their ideas to themselves. In some cases, they may feel that the idea could result in the loss of personal employment or that of a co-worker. At other times, they may believe that the idea would be viewed negatively by a superior, especially if there could be some inference that this individual should have identified the potential saving as part of his or her responsibility.

Table 6.5.   Major Barriers to Cost-Reducing Innovations

- Conservative management and supervisory attitudes
- Comfort with existing processes and procedures
- Perceived lack of management and supervisory interest in ideas; failure to respond; failure to reward
- Lack of a forum for employees to propose cost-reducing ideas
- Lack of employee understanding of how to propose ideas effectively
- Excessive management concern with direct costs and ROI
- Shortage of seed money and funding to explore ideas
- Lack of resources to implement ideas
- Excessive concerns over safety and hygiene
- Perceived negative rewards for proposing change
- Lack of information to focus employee efforts on high-cost areas and items
- Concern that a cost-reducing idea will cost other employees their jobs
- Failure to integrate separate groups and departments to explore common cost-reducing opportunities

In many cases, however, employees do try to share their ideas, but a lack of responsiveness or feedback from supervisors and managers causes them to give up in frustration. Nonmanagerial employees frequently cite examples of having proposed cost-reducing ideas, but in spite of repeated requests, never hearing back from their superiors. A common vow at such times is: "Never again." An even worse situation arises in cases in which a supervisor or manager brings forward the idea as his or her own at a later date.

These problems appear to arise more frequently in corporations that have adopted a lean and mean approach to business. In such organizations, managers, supervisors, and professionals perceive themselves to be overloaded, having no time to spare for working with other employees on their ideas. In traditional organizations in which nonprofessional employees have little or no power to implement changes, this situation effectively precludes them from active participation in cost reduction.

Creating an Appropriate Environment

The initial challenge for top management is to provide those people who have a propensity for implementing cost-reducing innovations with an environment in which they feel they can go ahead. These employees are likely to emerge from groups throughout the organization, and seniority and rank are not likely to be reliable indicators of potential contribution. Suggestions for cost reduction may come as often from people in the work force or clerical and technical groups as from professionals and managers.

Organizations frequently benefit from a flood of pent-up ideas from employees, once the appropriate conditions have been created. Establishing these can take a long time, especially if employees feel that there is substantial personal risk in being perceived as rocking the boat by suggesting changes. This feeling is especially prevalent in organizations that have experienced layoffs and down sizing.

Many of the cost-management activities already described contribute significantly toward freeing up the organization. Symbolic cost-reducing actions by executives and managers serve as examples for other employees to imitate. Improved communications and information on costs increase awareness of the need for action. Many of the activities described in the next chapter can provide vehicles for employees to participate actively in cost reduction.

Stimulating Action

Executives can vigorously promote an organizational environment in which employees feel that they can make change happen and bring about cost reduction. To a large extent, employee involvement depends on the creation of a do-it or can-do mentality.

In lean organizations, however, one of the most limited resources is the time available to work on important cost-reducing projects. Routine jobs absorb much of every employee's day, and the ability to free up a block of time to work on strategic issues is limited. In these circumstances, executives can promote the elimination of unnecessary activities through a stop-it campaign. Although this notion might seem at odds with the do-it approach, it is actually complementary, given that it eliminates time spent on procedures and administrative routines which may add little or no value and which prevent employees from working on more important projects.

A second way in which management can foster employee involvement in cost reduction is by ensuring that employees know what is expected from them beyond their routine responsibilities. Quite frequently, supervisors and operators fail to respond to executive exhortations to participate in cost reduction simply because they do not know what to do. One corporation distributed a short document entitled Cost Management and You to its employees during cost-management seminars. This short statement instructed employees on how they could reduce costs by changing their own attitude toward work (e.g., attendance, work safety, degree of effort), redesigning their own jobs, improving those of others on their work team, and facilitating those of people they service. Ways of reducing materials usage and substituting cheaper materials were also suggested.

Creating an action-oriented culture requires more than tokenism from executives. Good cost-reducing ideas sometimes need seed money so that the first steps can be taken. Supervisors, engineers, and professional staff have to be made aware that they must make time available to work with any employee on significant cost-reduction projects. A cost-management strategy is working well when an employee with a significant proposal can obtain a decision to proceed, requisite resources, and authority to take action simply by meeting with his or her immediate supervisor and any relevant experts. Implementation has to be championed and worked on by committed employees and not hindered by paperwork and committees.

Above all, executives can support the freeing up of the organization by personally dismissing and eliminating the barriers to change when they are manifested. Executives must act decisively to eliminate roadblocks when they see that good ideas are being stifled because of traditional ways of doing things, supervisory discomfort with change, administrative sacred cows, or bureaucracy. Executive sponsorship that results in visible actions to support individuals initiating change is a powerful lever for creating an appropriate environment in which a cost management strategy can thrive.

Operation Simplification

Marks and Spencers' Operation Simplification illustrates the potential of simplifying organizational procedures. This campaign, carried out in 1956, eliminated 26 million pieces of paper per year and reduced the company's staff from 32,000 to 22,000.

Lord Marks, Chairman of Marks and Spencer at the time, is said to have remarked to his partner Israel Sieff, "It's not a law of business growth that administrative costs continue to increase." The principles of Operation Simplification are still as valid for cost-conscious corporations today as they were for Marks and Spencer 30 years ago. They are:

1. Sensible approximation: the price of perfection is prohibitive; approximation often suffices and costs less.
2. Exception Reporting: events generally occur as arranged, and only exceptions need ever be reported.
3. Never legislate for exceptions: detailed manuals are unnecessary

(Marks and Spencer went from thirteen manuals to two), and local decision making enhances willingness to assume responsibility.

4. Decategorization: those below management and supervisory levels are more useful in a general staff category than as specialists.
5. People can and need to be trusted: eliminating checks and controls saves time and money, while improving staff self-confidence and sense of responsibility. Management control is more effectively exercised by selective spot checks.[3]

Operation simplification was aimed at freeing Marks and Spencer's staff, managers, and support services from paperwork. If Canadian and U.S. corporations are going to reduce overhead costs through leaner organizations, a similar exercise is essential, or the remaining employees will be swamped by the output from corporate MIS.

More recently, some corporations have taken to examining every task performed to look at its profit contribution. This approach, termed element analysis, is discussed in Chapter 8. Celanese used this approach as the basis for much of its cost-reduction activity. Among the benefits was a major reduction in the number of financial reports generated.[4] For many companies, however, the activity is perceived to require such painstaking reporting and analysis that they are unwilling to commit the time and effort required. Executives in these firms hope that much of the value can be obtained with approaches requiring less formality and rigor.

Organizational Simplification and Self-management

There is now considerable awareness that beyond a certain optimal level, increasing levels of management and supervision and larger staff units start to become dysfunctional. Multiple supervisory layers deemed to be necessary to ensure an appropriate span of control are often redundant, resulting in excessive control, policing, and reporting. Staff groups can become isolated from the realities of the business and operations, developing their own objectives and goals, which may have little to do with those of the business, particularly cost management. As one executive observed, "Staff groups seem to have a way of finding new ways to spend money, not save it."

Many corporations that are serious about cost management find ways to eliminate staff groups and excessive layers of supervision by encouraging self-managing employees. Some firms, which have relatively high locational flexibility, are closing old plants and starting up in different areas with new equipment and streamlined organizations, sometimes at a fraction of the cost of their former site. In some of the more advanced of these situations, not only are supervisory and staff roles eliminated, but functional structures are as well.

These firms are not merely redesigning the organization chart. Rather, they are virtually eliminating it, at least in a traditional sense. Operations of up to 200 people are being run by multidisciplinary teams of employees containing maintenance and engineering support. A single manager and a small team of staff specialists provide leadership and advice in specialized areas, as teams plan, schedule, and manage their own work and do their own recruiting and training.

In corporations that do not have such flexibility and must continue to operate in their traditional location with an exisiting work force, a self-managing approach to operating and cost reduction is more difficult and takes longer to implement, but many of the benefits can be obtained if management is willing to persevere.

Many successful cases can be cited. For example, Dupont Canada has introduced self-management at the hourly level in two plants at its Maitland operation in Ontario. With appropriate training, the work force in these plants has proved capable of performing the majority of the operating, maintenance, and administrative functions. Staff groups at the Maitland site have supported these developments, permitting the new concept to survive and grow. Labor productivity improvements of 100 percent have been attained, with attendant cost reductions.

Executives in some traditionally managed corporations view the transition that has to be made as proceeding from a situation of tight supervisory control and low work-force involvement through two intermediate stages to possibly self-directed work groups, as shown in Figure 6.2. In most companies, the major barriers to this transition are:

Staff and supervisory concern for the nature of their own role, and ultimately their job (self-managing work groups do not need supervisors)

Union resistance

Lack of management commitment and capability to sustain the process

Bureaucratic requirements

The accompanying organizational transition is shown in Figure 6.3. There is usually significant simplification as supervisory layers are eliminated and staff groups are reduced in size.

In many organizations, the attainment of fully self-managing work groups is so threatening to supervisors and staff, and in all probability so far out in the future, that executives see the attainment of supervised, participative work groups, along with the possible elimination of func-

Advantage compared to traditional work arrangements	Cooperative	Participative	Self-directed
Cost improvement potential	Moderate	High	High
Worker development	Little	Some	High
Training needs	Little	Moderate	High
Worker selection	No change	Selective	Careful choice
Support organization	No change	Minor reduction	Major reduction
Time for implementation	Months	Years	Decade (?)
Management commitment	Moderate	High	Extreme
Supervisory threat	Low	Moderate	High
Risk	Low	Low	High

Figure 6.2.   Stages in Transition to Self-managing Work Groups

tional barriers, as a realistic target. For many organizations, even these changes could result in significant cost reductions because of reduced overhead, improved labor utilization, and improved operational integration.

For most corporations, even these changes have a significant impact on organizational procedures, culture, and supervision. For example, moving from a control orientation to participation demands a significant change in supervisory roles. Control, policing, disciplining, and leading are no longer appropriate. Coordinating, motivating, problem solving, and coaching are necessary. Many supervisors, particularly those selected on the traditional criteria of being the best operator, find this transition difficult. However, because fewer supervisors are ultimately required (spans of control may increase from as low as 1:7 to as high as 1:50, or even 1:100 as at Lincoln Electric), early retirement and attrition can be used to deal with this problem.

A switch to more multiskilled employees often accompanies increased

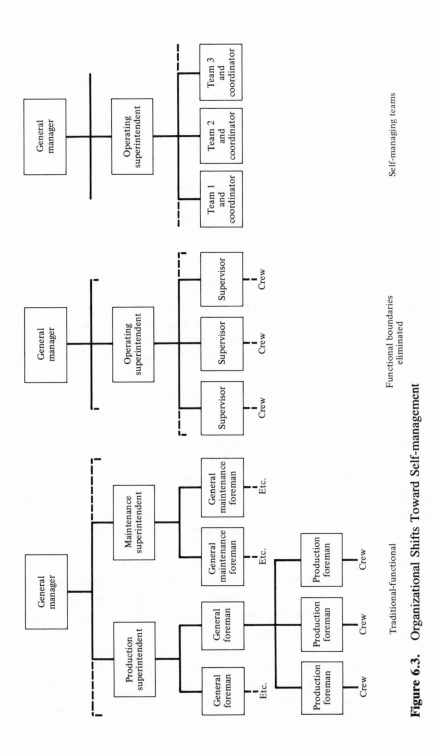

Self-managing teams

Functional boundaries
eliminated

Traditional-functional

Figure 6.3. Organizational Shifts Toward Self-management

137

involvement and greater self-management. Union resistance to the elimination of functional and jurisdictional job classifications and boundaries is likely, but many corporations are simply facing up to this challenge and going ahead anyway, often with the support of the employees involved.

Considerable job redesign and training are required for employees to carry out cross-skills roles, and this approach tends to be more effective when a single supervisor is responsible for all aspects of operations and maintenance in a specific area. Nevertheless, operators capable of routine maintenance and maintenance personnel who can operate plant equipment when they are not otherwise engaged will become common during the next decade.

Establishing a Cost-Reduction Budget

The cost-management strategy needs to have adequate resources provided, in terms of both personnel and finances. Cutting costs wisely involves spending money in order to save, and corporations have found that creating a budget for cost reduction is an important demonstration of management commitment to the initiative.

Establishing a budget should be one of the first tasks undertaken by the cost-management coordinator. Initial estimates are likely to be approximate, but as one manager commented: "If more is needed, especially for rewards and recognition, then it's likely we're getting the costs down." In one corporation, the cost-management budget for the second year of the activity was depleted by the end of April because employee incentive awards for ideas were being made at an unprecedented rate. Management was delighted when this budget eventually overran its initial forecast by 250 percent, because company savings surpassed these expenditures sixfold.

The major elements companies should include in their cost-management budget are shown in Table 6.6. The salary and benefits of the coordinator are normally included, as are specific training and development costs associated with cost management, promotion expenses, and amounts set aside for reward and recognition.

Some corporations also include a budget for nonmanagerial, nonprofessional employee travel to visit suppliers, customers, and competitors. Supervisors and operators can often pick up cost-reducing ideas on such trips which more senior employees fail to see and can generate considerable value for the corporation, especially if short reports are required from these employees on what they have seen.

Table 6.6.   Elements of the Cost-Management Budget

- Coordinator's salary, benefits, and associated costs
- Cost-related employee training and development expenses
- Cost-management strategy promotion and communication expenses
- Reward and recognition expenses for cost reduction
- Funds for employee travel on cost-management activities
- Seed money for funding inexpensive cost-reduction ideas and projects outside normal procedures
- Funding for special programs and activities

Amounts can also be included in the budget for cost-reduction seed money that supervisors and ordinary employees can access without having to go through the usual paperwork bureaucracy, especially if small amounts of capital are involved. Routine procedures often discourage employees from submitting their ideas, and a slush fund to facilitate low-cost initiatives, either at the discretion of the cost-management coordinator or individual supervisors, can be a major incentive.

Additional amounts can also be included in the cost-management budget for special programs the corporation wishes to pursue. One corporation invited all employees to a series of off-the-job, problem-solving dinner meetings held at three-month intervals, reasoning that production lost for such meetings held on company time was extremely costly. Such events are less likely to occur on a regular basis if they have to be funded by a line manager or supervisor who may be under continual pressure to reduce expenses.

After the initial year, the cost-management budget can be established as some percentage of annual savings, either realized in the previous year or projected for the current year. Consequently, management can view the budget as the investment necessary to keep the cost-reduction process moving along. In addition, budgets established in this way are unlikely to be trimmed substantially during periods when the corporation as a whole may be going through tough financial times. The more successful the cost-management process, the more important the budget becomes.

7.

Obtaining Employee Involvement

The Value of Greater Employee Involvement

There is tremendous value to be created in all firms from obtaining greater employee involvement in cost reduction. Foreign competitors of Canadian and U.S. firms, often with less-well-educated work forces, have gained significant competitive advantage by exploiting this potential. For example, in 1984, Toyota is reported to have obtained 900,000 process and product improvement suggestions from its 45,000 employees, saving the company an estimated $230 million.[1] Matsushita Electric received over 640,000 suggestions from its 80,000 employees in a single year. Many Canadian and U.S. firms are lucky if they receive an average of one suggestion per employee each year.

Suggestions are only one aspect of employee involvement in cost reduction. With slimmed-down management, engineering, and support staffs, many corporations are finding that product and process changes leading to cost reductions are bottlenecked unless work-force assistance with implementation can be obtained. In most newly lean and mean corporations, professional staffs are frequently overloaded and demoralized. Consequently, some corporations are delegating part of the responsibility for implementing cost reductions to operating employees. They are being asked to work alongside professional employees to reduce supplier costs, redesign processes, and improve products.

140

In contrast to Japanese industry, the approach of typical Canadian and U.S. companies to involvement tends to be focused and faddish. For example, many corporations are now starting to involve a broad cross section of employees in programs aimed at improving quality and increasing labor productivity. Concern with the cost of poor quality has forced many companies to involve employees in activities such as quality circles and statistical process control in an effort to be more competitive. Productivity and profit-improvement schemes such as the Scanlon Plan[2] and Improshare[3] have also received considerable attention.

Although such approaches undoubtedly create value, they are only partial solutions and have to be integrated with broader business and cost-management strategies before they can be fully successful and enduring. Failed attempts to introduce programs such as these can actually lead to declines in productivity and increased unit costs.

There is little doubt that the initial moves to involve employees in cost management are an act of faith for many executives. Substantive economic returns are difficult to establish at the outset, and the amount of effort required to change managerial and supervisory beliefs and attitudes often appears daunting. Visits to operations that are successfully implementing involvement activities are useful ways to create awareness and support, as well as to learn some of the initial steps to take. In addition, a variety of experienced consulting assistance has now developed in this area, although corporations should take care to ensure that this advice is tailored to their own needs and is not an off-the-shelf package.

Different types of implementation problems arise depending on the level in the corporation at which employee involvement is initiated. If the drive comes from the corporate office, the effectiveness of the activity can be limited should division and operating executives lack a similar commitment. In larger corporations, implementation in the corporation's different business units usually varies in the rate of adoption and effectiveness.

If divisions or plants start to implement this approach on their own initiative without complete corporate support, changes initiated at the corporate level can create problems. For example, the general manager of a division which had successfully gained greater employee involvement in cost-management was promoted and replaced by an executive who did not believe in the approach. In another case, an extremely effective divisional activity was destroyed single-handedly by a newly appointed corporate executive. He decided that he had to demonstrate a tough approach and initiated a series of layoffs in the division, which negated several years of effort by its management team.

Although involvement is usually perceived as a bottom-up activity, there is little doubt that it is best initiated from the top down. In many traditional businesses, both in the service and manufacturing sectors, noninvolvement starts relatively high up in the corporate hierarchy. Senior executives should recognize that one of the greatest challenges facing them today is to reengage supervisors and middle managers in the cost-management process. Previous approaches to cost management may have caused these key employees to abdicate any responsibilities in this area.

How Involved Do You Want Your Employees to Be?

Too many Canadian and U.S. organizations are at a zero level of employee involvement in cost reduction. In these corporations few employees other than senior managers receive information about costs on a regular basis, make any impact on cost reduction, or have the motivation to become more deeply involved. Cost management is perceived as an activity engaged in by "the bosses and the bean counters." Because varying degrees of involvement are possible, executives need to determine what contribution they wish their employees to make to cost reduction.

Why Aren't Employees Already Involved?

Frequently, few employees know anything about costs. Management often keeps much of this information to itself, due either to excessive concerns about secrecy or to its failure to understand how employees can use such information to reduce costs. It is not unusual to find purchase prices for materials and supplies blanked out on copies of purchase orders that are sent to the employee initiating a requisition. The message such behavior sends to employees is clear: keep out, this is none of your business.

Supervisors frequently have minimal direct involvement in cost management, which often comes a distant fifth or sixth on their agenda of concerns and priorities. They generally list safety, work allocation, production reporting, employee problems, and keeping superiors happy as the five activities that take up most of their time. Although these functions all have a cost component to them, little time is spent directly thinking about and managing the inherent costs.

If they are involved, supervisors and staff are often frustrated by a poorly implemented cost-management process. Cost reports can be an exercise in frustration. Cost-review meetings are also frequently perceived as a waste of time. Excessive management concern with accounting variances, large amounts of time spent on minor cost items, and interdepartmental squabbles over cost accountabilities can turn these meetings into monthly nightmares in which the challenge is to minimize personal exposure and risk. Outside these meetings, management interference in supervisory decision making relating to costs soon leads to abdication of responsibility.

Unfortunately, even in those corporations in which employee ideas are sought, their input is often limited to suggestions schemes that may be poorly implemented. Long implementation delays lead to frustration and result in a loss of interest. When one corporation objectively reviewed its suggestion plan, it found that the value of management time needed to evaluate employee proposals was greater than the savings, that the more valuable ideas took much longer to evaluate, and that some employees had gone up to eighteen months without hearing anything on the outcome of their suggestion. These plans and other implementation mechanisms are discussed in Chapter 9.

Differing Levels of Involvement

The extent of employee involvement sought in cost reduction can vary according to the overall level of participation desired by the corporation and the degree of interest across the work force. As shown in Figure 7.1, there are several different levels of employee involvement in cost management, each of which places different demands on managers and the corporation. Worker self-management accompanies the move toward a partnership approach.

The first level of involvement is attained when management makes a

Figure 7.1. Differing Levels of
Employee Involvement

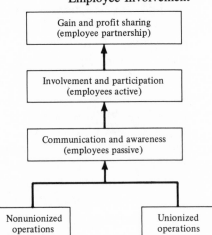

major effort to improve communications with the work force about costs to create greater awareness about economic realities and the competitive position of the business. In the absence of such communication, it is difficult for employees to have any continuing cost consciousness. Once aware of the cost position of their organization, employees may be more motivated to put in a fair day's work, although they may have little direct involvement in cost reduction other than making sporadic suggestions.

A second level of involvement is reached when employees from all parts of the organization start to take an active role in cost reduction. For this to come about, managers have to create an environment in which employees are encouraged to bring forward cost-reducing ideas and help in implementing them. At this stage, employees start to realize that cost management has a lot more to do with working smarter than harder. In addition to increased productivity, the organization is likely to obtain value directly from employee-driven innovations that reduce costs, and management has to start thinking about ways in which this value can be shared.

The third level of involvement is reached when a formal gain-sharing or profit-sharing agreement is adopted and management comes to view all employees as partners in the enterprise. This arrangement is most likely to work in organizations in which there is already an underlying culture of involvement and innovation. Timing and startup are critical determinants of the success of these types of activities.

All three levels of involvement can be achieved in both union and nonunion situations, although there is general agreement that the absence of a union makes implementation easier. In nonunion corporations and plants, employee associations may be actively involved in the cost-reduction drive right from the start.

Although each of these levels of involvement may be targeted, there will always be a spectrum of involvement in any specific situation. In operations in which labor-management relations have been traditionally hostile, the early stages of any attempts to involve employees in cost management may be met with indifference and suspicion by the majority of employees, including staff and supervisors. In many corporations, the immediate challenge is to gain the involvement in cost-management activities of supervisors and lower-level managers, who are likely to view their own roles as dealing exclusively with production and employee issues.

Typically, about 15 percent of the operating employees will initially be enthusiastic about the approach, seeing personal opportunities that they have always sought; 75 percent will be indifferent or adopt a wait-and-see attitude under the assumption that this is yet another management fad or short-lived program; and 10 percent may be hostile, perceiving the approach as management's way of achieving further down sizing.

As enthusiasm and acceptance grow, more employees are likely to become actively involved, and fewer will be openly hostile to the approach. In one such organization, about four years after the adoption of a full-scale employee-based cost-reduction activity, about 30 percent of the employees were active, and opposition had ceased. To get to this position, however, management had invested thousands of hours in gaining employee acceptance for the approach.

Even in nonunion businesses and operations in which initial employee reactions to this type of approach may be positive, a significant degree of active involvement early on is unlikely unless management creates specific vehicles and programs to obtain it. Most employees will be unwilling to take personal risks or invest significant amounts of time until they see how the initiative develops.

Selling Cost Management to Employees

The process of convincing employees about the importance of cost management can be difficult, but is an essential part of any strategy in which broad-based involvement is important. Without awareness and understanding of the value of the activity, employees are unlikely to appreciate its importance to both corporate survival and their own employment security.

In this initial phase, management is faced with four major issues that must be addressed. First, executives have to decide how they will create a broad awareness of the need for more effective cost containment. Second, they must determine how they will deal with employee fears about loss of job security that are usually associated with cost reduction. Third, management has to determine its initial approach to the union about this initiative. Finally, a decision must be made regarding whether to start small or with a full-scale organizational commitment.

Creating Awareness

Possibly the toughest time to sell the notion of cost management is when the corporation is profitable, as employees fail to appreciate why focusing on cost reduction is important. In tough times, everyone understands that costs have to be cut: the way in which these reductions are to be obtained is what causes problems.

A first step in this selling process is for top management to ascertain the level of information and education different groups of employees have about the business. In many cases, even quite senior managers do not have a grasp of the corporation's strategy, the nature of competition, and future challenges facing the business. Lacking this kind of information, they may fail to grasp the importance of cost management.

In addition, management must convince employees about the need for profits and explain their subsequent uses. Executives often communicate performance results only when times are tough and there is a need to take firm corrective actions. This approach has given rise to a belief among many employees that because results are communicated only when they are poor, there must be some dire reason for secrecy about high profits. It is not surprising that the work force then perceives cost management during good times as simply putting more cash into the owners' pockets.

Of course, the fact is that most corporations reinvest a substantial part of profits in new facilities, products, and processes. Once they are made aware of the uses to which profits are put, most employees are delighted and not resentful when executives tell them that the corporation is enjoying record profits. This situation is reinforced when workers are also sharing in these profits.

In the early stages of implementing an effective cost-management strategy, executives have implicitly committed themselves to creating a broad understanding of competition, business strategy, and the need for cost reduction among their employees. Some chief executives make presentations to small groups of their employees in which these topics are presented and discussed. This activity is important and should be carried out at regular intervals, perhaps every three months.

In some corporations, a series of one- or two-day seminars have been developed in conjunction with these presentations. In Falconbridge, for example, the objective of this type of seminar is to educate all employees from department managers down about the nature of competition in the minerals business, the corporation's business strategy, its need for profits to develop new mines and reinvest in new processes, and the importance of employee involvement in helping the corporation manage its costs. An executive who attended one of these seminars commented that he felt they were the best two-day course in capitalism he had ever been involved with.

Employment Security

A major concern when implementing a cost-management strategy based on broad involvement is whether job or employment security can be offered to employees. Generally speaking, employees will not offer cost-reducing suggestions if they believe that their proposals will result in either themselves or a fellow worker being put out of work. In corporations with relatively low work-force costs or sufficiently high labor turnover to accommodate possible reductions, such employment guarantees may be possible.

In most corporations, however, it is impossible to make unconditional offers of employment security to employees because of competitive and business realities. One approach that has met with some success is to make assurances that employees will not lose employment as a result of their cost-saving ideas. In such situations, the corporation usually commits to reduce staffing levels either through attrition or early retirement.

Nevertheless, there are limitations to this approach. For example, managers in one plant made such assurances to employees, and over the course of twelve months, built up a pool of about thirty employees who had been displaced by cost-reducing ideas and were supposed to be reallocated to new jobs as other employees left or retired. When corporate management heard about the existence of this pool, they insisted that these employees be let go. Trust between plant management and the remaining employees declined, and the broad involvement in cost management that had been developing was snuffed out.

Dealing with the Union

A third concern at the outset of a cost-management initiative is whether, and how, to involve the union. In some cases, if management-union relations are already cooperative and there is a mutual relationship of trust, management efforts can be strengthened by involving union representatives from the outset. In organizations characterized by confrontational relationships, which may already have been hit by work-force reductions, the union response to such proposals is likely to be either negative or ambivalent, at best. In these situations, the union is primarily interested in job security for its members and the maintaining of union dues, both of which could be perceived as threatened by an effective cost-reduction effort.

There is no doubt that active opposition to employee involvement by elected union representatives can nullify management efforts. Correspondingly, there is a widely held view that such activities should not proceed unless union cooperation has been gained. Realistically, this could mean a long lead time in many organizations before any significant benefits are gained, and also a great deal of compromise along the way.

Many managers are simply not willing to wait the length of time this approach implies to get results.

Some managers view the winning of union support for involvement as similar to the Democrats trying to win elections for control of the Senate by seeking to convince the Republican senators that Democratic senators could do a better job. The gulf in beliefs and ideologies precludes any reasonable chance of success, and it is far better to win the hearts and minds of the voters.

Executives should recognize that employee involvement has internal political overtones associated with it. Winning and building support for cost management by starting with employees who are most likely to go along with the approach, then subsequently building from this base, appears to be the most appropriate campaign tactic. Union representatives should be informed that the initiative is being undertaken as part of the corporation's efforts to be competitive, but formal requests for cooperation can be avoided, especially if management knows that the union's initial response is likely to be negative.

If management is successful in this approach, the attitude of the union is likely to change over time as elected representatives are influenced by emerging membership attitudes. For example, one Canadian mining corporation introduced an involvement-based cost-management scheme in 1978 in the face of considerable union displeasure. By 1980, many union members were actively involved in some aspect of cost reduction. In 1981, a short-duration cost-saving program obtained official union recognition. In 1982, this program was converted into an official gain-sharing activity with full union participation in steering committees and administration.

Starting Large or Small

There is a divergence of opinion on how to go about initiating more employee involvement in managing costs, quality, and productivity. A prevalent view is to start small and gradually expand the activity, thus minimizing risk. Certainly if a full-scale introduction is done poorly, then recovery is difficult. On the other hand, many of the initiatives that have started small have never grown, even when they have been a local success. Management attention moves on to other initiatives or the pilot activity becomes overwhelmed by the more entrenched traditional culture of the whole organization.

A preferable but admittedly riskier approach which offers faster returns and greater impact is to commit the total organization to the approach, but initially to allow individual departments, plants, and divisions to proceed at their own pace. Some managers will wish to move ahead rapidly and in so doing provide leadership and a basis of experience for those who are less committed and holding back until they see how the initiative develops.

Stages in Gaining Greater Involvement

Gaining greater employee involvement in cost management is a process with a distinct life cycle, which in its first few years closely resembles the development of an affectionate relationship intended to end in marital bliss. An executive in one firm that went through this process observed that wooing the work force is very much like marriage: you had better be sincere and willing to make it work once the romance has faded. Executives who are seduced by the apparent glamor of the participative approach should be aware of the underlying effort needed to build a long-lasting relationship.

The life cycle of a typical cost-management activity encompasses the following seven distinct phases:[4]

1. Gaining top-management commitment and establishing a supporting framework for the activity
2. Courting middle management and supervision
3. Wooing the work force
4. Consummating union involvement
5. A romantic interlude
6. Complacency
7. Sustaining involvement

The time periods for each of these may overlap, as shown in Figure 7.2, and the sequence may vary slightly depending on the culture of each particular organization. For example, the need to consummate union involvement will be irrelevant in nonunion operations, and it may take place earlier in the cycle in organizations with cooperative management-union relations.

Establishing a Supporting Framework

Once the top-management group is committed to implementing a cost-management strategy with greater employee involvement as a cornerstone and has decided on its objectives for the activity, the challenge is to get it up and running as rapidly as possible. One of the most important aspects of this task is to ensure that it is well championed and not ignored among the day-to-day pressures of business.

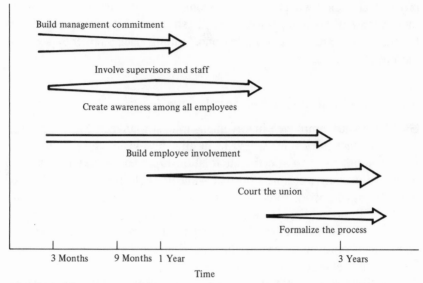

Figure 7.2.   Sequence of Stages in Gaining Increased Employee Involvement

Most corporations and businesses implementing such a strategy have found it critical to appoint a full-time coordinator (or director, depending on the size and scope of the activity) reporting to a senior executive to champion the startup of the cost-management activity. Cost management can be the sole concern of the coordinator, whose persistent probing and pushing keeps the attention of managers and supervisors on the activity. Implementation of one mining company's strategy stalled for twelve months until it was recognized that this role had to be filled.

In practice, championing cost management can easily take up to sixty or seventy hours a week of an individual's time, even in smaller operations. The coordinator spends a great deal of time promoting interest in the activity, resolving roadblocks and implementation problems, and serving as a source of information for all employees and as a resource for supervisors and managers. After the strategy has been in place for about a year, a major part of the coordinator's time can be taken up working closely with departments in which implementation is lagging.

The individual selected for this role is an important determinant of the strategy's ultimate success. Candidates to fill the position can be senior executives, but many corporations simply do not have talent to spare at this level in the corporation despite the importance of the task. More commonly, the champion is drawn from the ranks of middle management, and it should be someone having the potential for early promotion,

because this role turns out to be an excellent general management development vehicle. Personal qualities that are appropriate include an enthusiasm
for cost management, a willingness to work through influence rather
than a formal power base, a high energy level, a good rapport with a
broad cross section of employees, and a demonstrated propensity for
action.

To assist the full-time coordinator, some organizations find it useful
to appoint part-time departmental or functional coordinators to champion
the strategy in specific areas. Engineers, staff personnel, and highly
motivated nonsalaried staff are appropriate for this task, which is carried
out in addition to the individual's regular duties. The number required
depends on the size and complexity of the organization, but if there
are more than ten or twelve departmental champions, many of the advantages to be gained from teamwork begin to dissipate. As with the full-
time coordinator, the role of these individuals is to assist line managers
and supervisors in implementing the strategy in their own areas of responsibility.

Within departments and functional areas, a series of small committees
can be established to support cost-management activities, as is the case
with the Scanlon Plan.[5] These groups assist in planning their own department's cost-management activities and may even administer rewards.
They can include members from different functional areas, such as maintenance and production, as well as staff groups such as purchasing and
engineering. A broad employee representation can help integrate the
cost-reduction activities in different parts of the corporation and thus
avoid situations in which one department is reducing its own costs while
raising those in others. For example, it is not unusual for maintenance
to reduce overtime at the expense of lost production resulting from increased downtime.

Courting Middle Management and Supervision

The full support of middle managers and supervisors is needed if em-
ployee-involvement programs are to be successful.[6] Much resistance
can stem from these levels in organizations, and communication from
the top down often stops at these levels, with a corresponding filtering
process of what is allowed to percolate upward. Initially, supervisors
may view participative management with suspicion and resist implementation, seeing in it a potential loss of power, and ultimately, their own
employment if employees become self-managing.[7]

These issues appear to have been the cause of problems in General

Foods' experiment with a Topeka, Kansas dog-food plant designed to operate with a minimum of supervision. Workers were intended to schedule their own work, recruit their own teams, carry out their own engineering, and be self-managing in general. Economically, the plant appeared to be a success, but the result seems to have been threatening to other employees. Managers and staff personnel perceived their own positions to be in danger of elimination, and the initiative appears to be in trouble.[8]

A common complaint voiced by supervisors is that involvement is too unstructured or too democratic and that more effective results can be obtained from a traditional, directive style of management. Many supervisors prefer to work in an autocratic system with limited autonomy, even though stress and conflict levels may be high, because accountability for decisions can easily be passed upward to more senior managers.

If managers and subordinates begin making decisions in areas supervisors formerly perceived to be their domain, confusion and uncertainty about roles may result. Also, if some senior managers only pay lip service to participative principles and resort to traditional autocratic styles during periods of pressure, as is common in the early stages of employee involvement, considerable cynicism and mistrust may develop among supervisors.

Adjusting to Changing Roles

In most organizations, supervisors need time and assistance in adjusting to the increased autonomy and responsibility that broader involvement requires.[9] Their role becomes one of coordinating, facilitating, problem solving, and team building. Realistically, not all traditional middle managers and supervisors can play this role easily.

In firms in which little has been spent on management training and development, initial results will depend to a great extent on rapidly providing coordinators, supervisors, and staff with some of these essential skills. Corporations have found four areas to be central:

Cost management—many employees do not understand cost information and have little idea about which costs can be managed, how to go about reducing costs, and how to sell their ideas to management.

Presentations and communications—many supervisors do not feel comfortable making presentations to subordinates, especially if visual aids are required.

Problem-solving meetings—although many middle managers and supervisors are used to holding meetings in which they pass on information, they are not adept at holding meetings with their teams in which they try to resolve problems and determine courses of action.

Managing change—most employees in Canadian and U.S. firms are good at maintaining operations, but very few have developed skills in innovation and change.

Cost-management seminars can be developed to provide these skills, and outside assistance is usually available from universities, colleges, and consultants. Short one- or two-day courses are especially powerful ways of building commitment and involvement, especially if they explain the need for cost management, the approach the company is adopting, the role employees can play, and the tactics for implementing ideas. At the very least, they help reduce worker resistance, because awkward questions (e.g., "Will there be layoffs?") can be raised and discussed in a relatively nonthreatening environment. One company even asked every employee who attended such a seminar to bring along one cost-reducing idea to be developed further in the sessions and to try to implement on return to work.

Ensuring Continuity

Quarterly or monthly cost-reporting meetings can be held to discuss prior period performance and to hear how supervisors plan to reduce costs within their jurisdictions in the forthcoming period. Intangible cost items such as safety, absenteeism, poor quality, and equipment downtime can also be discussed at these meetings, as can problems and issues arising from the drive for greater employee involvement.

Small cost-management budgets, which supervisors can use at their own discretion for cost-management activities, can also be useful incentives. At first, many are reluctant to use these funds, often because they have been told for so long *not* to spend money. Once supervisors accept that management is not going to berate them for spending unwisely, they start to use the money for a variety of cost-management purposes: small rewards for their crews for outstanding performance, cost-management suppers, or even small pieces of equipment that they cannot justify within normal financial procedures but which they believe will lower costs. In a very short time, these budgets can become tangible symbols of the trust management places in supervision.

At the end of this stage in the involvement cycle, tangible evidence of progress should be evident in the following ways:

Supervisors are fully aware of the major issues facing the organization and of their own potential impact on these issues.
Supervisors should be taking more accountability for costs.
Supervisors are engaged in more open communication with superiors, peers, and subordinates.

Decisions are being made at appropriate levels in the organization, whereas previously they were being pushed upward.

If progress is measurable, then it is likely that a considerable degree of work-force involvement will already have been initiated, and more can now be actively sought.

Wooing the Work Force

Winning greater workforce involvement in cost management necessitates demonstrating that greater worker involvement will bring about mutual management-employee benefits, such as increased employment security through improved competitiveness, more challenges for employees in their jobs, and an improved work environment.

There are a variety of ways management can convey a sense of employment security, such as work-sharing arrangements during business downturns and guaranteeing minimum work periods of several years.[10] For example, Lincoln Electric guarantees no layoffs for employees who have been with the company for over two years, but uses reduced work weeks and job sharing to reduce labor costs (by as much as 25 percent) when demand is slow. In March 1984 Ford guaranteed workers at its Rawsonville assembly plant a minimum 32-hour work week for three years in return for productivity increases.

The business environment has been so threatening to workers in Canada and the United States in the last few years that most employees now accept shrinking work forces as a fact of life and are willing to help managers reduce costs as long as every attempt is made to mitigate the impact on individual employees. If work-force reductions are unavoidable, management must convince employees that layoffs will be avoided wherever possible through the use of early retirement and attrition.

In other words, management must gain work-force support and involvement by demonstrating an appropriate style (e.g., consultation, equity, openness) and not by preaching a doctrine. Seminars on cost management similar to those previously offered to supervisors can be used to educate workers about the need for cost reduction and how they can contribute. Other actions management can take to gain cooperation include:

Demonstrating a willingness to discuss the firm's operations by holding information sessions on competitiveness, financial results, costs, and major changes, then inviting questions and comments on these subjects

Encouraging supervisors to hold regular crew meetings (problem-solving and communication skills become important here)

Providing enthusiastic employees with a variety of opportunities to participate in cost reduction and problem-solving activities (e.g., suggestion schemes, cost-reduction projects, input into major capital expenditure decisions)

Recognizing and rewarding supervisors who demonstrate appropriate leadership styles and instituting remedial action when styles are inappropriate.

Rewarding individual workers and groups for helping to improve operations and reduce costs

Providing employees with information on high-cost items, activities, and operations can focus their activities. One approach that companies have found to be successful for materials and supplies is to put price tags on all warehouse supplies over a certain unit value. In Falconbridge employees play their own version of "The Price Is Right" when they are asked to guess the cost of specific supplies and components. They are frequently amazed at the cost of these items. For example, employees were asked to estimate the price of a box of 100 overhead transparencies made by 3M Corporation. Their estimates ranged from $8.00 (Cdn) to $150.00 (Cdn). The actual price was $51.95 (Cdn). Armed with such information, employees are much more careful in their usage patterns. Many may also try to come up with specific ways to cut back on waste and consumption rates.

Employee involvement should not be forced during this period. Such actions could lead to a negative union response, which might result in a withdrawal of support by the work force. Rather, management should seek and encourage greater involvement by recognizing and publicizing successes and not punishing failures. Publicly acknowledged successes may themselves create the peer pressure needed to stimulate other employees into trying out their own cost-saving ideas.

Consummating Union Involvement

Most experts agree that at some point the union must become a partner in cost management,[11] because gains from employee involvement are likely to be limited without union cooperation. Union involvement offers a number of advantages, including the possibility of easier implementation of cost-reducing actions, such as eliminating job jurisdiction restrictions, simplifying job classifications, and negotiating cost-management incentives such as gain sharing. Bringing the union on-side is also likely to silence an often vocal minority of employees who oppose management attempts to increase employee involvement.

Seeking union involvement can also be risky, because management has to be prepared to negotiate items that previously it was able to act

Table 7.1.   Sample Actions to Gain Union Involvement

- Opening the company's financial statements to union scrutiny
- Holding joint management-union conferences on strategic issues facing the corporation
- Ensuring union representation on crew committees in each workplace and on cost-reduction committees for the whole operation
- Initiating jointly with the union an annual cost-reduction drive, with small rewards for all involved employees
- Gaining union assistance in toughening up on well-known abuses of work practices
- Implementing a program to improve the general work environment

on unilaterally, especially when job reductions are involved. This process can result in slower decision making and loss of momentum in the cost-management activity. Some employees may also be disconcerted if they perceive that the union is "jumping into bed with management" and not protecting their best interests. Management should also recognize that this step is one that cannot be reversed without considerable loss of trust between management and the work force, and so there has to be a willingness to pursue the approach even in tough times.

A number of actions can be undertaken to involve union representation:

Management can clarify in which aspects of cost management greater union involvement is being sought (e.g., problem solving, quality, productivity increase, general operating decisions, or safety).

Union representation on a variety of operating committees can be sought.

Specific, high-profile worker-involvement activities such as gain sharing can be initiated.

Management has many options at this stage by which to demonstrate its good intentions. For example, one mining company initially sought union involvement in the ways listed in Table 7.1. Following initial successes with these activities, the company rapidly adopted a full-scale gain sharing program. Timing is critical, however, and the utmost caution should be exercised when deciding to make this move. For instance, it is not advisable to take this step in the period leading up to contract negotiations.

Ensuring a Lasting Relationship

The period after fairly broad employee involvement in cost management has been gained can be broken up into three quite well-defined periods.

Initially, a honeymoon period ensues in which cooperation between management, workers, and the union is high, and each group is especially sensitive to the needs of others. After one or two years, however, management may start to take the new approach for granted and relax the methodologies and disciplines that underpin involvement. If this change occurs, then the activity enters a third stage of either renewal or continued decline.

A Romantic Interlude

During this period, workers seem to express more interest in their jobs and take more care in the workplace. Many companies have found that their safety records improve as employees become more involved in cost management, especially if the high costs associated with a poor safety record are stressed. As unions become more involved, fewer grievances arise, job-jurisdiction disputes decline, and managers and supervisors waste less time on managing these fractious issues.

If cost management is properly structured, lower costs inevitably result for a variety of reasons. Workers make greater efforts to keep the operations going and minimize unnecessary downtime. Line operators often start to carry out routine maintenance activities themselves, and maintenance requirements are reduced. A profusion of suggestions to lower costs and improve productivity also emerge. Many of these are not new, but if an emphasis is placed on action, they can now be implemented.

The honeymoon phase of cost management can set the stage for corporate success, as was the case with Rubbermaid, a manufacturer of molded plastic products, which made Fortune's list of most admired companies three years running from 1984 to 1986. The company negotiated a contract with the United Rubber Workers that froze wages in return for a pledge from the company to try to maintain jobs. In 1986, employees in its housewares business generated 12,600 suggestions for cost reduction. Hourly workers have become tied into profits through their pension plan, which is based on profit sharing. These cost-reduction efforts, combined with close attention to customers and the market, have resulted in growth rates for sales and earnings per share of over 15 percent a year and a price-earnings record that ranks with those of high-technology corporations.

Complacency

After a year or two of successfully involving a major part of the work force in cost management, the honeymoon may draw to a close. The competitive pressures that led to the approach may have eased.

Although significant changes and improvements are likely to have been brought about, managers and supervisors start to take the activity for granted.

Employees find crew meetings and presentations routine, and the novelty of being involved wears off. The routine of involvement can start to break down if the frequency of crew meetings decreases, and the level of attendance declines. Managers find "more important things to attend to." Supervisors become less responsive to employee suggestions and ideas for change. Some issues of major concern to the work force may still not have been resolved.

In addition, involvement now enters a new stage of vulnerability. If operating results do not improve significantly, possibly as a result of deteriorating markets, managers and supervisors may feel tempted to revert to their former autocratic style of decision making. This tendency can be substantial during periods of low profitability, especially if senior managers perceive that the search for greater involvement has lead to overconcern with employee feelings and behavioral issues, resulting in a failure to address tough problems.

Any layoffs in such periods will almost certainly be attributed to the cost-management activity. Such actions allow work force skeptics of the approach to voice their opposition and can lead to a loss of union and employee trust in management, with a concomitant withdrawal of employee support. If payroll costs are significant and cost management is successful, then there will almost certainly be a need to reduce employment unless new growth opportunities (possibly arising from being a low-cost producer) have been created requiring additional staff. By this stage in cost management, corporations need to have developed a well-defined manpower plan and down-sizing strategy emphasizing early retirement and attrition.

In most situations, management is unaware that a breakdown in involvement is imminent.[12] At this stage, the ongoing participation of an outside consultant with an objective perspective can play an important role in making management aware of the problem.

Sustaining Involvement

As in a good, lasting marriage, there is a continuing need to work at involvement and keep the relationship fresh and vital. Consequently, corporations implementing involvement-based cost management have to ensure that the relationship with the work force continues to grow and evolve into a fuller partnership. Without resorting to fads and programs, executives can gradually introduce changes to the structure and format of the cost-management strategy to ensure that the interest and involvement of the work force is retained.

On a personal level, management must continually reinforce the values and philosophies embodied in cost management by its own actions and decisions. Identifying and resolving supervisory and work-force concerns about continuing involvement is one important aspect of this role. Frequent management visits to the workplace create high visibility with operators and provide accessability, which is important at this stage. In addition, through their personal attendance at crew meetings and problem-solving sessions, executives demonstrate their continued interest in the cost-reduction efforts of their subordinates.

A variety of minor changes can also be made at this time to keep cost management from becoming stale and routine. The format of communication presentations can be altered. Short-run, high-profile cost-reduction activities can be developed to maintain a sense of excitement and enthusiasm. More employees can be sent on visits to customer locations and other plants to search for new cost-reduction approaches. If the company is in a strong financial position, some of the savings that have been generated can be used to improve facilities provided for employees, such as lunch rooms and exercise areas. Many small changes of this type can be used to keep the attention of the work force focused on cost reduction.

In addition, managers can seek to delegate more cost-management functions to supervisors and their teams. Both the establishment of cost-reduction targets and the development of action plans can be left to these groups, with appropriate inputs from technical and other support functions. In some cases, managers may wish to move further down the road toward self-managing work teams by decentralizing other functions, such as recruitment and scheduling. In this mode of operation, management's main role is to provide the policy framework in which these developments can occur, resolve problems as they arise, and ensure that budgets and resources are appropriate.

Three to four years after the successful implementation of a cost-management strategy, when a strong base of involvement has been established, some form of gain sharing or profit sharing might be considered if it is not already in place. The successful implementation of one of these schemes takes involvement to the point at which employees start to believe that they are truly partners in the enterprise.

8.

Cost-Reducing Programs
and Techniques

The Search for New Ideas

A successful cost-management strategy requires that a stream of ideas
be translated into specific actions that reduce costs. An essential part
of the strategy is a set of techniques and activities that generate cost-
reducing ideas. In this chapter, the most important of these are described.

Many cost-reduction ideas are to be found outside the corporation.
Suppliers, customers, competitors, and firms in other industries can be
screened for ideas to reduce costs. Visits to other organizations by
employees at all levels in the organization can be a major source of
ideas for cost improvements. In addition, corporations have to find ways
that allow them to manage the costs associated with suppliers and customers.

Specific techniques can be adopted by organizations to help reduce
certain types of costs. For example, value analysis, product simplification,
and reverse engineering are widely used to reduce product costs. Element
analysis is gaining increasing acceptance as a method for analyzing and
reducing administrative costs.

It is unlikely and inappropriate that these activities will all be adopted
and implemented simultaneously. To be seen as important, cost-management activities must focus on high costs in each area of the corporation

and involve those people who are in a position to do something about reducing them. In the lean and keen corporation, the time available for employees to work on cost management is relatively scarce, and it is vital that activities focus and refocus on those areas that can have a maximum impact on the cost structure. Bringing a few approaches to bear on a limited number of important costs is likely to create more value than a smorgasbord of activities aimed at no particular set of costs.

As the cost-management strategy becomes established, a series of new initiatives can be implemented over several years. These will typically take one or two years to become fully effective, as organizations take this amount of time to learn how to use them (it is often just at this point that faddish managers lose interest and move on to something new). Properly implemented, most approaches remain effective for a further four or five years, but then start to become stale and either need to be revitalized or replaced with a new approach.

External Sources of Cost Reduction

Many sources of cost reduction are external, and strategies should explicitly include activities and mechanisms ensuring that employees at all levels in the corporation are able to investigate these possibilities. A major part of the industrial success of the Japanese has been their willingness to comb the world for new technologies and implement them, often in an improved version, in their own operations and products.

In the past, Canadian and U.S. firms have typically gone to suppliers for new process hardware, but have tended to develop their own know-how or software internally. General technical and business information has been obtained from attending conferences and industry trade shows, but too often the benefits have not been seen in lowered costs. In contrast, the Japanese have been willing to import technical and managerial methods and approaches to enable them to utilize their hardware more effectively than the competition. They obtain these ideas from well-organized, focused activities that are designed to obtain and use specific types of competitive information and intelligence.

In Canada and the United States, corporations have tended to shun the know-how of competitors or suppliers, believing that there is little to learn from these sources. The NIH (not invented here) syndrome has been a major contributor to this failure. As a result, corporations have invested many person-years of effort in reinventing what is already being done elsewhere. Employees either have not known what is available

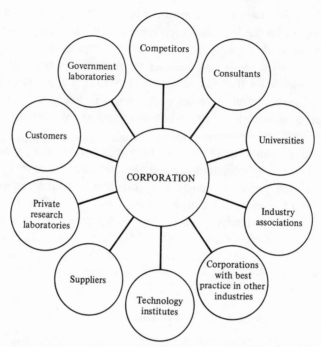

Figure 8.1. Network of External Cost-Reduction Sources

from outside or have preferred to think that developing their own internal solutions will produce a better result. R&D departments have been particularly prone to this line of reasoning.

As shown in Figure 8.1, there are a rich variety of external sources for corporations to draw on in their cost-reduction efforts. Each offers something different, and each needs to be approached and utilized in a focused manner. Sometimes extensive assistance can be expected, but in other cases, such as with competitors, the required information may be hard to obtain.

Customers as Sources

Working with existing and potential customers is an extremely useful way to obtain not only market and sales information, but also valuable cost-reduction insights throughout the cost chain. In many corporations, only sales, marketing, and possibly technical personnel visit customers, but it is clear that considerable value can be created by having even production employees meet with consumers.

These meetings can be particularly important in emphasizing the high costs of poor quality and identifying specific problem areas causing low customer utility and satisfaction. In a price-competitive market, visits to potential customers can yield valuable data on cost levels needed to obtain business and on product characteristics that may affect the cost structure.

Product teams made up of employees from different groups and levels within the company are extremely effective ways of carrying out this activity. One consumer goods corporation that put together a series of teams for each of its major product lines required that visits be made at least every six months to customers by each team. Not only did customer relations improve markedly, but on each visit the teams were able to identify a number of ways to reduce quality costs and improve customer satisfaction.

Competitors as Sources

Significant value can be obtained from competitors, although generally not a lot of cooperation can be expected. The exception is in industries in which extensive cross-licensing of technology is prevalent. Although competitors may not be forthcoming about their products, processes, and cost structures, a significant amount of useful information can be obtained without stooping to devious and unethical behavior.

A major source of cost reduction can be obtained by reverse engineering of competitive products, a technique used extensively by corporations such as Xerox. This approach is described in detail later in this chapter. Over time, developments in competitive products can be tracked, an activity known as competitive benchmarking, to develop estimates of rates of technical progress being made by the competition and to determine areas of competitive strength and weakness. This analysis can be used as one input to determine a company's own level of technical effort and the spending required to remain competitive.

These activities can spread throughout the entire organization. Once competitive products have been reverse engineered, they can be turned over to manufacturability teams, and even displayed on the shop floor, to demonstrate areas where the competition has superior quality or lower product cost. Employees can be galvanized into action by such demonstrations of growing competitor cost and quality superiority.

Besides information obtained directly from competitive products, a variety of inputs to cost management can be obtained from competitive information. New marketing and distribution channels can be examined for their impact on costs. Industry studies put out by trade associations and industry consultants can provide valuable information on cost structures which can assist in developing targets for cost reduction.

In some industries, limited cooperation on cost reduction can be developed between competitors. Plant tours and visits can be arranged in which useful information on processes and methods can be derived. Such visits should include employees at all levels in the corporation, although typically only managerial and technical staffs have been involved in the past. However, companies are finding that when supervisors and operating employees visit competitive plants, they look for and notice things quite differently than professional staff, and these can often result in substantial savings if followed up and implemented back in their own operations.

Other Industries

A failing in many corporations is looking only to their own industry for cost-reduction ideas and opportunities. Standards in specific industries may not be representative of best practice across industry in general, and sometimes companies can obtain major cost-reduction ideas by looking beyond their traditional boundaries for new ideas. This approach requires a broad search for cost reductions suited to specific applications.

One senior mining executive described how he sought out cost-reduction ideas for specific areas by looking at the best firms in industries that depended on that specific aspect of business for their competitiveness. His corporation did not look and see what other mining companies were doing to manage inventory costs, but instead looked at the systems employed by department stores and discount retailers, reasoning that this aspect of their business was so important that they would have advanced systems and procedures. In this case, not only were warehouse inventories substantially reduced by adopting a similar system to that used by retailers, but the mining corporation adopted a whole new approach to delivering materials to its working areas which saved large amounts of queuing time for employees.

Rather than developing its own reservation system, Canada's national passenger railway, VIA rail, went to the airline industry and purchased the system used by Air Canada, resulting in a considerable saving of time and dollars. Executives in a major food corporation looking for ways to develop better process control recruited staff from the chemical industry to develop systems, recognizing that process control is probably further advanced in chemicals than in most other industries.

Consultants

A broad range of consulting services are available to help corporations with cost reduction. Some engineering consultants may specialize in specific industries and be able to provide insights into particular process and product technology opportunities to reduce costs.

Although consultants can be extremely useful, considerable caution has to be exercised to avoid negative results from their involvement. Frequently, narrow cost-reduction programs and products offered by some consultants can reduce costs in one area, but increase others. For example, one corporation found that while maintenance costs were considerably reduced when it adopted a specific approach recommended by a consulting firm, over the next year breakdowns and lost production more than offset the savings.

Consultants are most useful when they know something about the company and its business. Otherwise, considerable time and expense is incurred in simply helping the consultant gain the necessary understanding of the firm, its strategy, and the industry. Executives also find that consulting firms offering techniques and products that are not tailored to specific company needs have a much lower success rate than those that modify their approach to suit each client. Recognizing that cost reduction is an ongoing organization process, rather than a specific technique, also suggests that consultants who are prepared to help the corporation develop a process and work alongside during implementation (as coaches, facilitators, and educators) are likely to be more effective.

A few companies have enjoyed considerable success when they select a consultant with whom they propose to develop a continuing relationship for several years, rather than on a specific project basis. The consultant then has a considerable incentive to learn all about the corporation's approach to cost reduction and once aware of the business problems and issues, is in a much better position to provide useful advice and assistance.

Other Sources

As shown in Figure 8.1, cost reductions can be derived from several other external sources, both in the public and private sectors. Corporations are increasingly using universities for their basic and applied research capabilities, and these can be equally well applied to cost reduction through the development of new products, processes, and materials. A number of corporations are currently using materials science departments in universities to examine the potential of advanced ceramic materials and coatings to cut costs, as well as for their new product opportunities. In some cases, universities possess testing facilities that can provide fast answers to process problems, especially if university researchers and corporate technical people have a good working relationship.

Similar contributions to cost reduction are possible from a variety of government and private research laboratories which can often provide specialized help in specific areas, such as lowering energy costs or developing new materials. Very often the only barrier that prevents corporations from using these resources is the simple fact that no one in the corporation knows of their existence.

Industry associations and specialized technology institutes are springing up to help firms adopt specific new cost-reducing technologies. National productivity centers have been established in the United States and Canada, and both countries contain a variety of institutions devoted to the diffusion and application of new technologies such as computer aided design and manufacturing (CAD/CAM), robotics, advanced ceramic materials, and artificial intelligence.

Part of each corporation's cost-management strategy should be the identification and establishment of links with these kinds of external agencies. Corporations usually find that a limited number of contacts focused on areas of potential competitive advantage are most effective.

Taking Costs Out of Inputs

Purchased materials, supplies, and services can be a major cost item for manufacturing and service corporations. In some consumer goods assembly operations, purchases can account for as much as 80 percent of total costs. In service businesses such as the retail sector, purchases often account for similar amounts. Even relatively small savings in this area can make a significant contribution to profitability, yet many corporations pay little attention to purchasing in their cost-management efforts.

Purchasing is a function that, unlike marketing or finance, has not been seen as glamorous, exciting, or one of the routes to the top of the corporation. Consequently, many executives know little of the function and do not take much interest in it, except when there are problems. Procurement people tend to compound this situation by being excessively procedure bound and guarding their vendor contacts as jealously as sales people treat their customers. As a result, broad working relationships with vendors do not develop, and major cost-reduction opportunities can be lost.

The costs of ignoring this end of the business can be high. Some businesses create a substantial cost for themselves by treating supplier performance as a given, then creating their own systems to offset poor service. Too much time is spent inspecting incoming supplies and components because the supplier quality cannot be trusted. Excessive inventories have to be carried because unreliable deliveries threaten to close down lines and plants. Extra warranty and goodwill costs are incurred because defective inputs that slip through the inspection screen ultimately cause the end product to fail in the hands of the consumer.

Corporations are now starting to realize that if supplier-related costs are a significant part of total costs, they have to be managed as tightly as those incurred internally. In the past, companies have attempted to meet this requirement through hard bargaining, double sourcing, and cutting off suppliers that fail to perform. Although these tactics are appropriate in some situations, they have not proved totally satisfactory, and both quality and delivery remain problematic for Canadian and U.S. manufacturers.

A more strategic and effective approach has been demonstrated for many years by the British retailing giant Marks and Spencer. Residents and visitors to Great Britain know that this company stands for value and quality in clothing and food products. What they may not know is the remarkable system that the company has developed over the years to ensure that its purchased inputs meet its exacting quality and cost standards. The company has a strategy, as well as an integrated engineering and purchasing organization, to manage the supplier network.

Although it offers a broad range of clothing and food products, Marks and Spencer uses relatively few suppliers, and it is usually the major customer for these firms. In addition to guaranteeing a long-term relationship with these companies in return for outstanding performance, Marks and Spencer provides them with a great deal of assistance. Purchasing, engineering, and accounting personnel from the retailer visit suppliers regularly and work jointly with them on product design, quality assurance, process improvement, and cost reduction. The directors of the corporation informally reinforce this system by routinely visiting stores on weekends and asking shop assistants and customers whether they are happy with the quality and value of the products on the shelf.

The effectiveness of the Marks and Spencer approach is demonstrated in its diversification into Canada in the early 1970s. The Canadian Foreign Investment Review Agency permitted the move on the condition that the company obtain 90 percent of its requirements domestically within five years. At the time, the Canadian textile industry was known for its appalling quality and high costs. Marks and Spencer replicated its British system in Canada, induced a few British suppliers to set up subsidiaries in that country, and within the allotted time frame was sourcing the required quota of high-quality, competitively priced purchases within the country. In contrast, its major Canadian retail competitors obtain about 30 percent of their products from within the country.

Canadian and U.S. automobile manufacturers are now adopting a similar, and possibly more structured, approach to managing supplier costs. Creating strong relationships with reliable, single-source suppliers is now considered to be preferable to double or triple sourcing. Vendor certification programs are being developed that are resulting in a tier system for suppliers. First-tier suppliers must meet a variety of stringent performance criteria that are intended to ensure they have world class manufacturing and engineering capabilities. These include:

1. Having 100 percent of processes under control (usually through the adoption of statistical process control)
2. Having less than 500 production rejects per million
3. Having greater than 90 percent equipment uptime
4. Having a product development lead time of one year or less
5. Reducing production lead time to three days or less
6. Increasing annual inventory turnover to at least 50 times

To meet these stringent requirements, tier-one suppliers have to adopt an array of new manufacturing techniques and approaches which typically include statistical process control, just-in-time deliveries, and flexible manufacturing systems. Recognizing that many suppliers do not have the internal capabilities to develop these approaches by themselves, automobile companies are working closely with them to provide the necessary training, skills, and technological support.

Most corporations do not have the purchasing clout with suppliers that is possessed by automobile companies or large retailers such as Marks and Spencer, but there are nevertheless a number of cost-reducing actions that smaller firms can use that have a similar impact. Vendor selection and certification can be practiced by smaller corporations as well as large ones, and much can be gained by limiting the number of suppliers that have to be managed, especially in lean corporations, where purchasing and engineering staffs are small.

Establishing a continuing dialogue and working relationship with the most important vendors is also important. Typically, 80 percent of purchases will be made from fewer than 20 percent of the total supplier group. Inviting executives from these suppliers to annual vendor conferences at which needs, issues, and problems can be discussed is useful. Creating purchased materials task teams to work with these key vendors on quality, cost, and delivery problems is also important.

Relationships with suppliers at multiple levels in the company can be extremely useful. Executive contacts can be used to define and build long-term relationships and negotiate important issues relating to contracts. At the professional level, purchasing personnel, product engineers, and process engineers can be used to help vendors provide better service in ways described above.

In some corporations, routine contacts with vendors to resolve minor delivery and quality issues are handled by the operating employees themselves. Unfortunately, too many managers and purchasing people are scared of what they perceive to be a surrender of control to the work force. With appropriate training, however, this step can actually provide a significant increase in the leverage and influence corporations can bring to bear on suppliers.

In addition, having operating personnel handle routine contacts eliminates the procurement bottleneck that is created by lean staff departments, and it also frees the professional staff to work on important issues with vendors, rather than spending their time firefighting. In these situations, groups of production or operating employees will often visit suppliers to resolve problems and create personal contacts.

As indicated above, a variety of approaches to reducing supplier costs are possible, and a well-thought-out strategy that defines appropriate roles in this effort for different employee groups can result in considerable involvement and delegation of decision making to hourly paid employees. The approach of Sikorski helicopter which is described at the end of this chapter demonstrates the range of possibilities that exists when management thinks and acts strategically in this area.

Taking Costs Out of Marketing, Sales, and Distribution

Cost reduction in sales and marketing is a relatively neglected area, frequently ignored by practitioners and writers alike. Most marketing and sales cultures are oriented toward increasing revenues rather than decreasing costs. Executives in these functions generally argue that an increase in sales and marketing expenditures will do more for the bottom line than a reduction in their budgets.

In fact, increased gross margins brought about by cost reductions in manufacturing and operations are often not reflected in improved bottom-line profitability, as higher levels of marketing, sales, and distribution expenditures swallow up the savings. Very little has been written on marketing cost reduction, even though corporate spending increases in this area have created substantial potential for savings.

Cost reduction in these areas is difficult to generate effectively. In some corporations, the brand management system results in resource allocation procedures that merely shift expenditures between products, rather than creating real savings. A continuing power struggle in many corporations between sales and marketing tends to mean that reduced advertising expenditures (usually controlled by marketing) are frequently offset by increased sales promotion activities.

There are undoubtedly considerable business risks in reducing costs in these areas. Reduced advertising and promotion expenditures could result in the loss of profitable market share. Focused cost-cutting activities, such as product-line pruning, are difficult to bring about because of the problems in accurately measuring product profitability. The allocation of all types of cost to individual products is a very hit-and-miss affair in most corporations (see Chapter 4). Consequently, reductions in marketing and promotion expenditures tend to be subjective, because of the lack of concrete data on the value creation of these activities. These problems, however, only make the cost-reduction challenge more interesting.

In spite of the difficulties, some corporations are taking a hard look at sales, marketing, and distribution costs. For example, Heinz is actively pursuing ways to reduce all three as part of its overall strategy to be a low-cost producer in the food industry. Between 1980 and 1984, Heinz increased gross profits from 35.2 percent to 38.1 percent, but put 60 percent of the proceeds into increased marketing expenditures.[1] Since 1984, Heinz has made a variety of savings in these areas, among them $4 million from simply eliminating the label on the back of its large jars of tomato ketchup.

Other corporations in the food industry have joined forces to manage costs under the umbrella of the Direct Product Profit (DPP) Institute. This initiative is intended to provide suppliers, wholesalers, and retailers in the industry with standardized approaches to individual product costing so that opportunities to reduce costs and increase profits can be identified. As with total loss control, DPP is a management tool that requires considerable training and development of procedures in organizations that adopt the approach.

Initiatives such as these demonstrate the recognition that bottom-line profits will only increase if the benefits of improved gross margins are passed on through the marketing and distribution chain. The strategic challenge in cutting marketing, sales, and distribution costs is to make savings while maintaining or increasing the value and utility of the product to the customer and the end consumer. Cost reductions that reduce perceived value, quality, service, or other product characteristics are likely to result in reduced sales, all else being equal.

Strategic cost management in these areas employs the same framework and the same five principal sources of cost reduction described in Chapter

3. Capital investment, economies of scale, new technologies, the learning curve, and simplification are all relevant. There are, however, greater opportunities for corporations to use cost reductions as a competitive advantage in these areas if, in addition to reducing their own costs, they can cut those of their customers as well. Figure 8.2 shows a framework for marketing, sales, and distribution cost containment adopted from a marketing model developed by Joe Magrath and Kenneth Hardy. This framework provides a unifying approach within which various sources of marketing cost reduction can be integrated.[2]

Capital investment can make an important contribution to reductions in distribution costs. Automated warehousing and distribution systems, palletization, and container shipments all still hold tremendous potential for cost reductions in a variety of industries. Ross Stores, a large California retailer of women's off-price clothing, increased the productivity of its distribution center by 50 percent through the introduction of computer

Figure 8.2. A Framework for Reducing Marketing, Sales, and Distribution Costs

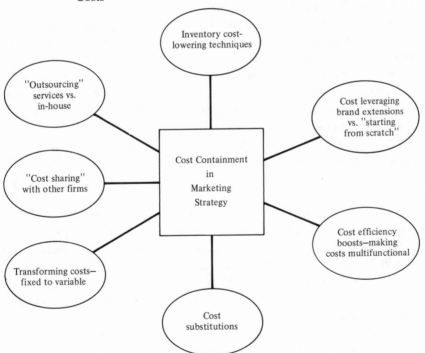

controlled materials handling systems to sort, bag, and price garments.[3]

Different ways of increasing volumes are possible through nontraditional routes, even in mature markets where increasing share points is likely to be costly. For example, Magrath and Hardy point out that cooperative sales and promotion programs between noncompeting firms can reduce the unit costs of these activities. Unit transportation costs can be significantly reduced by increased use of backhaul, thus spreading freight costs over a greater volume of goods.

New technology can be used to reduce sales, marketing, and distribution costs in a variety of ways. Telemarketing can reduce sales costs. For example, Louisiana Oil and Tire Corporation eliminated most of the travel for their salespeople by moving to this approach. Sales expenses fell 10 percent, while sales doubled.[4] Video-conferencing can reduce the cost of sales and marketing meetings. Packaging and distribution costs for bulky products such as diapers and feminine hygiene products can be reduced by the development of more densely packed materials. Computerized ordering systems and electronic communication links between customers and suppliers have the potential to effect major reductions in all marketing-related costs.

Many cost improvements arise from employee learning that takes place over time throughout the marketing and distribution chain. For this reason, inputs obtained from individuals at all stages in the distribution process are important. Customers may provide ideas that reduce both their own costs and those of their suppliers. For example, many large corporations now insist that their suppliers be able to accept and process purchase orders electronically, which substantially reduces the costs associated with generating these orders, as well as reducing delivery lead times. Suppliers affected by these requirements have found that such changes to their systems also reduced their own selling, order entry, inventory, and distribution costs.

Simplification can play a variety of roles in reducing marketing and distribution costs. Reductions in product lines can produce major savings by eliminating either low-profit flanker brands or redundant packaging sizes and forms that lose money and add little to strategic market positioning. Advertising can also benefit from this approach, sometimes in unexpected ways. For example, shorter commercials cost less and may actually have more viewer impact.

Product and packaging simplification in the consumer products industry has increased case-cube efficiency and reduced distribution costs. Procter and Gamble saved its customers 32 cents per case by redesigning the shape of its Crisco oil bottle. Colgate Palmolive eliminated the handle from its small bottles of Liquid Ajax cleaner sold in Europe. Retailers were able to save shelf space, and Colgate saved approximately $2.5 million per year from the change. When Proctor and Gamble switched the packaging of several of its leading brands of soap from single bars to bundles, it reduced manufacturing costs and also saved $1.00 per case for its customers.

Specific Cost-Reducing Techniques

A variety of techniques have been developed that can help both to identify and to implement cost reductions. These include well-used activities such as value analysis and more recent developments such as reverse engineering. Such techniques have traditionally been viewed as largely in the domain of engineering or manufacturing, and thus not incorporated into an overall strategy. In a total-cost approach, they can be integrated into a broader set of corporate and business activities, and with appropriate training a wide spectrum of employees can use them effectively, especially within team settings.

Some of the most commonly used cost-reduction techniques are summarized in Table 8.1. This list does not include several operating management tools and approaches that are gaining increased acceptance, such as just-in-time delivery systems, materials requirements planning, and statistical process control. These approaches have a far broader purpose than cost management, although if they are implemented and managed well, they can reduce production costs substantially. These concepts have already

Table 8.1. Cost-Reduction Techniques

TECHNIQUE	PRIMARY APPLICATION	AREA OF COST IMPACT
Value analysis	Products, materials, components	Purchase costs, process costs
Reverse engineering	Products, components	Material costs, quality costs
Competitive benchmarking	Products	Materials, development and engineering costs
Element analysis	Administrative and clerical tasks	Overhead costs
Paperwork simplification	Reporting and information systems	Administrative costs
Total loss control	Processes, safety, waste	Operating and intangible costs

been described at length in a variety of other books and publications, and readers are referred to such sources for further information.[5] In this section we focus on techniques that are specifically intended to facilitate cost reduction.

Consulting firms offer these techniques and a large set of variants under the same or different titles. Since executives from nonmanufacturing backgrounds may not appreciate the potential contribution or understand the appropriate application of these tools, the purpose of this section is to provide a brief overview of their use and provide readers with a managerial perspective on how to fit them into cost management activities.

Value Engineering and Analysis

There are many opportunities to cut the cost of products and services by either reducing the cost of materials and inputs or by simplifying the overall structure of the item being delivered. Estimates suggest that Northern Telecom Limited reduced the number of components in a telephone by 60 percent and the manufacturing cost by over 50 percent using this approach. Value engineering is usually undertaken during product planning and design, and value analysis is carried out on existing products and services.

Value analysis is generally conducted by multidisciplinary teams drawn from across the corporation and may even include customer representatives. Members of the value analysis team have a variety of roles to play: product and manufacturing engineers provide specialized technical information as well as design knowledge; sales and marketing people can advise on the impact changes will have on customers (as can any customers on the team); purchasing personnel supply cost and availability data on materials and components; accounting personnel can present product and process cost breakdowns for alternative designs; production management personnel provide input on the impact of design changes on manufacturability. Many corporations also include production workers in these groups. The value analysis team first examines the use and function of the product and then investigates the utility of its features. The value of the product to the customer is compared to the delivered cost. Specifications, components, materials, and product structure are then analyzed in a process similar to zero-based budgeting.

The principal questions asked include:

Can components be eliminated without reducing performance?

Can materials be replaced by either cheaper substitutes or possibly more expensive ones that will improve performance and that customers are willing to pay for?

Can specifications be relaxed without affecting quality?

Can the product or components be redesigned to reduce manufacturing costs?

Can the product be redesigned to provide greater customer utility and value?

Component and materials standardization across product families is a useful extension of value engineering which has been facilitated by CAD/CAM. Inventory costs can be significantly reduced, customer service improved, and purchasing economies obtained if different products can use the same components. One manufacturing corporation analyzed the number of different screw types used in its products and found that there were over a thousand. Product redesign, facilitated by the standard recipes available on CAD/CAM systems, reduced the number to less than 200 within a year.

Reverse Engineering and Competitive Benchmarking

Reverse engineering focuses jointly on product improvement and cost reduction. By analyzing the design and construction of competitive products, companies can avoid some of the costs of having to develop their own improvements, and also greatly shorten the time necessary to incorporate these into their own product lines. This analysis reveals how far behind or ahead competitors are in developing particular aspects of the product technology. In addition, quite accurate estimates can be made of competitive manufacturing costs, which can then be used to set targets for the corporation's own operations.

In reverse engineering the latest models of competitive products are purchased and physically inspected to determine what components, design aspects, or inferred manufacturing processes have been improved or changed. This analysis is performed by teams of engineers trained to carry out reverse engineering. Some organizations insist that the engineers responsible for designing products also carry out reverse engineering on those of the competition, so that they are constantly made aware of new developments.

The information gathered in this process can be used in two primary ways. First, specific cost and performance improvements in components and design can be studied for their applicability to the products of the corporation carrying out the analysis. Patent searches can be used to reveal if proprietary barriers prevent or limit this course of action. Even if barriers exist, developments can be initiated to find alternative ways to obtain the same result without infringing the patents.

A second use for the information is to benchmark the progress of competitors on specific aspects of product technology, as well as on cost improvements. Data gained from this activity can be used to project likely trends in the design and cost of competitive products. This information can then be used as input for a corporation's own cost improvement and technical development strategies.

There is no reason why this concept should not also be more widely used in service industries than it is at present. Although products in these businesses are generally intangible, corporations can periodically monitor the services provided by other firms and evaluate them on a variety of performance criteria including cost, quality, delivery, and convenience. Marketing and operations personnel can then analyze the results to determine ways in which their own corporation can improve or maintain its service characteristics at the same or lower cost.

Element Analysis

In element analysis, employees are asked to record every activity they carry out over a period of weeks or months. Carried to its logical extreme, element analysis can be a boring, mind-stultifying activity that can cause significant employee alienation, particularly if they feel threatened or if the purpose of the activity is not well explained. The technique is largely used to extend traditional time and methods studies to administrative activities. Instead of using industrial engineers with stopwatches, however, employees are asked to monitor their own activities.

The purpose of this technique is to identify every task carried out in an organization and subsequently evaluate its value and contribution. Consultants are often hired to establish and direct the process. Once data have been accumulated, teams of employees assess each job and task performed, asking whether the activity is necessary, and if it is, whether it can be simplified. If spare or waste time is identified, the possibility of combining jobs is examined. For example, many reception employees now are expected to carry out routine clerical activities when they are not dealing with visitors. Alternatively, some plants and offices have eliminated the receptionist entirely by providing a telephone and directory in the reception area.

Element analysis can make a major contribution when it is applied to routine clerical or administrative functions, which frequently can be modified for computer applications and in some cases, even eliminated entirely. This approach can be extremely powerful if it is combined with a procedure simplification activity such as that carried out by Marks and Spencer, as described in Chapter 6.

Paperwork Simplification

Over time, organizations build up tremendous volumes of reporting and administrative procedures that create paperwork, as well as additional costs. Furthermore, they can dramatically slow down the speed of organization response. In some large corporations it may take up to a year for a capital request to pass through all the various stages of review and approval, gathering weight and bulk as it does so.

Special reports are often created to deal with specific situations that then become part of the routine. For example, during tight financial periods, authorization controls are added to spending, which then become standard procedure. Every purchase order may have to be reviewed and signed off by a plant manager, even if it is only for $10. Items costing over $100 may have to be capitalized.

In this manner, many procedures evolve in which people simply exchange pieces of paper. Fundamentally, they add no value to the corporation or its products, and yet it generally proves extremely difficult to eliminate them. Institutionalizing a corporate control over this process rarely works, because the departments established to manage the problem usually end up being the worst offenders, sending out sheaves of paper exhorting other employees to use less.

Reducing paperwork costs is an area that is amenable to specific task force approaches, such as Marks and Spencer's Operation Simplification. In Canada, the federal government established a temporary office of paper burden that was quite successful in eliminating some of the worst excesses of bureaucratic redtape during its few years of existence. A periodic blitz is often most effective. Some companies establish task forces of people they know hate paperwork and turn them loose.

Another approach employed in some corporations is periodically to stop sending out reports and see if complaints are received. A third approach is for executives, managers, and supervisors to detail the reports received over a period of time (as in element analysis) and indicate whether they are useful, timely, and well formatted. Most important, employees should be asked to identify clearly which can be eliminated. Although such approaches are useful, it should be recognized that much of the value from eliminating paperwork is derived from eliminating the associated payroll costs. If reports are eliminated but not the jobs, new documents will be invented to fill both the vacuum and the time.

Total-Loss Control

This technique is a highly structured program intended to involve all employees in the elimination of all types of loss within a corporation, including those associated with safety, materials wastage, lost machine time, and absenteeism. In many respects, this approach complements the thrust of a corporate cost-management strategy, especially with respect to intangible costs. Some corporations use the technique as the core of that part of their cost-management strategy dealing with hard-to-measure costs, especially safety and health.

The total-loss control program is administered nationally in the United States by an institute that provides training and documentation to companies adopting the approach. In addition, the institute performs audits in the operations of participating corporations and awards a rating of from one to five stars based on the quality and effectiveness of the program.

Employees using the total-loss control system receive training that helps them analyze and decide on appropriate action to eliminate potential or actual loss conditions. Estimates of different types of loss within the corporation are then made widely available. For example, in one corporation, the cost of simple medical aid accidents was estimated to be $100, lost time accidents averaged $3,500 each, and broken legs $17,500. Following each reported incident of a major loss, a team was established to determine the cause, analyze the situation, and make recommendations to prevent a recurrence.

In most companies, total-loss control has not drawn much interest or support from senior management and is usually confined to the operations level in corporations that adopt it. Carried to its extreme, the procedure can be excessively bureaucratic and time consuming because of the paperwork involved, especially if its scope extends beyond major incidents. In addition, if interest and commitment to the program is lacking among more senior levels in the corporation, difficulties can result in implementing the recommendations that follow investigations.

Periodically Rejuvenate Activities

Although cost management eventually becomes part of the ongoing routine of corporate life, its effectiveness will be improved by periodic changes in focus and content. In a corporation using cost management strategically, these changes will parallel shifts in the business environment, as well as changes in the firm's own strategy. Even when these factors remain relatively stable, there is usually a periodic need to change the activities, communication vehicles, and promotional techniques of cost management simply to retain employee interest.

As noted previously, when demand is slack, margins thin, and surplus capacity exists, management is likely to focus activities around the reduction of direct cash costs. In boom times, when the firm is operating at full capacity, the firm may deliberately spend more to avoid the opportunity costs associated with lost capacity and forgone sales revenues.

The difference in cost management approaches required under each of these conditions is frequently ignored by managers and not appreciated by other employees. For example, after several years of depressed order books, a small shipyard received an influx of orders that ensured full capacity operations for at least two years. Late delivery of the vessels under construction could wipe out any profits on the orders. The company had been surviving by implementing a cost-management strategy that stressed minimizing direct costs and cash outflow.

Two months after the orders were received, it was apparent that the yard was already falling behind schedule. When executives reviewed the situation they found that their managers and supervisors were still operating under the old cost-management style. Materials were being ordered on a hand-to-mouth basis, which meant that workers were frequently waiting for delivery and not putting in needed overtime.

Having recognized this problem, the senior executives spent the next three months changing the focus of cost management away from direct costs to those associated with delays, lost production time, and late delivery. Cost-management symbols were changed, rewards were offered for ideas that increased the build rate, task forces were formed to develop approaches to reduce lead times, and an on-time/on-budget bonus was developed for the entire work force.

Similar problems arise during periods of growth. When new capacity is being brought on stream through major capital investment programs, executives may wish to emphasize minimizing the costs associated with poor facility design, late commissioning, and slow start-up. Even employees who are extremely cost conscious in day-to-day operations often ignore the opportunities to reduce the costs associated with capital. For many, capital is a costless " free good" provided by senior management, and there is little incentive to reduce spending in this area. Clearly, this is not the case, and major savings can result from extending cost-management strategies to capital.

Executives may also wish to reemphasize the importance of managing costs in the core business during expansionary periods, because it is at these times that cost control frequently goes out the window while management focuses its attention on growth. In such periods, it is especially important to ensure that the routine activities associated with cost management continue to happen. Special promotional blitzes, including presentations, posters and incentives, can be undertaken to maintain a high profile for the activity.

The East Greenville, Pennsylvania division of Knoll International, the furniture manufacturer, is an outstanding example of how keeping activities fresh can work without resorting to fads. As a part of its broad employee incentive scheme, the division has a special quarterly involvement theme throughout the year. In one period the theme might be reducing scrap costs, in another, those associated with accidents and lost time. These periodic changes keep the nature of involvement dynamic and continually provide new challenges for the division's employees.

The cost-management coordinator/director plays an important role in this respect, as can an outside consultant who can objectively monitor the effectiveness of various elements of the strategy and advise management when change is needed. Activities need not be abandoned completely, merely upgraded and modified to reawaken interest. For example, the format and content of crew meetings can be varied occasionally. Some of the savings can even be used to sponsor special social events for employees and their families. As Jim Moore, the cost-management coordinator at Brunswick Mining and Smelting once remarked, "The only limit to what we can do with cost management is our imagination."

Cost-Reduction Activities at Sikorski

Sikorski Aircraft Division of United Technologies Corporation is a primary supplier of helicopters for military and civilian applications. Executives in this division have used their imagination to develop and implement a comprehensive cost-reduction strategy which has resulted in reduced unit costs on a number of government programs. Changes in manufacturing methods, cooperation with suppliers, and activities to involve the total workforce of 12,000 in cost management have been cornerstones of their approach.

A major part of Sikorski's cost-management strategy was to identify and eliminate high-cost bottlenecks in resources and facilities throughout its manufacturing operations. A variety of techniques were used in this effort, including infinite and finite shop loading systems that provided a modeling capability. As a result, processes and methods were improved and accurate time standards developed for the facility, thus providing the basis for reliable costing information.

In addition, the factory was physically reorganized into individual manufacturing cost centers that operated as relatively autonomous plants within a plant.[6] The incorporation of some flexible manufacturing systems resulted in a variety of direct and overhead cost savings. Each center included manufacturing and industrial engineers, as well as production control and manufacturing personnel. These individuals operated as a team identifying problems, implementing solutions immediately, and carrying out long-range planning.

Because 65 percent of the cost of one of Sikorski's helicopters was contained in purchased supplies and components, the division's material department launched a four-point program of working with suppliers to reduce costs. The plan involved:

The formation of a *should cost* team, a cooperative program aimed at obtaining cost improvements without any reduction in quality. A specially selected team of senior Sikorski technical and manufacturing personnel visited suppliers and brainstormed on ideas for cost reduction. The aim of this activity was to develop changes that were simple to implement. Annual cost savings as high as $11 million have been generated by this activity.

A supplier recognition program, implemented to reward employees of Sikorski's suppliers for their cost-saving ideas. In return for an idea, the employee received a generous gift, and the Sikorski-supplier relationship was improved.

A target zero program, launched with the objective of reducing all manufacturing nonconformities to zero. Initially, this program was aimed at Sikorski's own operations, but it was extended to include suppliers. An instructional team from Sikorski worked with suppliers to implement the program in their facilities.

A curve busting program, designed to ensure that Sikorski exceeded the conventional learning curve for the business. Curve busting teams worked within Sikorski and with suppliers to find ways of obtaining greater than normal decreases in direct labor and purchased material costs, as well as improvements in yield.

Sikorski's operational employees have also been broadly involved in cost reduction. Workers in the plant were challenged to find ways of analyzing and simplifying operations through the implementation of a well-thought-out suggestion plan. Results and the names of people who submitted ideas were posted on bulletin boards throughout the plant. As this short case study reveals, executives at Sikorski are extremely people oriented and see employees as key resources in the division's attempts to remain a world-class leader in an increasingly competitive marketplace.[7]

9.

The Lean and Keen
Corporation in Action

A Framework for Implementing Successful
Cost-Reducing Innovations

The activities and techniques identified in the previous chapter have to
be facilitated by organizational mechanisms to ensure implementation.
Ideas have to be generated, selected, evaluated, and then implemented.
Because new ideas necessitate change, and change invariably meets resistance, certain barriers have to be overcome.

Corporations have found that there are a variety of mechanisms including employee circles, suggestion plans, and task forces that generate
ideas for cost reduction. The choice of which to use depends on the
circumstances, because each has its own advantages and disadvantages.

Having the appropriate mechanisms to generate ideas is not enough,
however. For these to work effectively, a good process is necessary
that allows employees to make proposals to management, run projects
effectively, and transfer ideas to operations successfully. Unsuccessful
innovations often fall into a management vacuum in which no one feels
responsible for moving the development along. Post-audits undertaken
by management groups have demonstrated that the most important causes
of failed developments, cost overruns, and late completion are the absence

of a well-understood project management methodology and discipline. Furthermore, key roles necessary for innovation, such as sponsor and champion, are either ignored or left vacant.

Recent research has identified the elements shown in Table 9.1 as key in successful innovation and change. Each has relevance for how corporations implement cost-reducing techniques and innovations, especially those originating in the technical system.

Change is an extremely emotional and political process, and because of its inherent uncertainty, is not logical and linear, but instead contains major elements of intuition and iteration. The discovery of new directions during research, the encountering of unanticipated barriers and obstacles, and the changing needs of an ultimate user all combine to result in a process that is iterative and fluid.

In addition, the traditional sequential model of innovation implies lengthy time frames for implementation of major cost-reducing technologies. If research, development, engineering, piloting, and commercialization are undertaken serially, then cost-reducing projects such as process developments will take many years to commercialize. In some large companies, ten years is not unusual for bringing a new process into operation. With an urgent need for cost reduction in many industries, however, developments have to be implemented more rapidly. Accordingly, mechanisms such as technology packages are required to facilitate the smooth introduction of cost-reducing ideas into operations.

Table 9.1.   Elements of Successful Cost-Reducing Innovations

1. No one source is likely to develop all the innovations required for a corporation to remain competitive: multiple sources have to be encouraged and used.

2. The potential value and ultimate use of many innovations is often hard to predict: apparently small developments ultimately have a major impact.

3. Corporations that obtain development proposals from employees throughout the organization usually possess a widely understood way for employees to sell their ideas to management.

4. Innovations tend to be more successful if potential users and clients are involved early in the process.

5. Innovations can be commercialized more rapidly if process, product, and market development activities occur in parallel, rather than sequentially.

6. Multiple sources of seed money for innovation increase the likelihood of success.

7. Successful innovations tend to have a strong management sponsor and a committed champion associated with them.

8. The transfer of new technology to operations is a critical step which can be facilitated by the creation of a technology package.

Organizational Processes for Reducing Costs

Increasing management concern for cost reduction has led to the development of a number of different organizational activities that lead to implemented cost reductions. Some of these activities, such as quality circles, are highly focused on specific areas of cost, while others, such as suggestion plans, are relatively broad. Cost-management strategies should be built around a set of such mechanisms that lead to appropriate employee involvement at different levels in the corporation as a way of ensuring that the desired results are achieved.

Cost-reducing mechanisms are known by a variety of different names, and frequently each approach is used in a number of different applications. For example, the quality circle methodology can be applied to safety, productivity, and cost improvements equally well. Table 9.2 lists these activities, each of which is discussed in the following section, and compares their applicability and value creation potential.

Profit/Cost-Improvement Groups

A powerful way to involve senior executives in cost management is to create what some corporations refer to as profit or cost-improvement

Table 9.2.   Organizational Cost-Reduction Activities Compared

MECHANISM	PRIMARY PARTICIPANTS	PRINCIPAL ROLE	TIME FRAME
Profit or cost-improvement groups	Executives and managers	Identify ideas; audit cost-management process	Periodic (yearly)
Cost management by walking around	Managers and engineers	Symbolic information gathering	Frequent, informal
Quality/productivity circles and crew meetings	Supervisors and operators	Cost reduction in specific work areas	Daily, weekly, monthly
Task forces	Multidisciplinary groups	Specific problems and opportunities	Ad hoc
Product/process teams	Members from functional and staff areas	Product and process cost reduction	Ad hoc
Cost/productivity-improvement drives	All employees	Short, intensive burst of cost-reducing activity	Annually
Suggestion plans	Work force and possibly supervision	Unfocused	Ongoing

groups. These executive groups can be formed to carry out general cost reviews of company operations or to carry out specific investigations of high-cost areas of concern. Depending on the severity of specific situations, the group can either be charged with responsibility for implementation or with simply providing recommendations to the appropriate management team. The H.J. Heinz corporation has adopted this approach in its profitability improvement program (PIP) in which teams of managers from different disciplines are organized to identify and prioritize cost-reducing projects throughout the corporation.

Membership in these groups is typically drawn from the corporate or division headquarters, although some operational executive input is useful. The inclusion of too many operating executives in the group can result in a failure to be sufficiently critical of any operation in order to avoid the same fate on home ground. An exercise of this type carried out by line executives alone can degenerate into a "you scratch my back, I'll scratch yours" kind of exercise. The involvement of an outside consultant can provide additional objectivity and can also enhance the process if this individual possesses skills that facilitate group problem solving.

Falconbridge Limited, the Canadian nickel producer, implemented this approach in 1983 and mandated that each operation in the corporation should undergo the scrutiny of its profit improvement group (PIG) at least once every two years. The typical composition of the group included the chief engineer of the corporation, the vice-president—technology, an outside consultant, a member of the corporate controllers group, and one operating executive.

Initially, such groups can be both resented and feared, especially in corporations that have cut employment levels. Resentment from operating executives can arise if they perceive a loss in managerial autonomy. Lower-level employees who are not well informed of the role of this group can perceive it to be yet another hatchet team. Consequently, the terms of reference of the group have to be clearly defined and communicated from the outset.

The group's methodology for conducting a cost audit can vary according to the situation, but typically it involves a considerable amount of prework in reviewing available cost information on the operation to be examined. This preparation is followed by interviews with all employee groups in the operation, during which the overall cost management process is discussed, high-cost areas identified, and ideas for cost reduction solicited. A short report or presentation should then be made to the local management team, focusing on recommendations for cost reduction and improvements to the cost-management process. Implementation is usually left to the local team, but a follow-up report or memorandum listing what actions have been implemented should be requested about a month after the review.

Falconbridge Limited found this approach to be an extremely effective way of demonstrating corporate commitment to its cost-management strategy. As well as identifying many opportunities for cost reduction within each operation, the PIG team was able to help eliminate numerous cost-increasing policies and procedures emanating from the corporate office. The approach was also used effectively to address specific issues such as working capital reduction and maintenance cost management across the corporation. In time, a positive PIG culture developed in the company, once local management groups learned that the group was a resource to be used to assist their own efforts.

Cost Management by Walking Around (CMBWA)

Most executives realize that costs cannot be reduced effectively in the office or going by the numbers alone. Especially in the early stages of a cost-management strategy or during crisis periods, management and professional staff can contribute by visiting operations, observing what is going on and soliciting cost-saving ideas directly from operating employees. In one situation, Jim Henderson, the president of Cummins Engine, noted that through such tours his relationship with hourly warehouse employees developed to the point that they would telephone him when they felt there was something he should know about the specific inventory problems concerning him.

Although this activity is unlikely to make large direct contributions to cost reduction, it is important as a symbolic gesture and can be used informally to reinforce the message that cost management is important. Such visits can be used to discuss cost management with operating employees and to identify cost problems that do not show up on monthly statements. High-cost activities or areas can be pointed out to individuals or groups of employees and their attention focused on how to reduce these.

Some corporations, including Lincoln Electric, have designated specific process and product engineers to patrol plants to generate informal discussions with operators in order to encourage potential cost savings. These engineers might work with an individual operator or gather small groups of employees together to discuss particular problems and opportunities to cut costs. In addition to generating specific savings, this activity can strengthen links between the shop floor and support groups.

Quality and Productivity Circles/Crew Meetings

Quality circles have been widely adopted as corporations seek to involve a broad spectrum of employees in reducing costs associated with poor quality. A well-defined methodology has been developed for the activity, and a variety of institutes and consultants have sprung up to service the growing demand for training and development.

Although the concept has been generally accepted, there are a disturbing number of problems with the approach. In some cases, quality circles have become major issues with unions and have had to be abandoned because of opposition and hostility. In other situations, quality circles have been perceived as just one more management fad and have encountered significant middle management and supervisory resistance. Worst of all perhaps, quality circles are treated as an end in themselves in too many corporations, relegating other important activities to the sidelines.

One senior executive with an ingrained scepticism of management fads observed that so far as he could see, his corporation had been doing quality circles for years but as part of a broader strategy and set of activities. In his view, a well-run crew meeting held either periodically or to address specific problems and opportunities provided 90 percent of the benefit of quality circles without all the ballyhoo and hype. In addition, employees in his crew meetings were expected to address a full range of operating and safety issues.

The circle or crew meeting concept can be a powerful weapon in lowering operating costs if used as a routine way of allowing work crews or teams to participate in cost-management. There is, of course, no reason why such activities should be limited to the shop floor: administrative, technical, marketing and sales employees can contribute through this approach.

A variety of factors determine the effectiveness of the approach, including the power and autonomy delegated to the group, membership in the group, and the nature and extent of meetings. At one end of the scale, members can feel powerless to change things, even if they identify major opportunities and problems, because management does not provide either the freedom or the resources to act. At the other end of the spectrum, these groups can be self-contained action teams with the authority and resources to implement change immediately.

To be most effective, circles or work groups have to contain the blend of skills and knowledge that permits good problem identification and analysis and facilitates action. This requirement suggests that engineering and even procurement assistance be either in the group or readily available. Many employee improvements appear to be held up for considerable periods of time because of the lack of a small amount of drafting or engineering assistance. Similarly, manufacturing groups should include maintenance as well as operating personnel.

Leadership within these groups is essential if an effective process is to result. In traditional workplaces, supervisors should be expected to provide this leadership. Facilitators may, however, be necessary to promote activities and ensure an effective process, because supervisors typically have little time for such activities, even in "enlightened" workplaces. Within the context of a cost-management strategy, this role can be played by the cost-management coordinators described in Chapter 7.

Employee development and training in a variety of management skills is necessary for circles to be effective. In particular, supervisors need to be introduced to the rudiments of participative management, and then typically need additional skills in running problem-solving meetings, making presentations, and other communication skills. All employees need to be provided with basic cost-management concepts and information, as well as skills in group problem solving.

Task Forces

Most organizations employ task forces at some time or another to achieve specific goals, but they are usually created on an ad hoc basis, with little or no prescribed methodology to guide their actions. As part of a cost-management strategy, specially created task forces aimed at reducing specific high costs can be extremely effective, especially if the concept is developed to the point where a well-understood approach and methodology is shared by corporate employees.

In one nonunion manufacturing company, executives decided that task forces would be a useful way of involving employees from all levels in the organization and from different employee groups in an integrated attack on costs. Rather than let employees adopt an unfocused approach to cost reduction, senior executives identified a number of high-cost areas and items and created a series of task forces to identify problems and opportunities, examine alternative solutions, and initiate appropriate action. Identifying areas in need of attention and creating the task forces was perceived as one of top management's most important cost-management roles in this company.

The task force program was coordinated by a middle management employee with considerable project management experience. Task forces were made up of employees from all aspects of company operations: manufacturing, engineering, purchasing, and administration. A single employee was selected to head each task force, usually from either the supervisory or professional groups, but occasionally an hourly employee with the appropriate skills was appointed. A senior executive usually monitored task force activities, primarily to provide advice, help break down roadblocks, and provide assistance in obtaining access to necessary resources.

These task forces proved extremely effective in reducing costs. The multidisciplinary approach provided an integrative problem-solving perspective. Hourly employees included in the teams sought out the advice of their co-workers and provided a practical shopfloor perspective. Sales and marketing personnel ensured that changes to products and processes enhanced or at least did not detract from customer service and value.

Over a period of two or three years, a shared understanding of the role of these task forces evolved, in part due to training and development activities provided by the program coordinator. Adjustments to work patterns had to be made to allow operators to attend meetings and take part in related activities. Task forces came into existence, did their work, and were disbanded. At any point in time approximately 10 percent of all employees were involved in a task force of some kind. The direct savings from these task force activities were substantial, but management stressed that the team building that took place throughout the corporation probably had an equal, though intangible value.

Cost/Productivity Improvement Drives

Some corporations have taken the task force idea and incorporated it into a short-run cost or productivity drive that, if done well, can eliminate the need for suggestion plans. In Canada, Brunswick Mining and Smelting developed its PLUS (acronym for prevent loss and unnecessary spending) program, and Black and Decker Canada its FOCUS (fend off costs and unnecessary spending) program around this concept.

Considerable preparation is required to make such activities effective, and a steering committee (preferably with union and operator representation) is usually organized to plan and manage the activity. Because considerable time can be involved, corporations usually try to hold these drives during slower business periods.

At Brunswick Mining, employees with cost-reducing ideas were asked first to sell these proposals to fellow workers and form groups of three, four, or five people to develop and investigate them. The group was required to submit its proposal on a single-page summary form and, after a brief review, was accepted for the program. Management and senior professional staff were not allowed to enter, because cost reduction was perceived as part of their routine work, and they were also expected to provide assistance to employee teams during the drive. Entries by single employees were excluded from consideration, because it was reasoned that if they could not sell fellow workers on their idea, it probably was not very practical.

Following acceptance of the idea, teams were given six weeks to work on their proposals. In this period they were expected to develop the concepts, evaluate the feasibility, and estimate the direct cost saving or revenue generation (improved yields, reduced lost time, increased output) potential. Groups were allowed one hour of work time per day per member (usually taken at the end of shifts) to work on their proposals. Management, engineering, drafting, and costing assistance was made available as required.

At the end of the six weeks the proposals were distributed into four classes, depending on whether or not they required capital and either direct cost saving or revenue generating value. The steering committee then reviewed the completed proposals, selecting a top prize winner in each class, based on the estimated value of savings. Generally, most proposals required little or no capital to implement. Wherever possible, work started immediately to implement the proposals, especially those showing a high return.

A month after the proposals were submitted, a banquet evening was held to which all employees who had entered and supported the program were invited, together with their spouses. Grand prizes for members of teams heading each class included televisions, cameras and microwave ovens. Every employee entering received a nominal award. Perhaps more important, photographs of the division vice-president shaking hands with every employee were later published in the local paper.

The first time the PLUS program was run, approximately 100 employees (out of 1,350 eligible) entered, and over $1 million in savings were identified. In the second year, twice as many employees were involved, and savings doubled. In addition, to start off the second year's effort, management used some of the previous year's savings to bring a well-known entertainment group into the isolated community where the mine is located and provided tickets for employees' families to attend their concerts. Considerable goodwill was generated by this gesture alone. After two years, the PLUS program was sidelined in favor of a comprehensive gain-sharing program at Brunswick.

The FOCUS program at Black and Decker Canada operated for seven years on very similar lines to that at Brunswick. In this case, employees were asked to volunteer for the program and were then assigned to groups that included engineering staff and asked to evaluate cost-saving opportunities in specific areas of the corporation (including sales and administration). Substantial savings were generated through this approach, but it was ultimately discontinued by a new management team who felt that it was becoming less effective than in earlier years. Some hourly paid employees who were subsequently interviewed stated that they felt management made a mistake when they took this step, because they did not replace the program with anything that continued to encourage employee involvement in cost reduction.

Suggestion Plans

Suggestion plans are the most common device used to obtain employee involvement in cost reduction. The National Association of Suggestion Systems represents over 1,100 Canadian and U.S. organizations with this type of program. Their membership spans a variety of industries, from the largest industrial corporations, such as General Motors and Eastman Kodak, to hospitals and bakeries. Their annual statistical survey reported that employee ideas saved reporting companies in the association $1.82 billion in 1986. The association provides a variety of educational and support services for its members, as well as for companies interested in setting up their own programs.[1]

Some suggestion plans work superbly, such as those at Hewlett Packard, Anheuser Busch, and IBM, yet most are implemented poorly and create little value. A suggestion commonly found in the boxes provided for employees to submit their ideas is to use the space on the wall for a more useful purpose. Employees perceive suggestion plans to be symbolic of managerial tokenism, and they rarely obtain the satisfaction of prompt responses to their ideas. Managers often view the administration of these schemes to be more trouble than they are worth.

Suggestion plans are an unfocused way of garnering a variety of employee ideas dealing with safety, product, and process improvement and cost reduction. Usually, these plans are administered by committee and can be quite bureaucratic. In companies that are determined to be absolutely fair and equitable in their administration of their scheme, processing and responding to employee ideas can be a lengthy process. Frequently, the greater the potential saving, the more exhaustive the evaluation, the greater the delay before implementation, and the greater the frustration for the employee before recognition or a reward is forthcoming.

There are, however, many examples of successful suggestion plans. In these case, corporations have avoided a series of common pitfalls which seem to ensnare the majority of such approaches. The most common of these problems are listed in Table 9.3. Most can be avoided if the program is designed and administered appropriately and if it is well promoted and understood throughout the corporation.

In 1982, the suggestion plan in Falconbridge's Sudbury operations suffered from many of these deficiencies. An excessively bureaucratic administration process meant that the value of management time expended on the program alone exceeded the value of the savings generated. Many of the ideas submitted were worth less than $100.00. More valuable ideas often took twelve months to evaluate and reward. Two years later, after the program had been redesigned and relaunched, annual savings worth over $2 million were being generated.

To turn its idea award program around, Falconbridge made some simple changes. First of all, rewards, amounting to 15 percent of the first year's after-tax savings were only paid out after an idea had been implemented. First-line supervisors, as well as hourly employees, were made eligible for awards. No ideas with potential savings of less than $1,000 were considered for an award, because the time involved was not worth the potential return. For practical ideas worth less than this amount, recognition was provided through the token award of a gift voucher, and employees were told to implement the idea on their own.

The idea award program was decentralized. Small departmental committees, created to support the operation's cost-management activity, were also given the responsibility for handling the suggestion plan. Senior

Table 9.3. Common Suggestion Plan Failings

- Management does not believe significant value can be created.
- There is inadequate promotion and championing.
- Supervisors do not support the program.
- There is no readily available format for submitting ideas.
- Excessively rigid and bureaucratic administration exists.
- Employees deluge management with a multitude of small, irrelevant proposals.
- Employee ideas create excessive work for managers and staff.
- There is a failure to follow up and implement ideas.
- Managers and supervisors fail to provide rapid feedback to employees on the fate of their idea.
- Payment is made for ideas rather than implementation.
- The costs of the program outweigh the value created.

departmental managers were permitted to make awards of up to $10,000 for ideas without requiring senior management approval. Over this amount, ideas had to be scrutinized by a central review committee before payment was made. Ideas with larger potential savings were accorded priority over those with smaller benefits.

To maintain employee support, a policy was adopted that feedback would be provided to every idea originator within one month of submission of the idea. If an idea was rejected, supervisors both explained the reason to the employee and attempted to suggest ways in which the proposal might be modified to make it feasible. If savings were difficult to evaluate, an interim award was authorized, and payment was made in full after annual savings had been estimated, based on the first year's experience.

As part of a cost-management seminar, all employees were given an explanation of how the idea awards program worked. A clear procedure for submitting proposals was developed in which originators submitted their idea to their immediate supervisor. If this initial proposal was rejected, alternative routes could be used to resubmit the proposal. In addition, employees were provided with skills to enable them to sell and evaluate their own proposals better, thus reducing the amount of managerial and engineering time consumed in evaluation. Wherever possible, employees were encouraged to make group rather than individual submissions. Most important, ideas were turned back for implementation to the individuals originating them wherever possible, creating a real sense of ownership.

The program was redesigned by a small task force assisted by an outside consultant. Individuals from this group then helped relaunch the scheme throughout the operations. Initially, a few complaints from professional staff who were not included in the plan were voiced, but these faded quite quickly, once it was made clear to these employees that such activities were considered by management to be a part of their routine jobs. Interest in the program grew as substantial awards as high as $40,000 were announced, and a poster campaign was developed to sustain the increased level of idea generation. As a result, the idea awards program rapidly became a useful contributor to the operation's cost-reduction strategy.

Implementation Methodologies and Roles

The importance of sound project-management methodologies for cost management have been alluded to on several occasions in this chapter.

Many innovations fail not because they are inherently unsound, but because they are poorly proposed and managed. A project-management methodology should be one of the shared mechanisms linking employees in such diverse activities as marketing, operations, R & D, engineering, and information systems.

The major building blocks for a sound project-management system are an effective selection process so that employees know how to advocate their proposals and what criteria they have to meet; a set of simple guidelines for setting up a project, which cover accounting, organization, and planning; a good periodic project review procedure which ensures that either progress is made or that the activity is terminated; a well-understood methodology for transferring projects to operational status; and a process for follow-up and review.

Proposal Methodologies

An objective review of ways in which employees can convince management of the value and practicality of their cost-reduction developments sometimes reveals the surprising (at least to managers) fact that there is not a well-understood way for accomplishing this task. Managers often complain about the poor quality of suggestions, proposals, and presentations, but they then fail to do anything about it. As a result, many potentially valuable developments lie dormant because they are not effectively sold to management.

In corporations in which management has resolved to tackle this problem, two major actions are mandatory. The first step is to create a simple document format that forces employees wishing to propose a development to "do their homework" before they approach management. This document is usually different from the one normally used in the budgeting process for capital requisitions, because the latter tends to be designed by accounting or finance personnel to suit their own needs. Many such documents are overly quantitative, short on description, and have a horrendous approvals process associated with them which deters all but the strong-willed or foolhardy.

A suggested format for a proposal document is shown in Table 9.4. The logic of the format forces employees to work through those major elements of their proposal that management will want to know. Most important, it asks the employee to consider why the development is useful for the corporation at this time, a question that is often not addressed. The proposal can be as short as one page or supplemented by additional detail for complex developments. It can be used with equal ease by technical staff or operators, and it can be reviewed quickly.

Table 9.4. Format of Proposal Document

- A descriptive title
- A short description of the proposal
- An assessment of the potential cost savings
- An estimate of the cost of implementing the proposal
- A justification of why the proposal is relevant to the corporation at this time
- An assessment of the resources and time required for implementation
- A brief description of any uncertainties and risks associated with the proposal

The second step is to put in place a process that facilitates the presentation of proposals to appropriate supervisors or managers and provides a quick review procedure. A series of seminars on presentation skills can provide employees with a basic ability to put together a visual and verbal proposal for management.

In addition, a shared understanding of simple procedures for gaining approvals for cost-reducing projects has to be established. Employees can be instructed where to go for advice, who to discuss their ideas with, and what to do once a project has been approved. Many corporations encourage employees to prescreen their proposals with their colleagues before seeking approval. These processes can eliminate many impractical ideas, and it also improves those that do survive.

Required Roles

As shown in Table 9.5, a variety of roles have to be played out in corporations if a stream of cost-reducing innovations is to flow into the business. Some of these roles are executive and strategic, having to do with the continuity of cost management and the sponsorship of major innovations. Others are operational, having to do with the acquisition, development, and implementation of specific cost-saving innovations.

Strategic Roles

The major strategic roles are those of the visionary, sponsor, and facilitator. Who plays these roles can vary from corporation to corporation and over time. In small firms, they may all be combined into one person. In larger corporations, the CEO and other senior executives may share them.

The visionary is able to perceive the contribution that proposed changes can make to cost reduction and communicate this view to others in the

Table 9.5.   Critical Roles in Innovation

ROLE	CONTRIBUTION
Strategic	
Visionary	Provides mission and direction
	Challenges employees and gains commitment
Sponsor	Ensures business acceptance
	Provides funds
	Supplies political clout
Facilitator	Knows organization processes
	Provides contacts and information
Operational	
Idea generator	Identifies opportunities
	Contributes creative solutions
Champion	Promotes specific projects
	Provides continuity of effort
	Excites colleagues
Project leader	Provides leadership and coordination
	Possesses project management skills
Gatekeeper	Brings ideas from outside the organization
	Knows potential internal applications
	Possesses broad networks
Implementer	Carries out tasks
	Provides pragmatic inputs to new approaches

corporation. If this role is played by the CEO, then it should not be too difficult to gain the support of other senior executives, although there will be considerable testing to see if there is real commitment to this vision or whether it is mere rhetoric. Real commitment will be backed up by appropriate resource commitments, sponsorship of specific innovations to symbolize direction, and a willingness to make sure an effective process is in place.

The second strategic role is that of sponsor. Because radical innovations are costly, complex, and contentious, they require continuing involvement from the top of the business to ensure that they continue to progress. Sponsorship is particularly important at the point when significant funding is required to pilot and commercialize a new development.

Executives often lose interest when R & D personnel ask for $5 or even $50 million to commercialize a new process that they believe has significant cost-reducing potential. In part, the fault lies with lower-level managers who often fail to keep executives fully informed about major developments that could require significant funding. When a proposal is ultimately made, there is no commitment to proceed at the senior levels of management. On the other hand, asking executives the question: "What major technical developments to cut costs are you currently sponsoring?" often brings a blank stare.

An effective sponsor is generally an executive who has access to the financial and human resources and the political clout in the organization to drive these innovations through to success in a reasonable time frame. Most sponsors of this type are relatively accessible to technical and operating employees with new ideas. Once a development is underway, the sponsor generally remains informed and in touch with progress and is available on an as-required basis to provide help when the going gets tough.

Facilitating an effective change process is a third important strategic role. If the visionary creates a sense of direction, the facilitator provides the means and the route to achieve objectives. An effective management of change process requires that a variety of organizational activities take place at the strategic level, including strategy planning sessions and cost-management reviews. In addition, the facilitator ensures that the type of roles described in this section are adequately staffed.

Operational Roles

In addition to the strategic roles described above, Table 9.5 lists a number of operational roles that need to be fulfilled for the cost-management process to work. These roles were initially described by Roberts and Fusfeld in their study of technical innovation.[2] Effective program and project teams are usually found to contain individuals displaying most of these attributes.

Anyone can be an idea generator, from the shop floor employee to the chief executive. Cost-reduction ideas flow from a variety of sources both inside and outside the corporation. Generally, these people are not in short supply, and there are more ideas for cost reduction than corporations have the ability to deal with. There are, however, a few individuals throughout any organization who especially enjoy being creative and are responsible for a continuous stream of suggestions for potential cost reductions. Although their ideas are often impractical, once in a while they bring out an important breakthrough for the company's way of doing things.

Such individuals are important to bring into brainstorming and problem-solving sessions, but they are often not appropriate to lead or champion a project subsequently. Once the idea is developed, these individuals are usually on to the next challenge. Provided that they are not threatened by organization values that penalize either nonconformance or ideas that challenge established processes and procedures, these individuals tend to obtain their rewards from recognition provided through seeing their ideas implemented.

Most successful projects have a champion. This activity is best carried out by individuals who are willing to take risks to obtain the application of a development that they believe strongly about. The idea itself may be obtained from someone else, but the champion is the person who sells it to the organization, obtains the resources, and ensures implementation.

Strong champions will often go to great lengths to promote their project. They will find ways to win the support of influential sponsors and obtain adequate resources to proceed. Failing success through formal channels, these individuals may well use informal processes and boot-legged resources to achieve their goals.

Project leaders require skills in planning and coordinating the activities and resources involved. A good leader has a broad enough perspective to be able to balance the specific needs of the project with overall organization goals and resource constraints. In most cost-reduction projects, this task requires broad disciplinary skills to provide the necessary integration. In many organizations, the project leader is the single person accountable for ensuring that milestones and deadlines are met, that cost projections are kept, and that the development meets its overall performance targets.

Gatekeepers make important contributions to cost reduction. This role is played by individuals who have a good sense of what is happening in the world outside the corporation. These are people who read widely, attend conferences and trade shows, and are provided with the opportunity to travel. An investment in gatekeeping can avoid much of the NIH factor associated with innovation. Faced with a problem or opportunity, these individuals can often either think of companies that have dealt with similar situations or of references and people that might provide solutions.

Well-managed gatekeeping activities are likely to have a very high return associated with them. For example, when one small insurance company faced with the challenge of upgrading its policy administration systems sent its executives to visit other insurance firms and software companies, it found that nearly everything it needed could be bought outside and used with very little modification. This simple step avoided large financial outlays on internal systems development and reduced the time required from an estimated four years to eighteen months.

One role that is often neglected, and which differs substantially from any of those mentioned above, is that of the implementer. These are usually hands-on people who obtain great satisfaction out of physically creating something new or improving the performance of what already exists. These people range from scientists who are willing to spend seven days a week, eighteen hours a day in the laboratory, to project engineers, to skilled tradespeople and operators who are sometimes willing to work far beyond the requirements of a collective agreement.

From a management perspective, idea generators, champions, project leaders, and gatekeepers are necessary, but in all projects the ultimate outcome rests largely on the quality of the implementation team. Even great champions are powerless when they are given weak support. Most companies will have far more success in reducing costs through innovation if they build up a cadre of these implementers and provide them with appropriate recognition and reward upon successful completion of major projects.

Facilitating Innovation

Corporations with a history of successful cost reduction have placed significant reliance on technological innovation for achieving results. These corporations have succeeded in spite of the numerous barriers to innovation which exist in most organizations. Other corporations do not fare so well and fail to overcome these obstacles that stand in the path of cost savings.

Failure to use the corporation's technical organization effectively is a major impediment to innovation. Established priorities, resource allocation, cultural values, and organization structure can pose obstacles throughout the corporation. These barriers can be substantially reduced by four major actions to be described in this section:

1. Creating a cost-reduction mission for the technical organization
2. Providing adequate resources for innovation
3. Facilitating the transfer of innovations to operations
4. Creating a climate of acceptance for innovation

Providing a Mission for Technology

The technical organization often lacks a sense of direction and mission with respect to cost reduction. Given the potential contribution of this area to cost reduction, this omission is serious. R & D managers may lack the skills to be proactive in strategy formulation and wait passively for senior executives to provide direction.

A variety of imaginative approaches can be adopted to elimimate this barrier. One approach that is gaining considerable attention is to involve professional and technical staff in strategy formulation sessions for cost management. In addition, some chief executive officers ensure that they periodically spend time in R & D finding out what is going on and using the opportunity to inform technical personnel about cost-reduction opportunities and concerns they can influence.

In larger corporations, geographic and organizational barriers can cause technical organizations to lose touch with the challenges, priorities, and time pressures confronting their operational clients. As far as operations are concerned, R & D becomes a black box about which little is known, and from which even less emerges. Frequent face-to-face contacts between personnel in these areas is necessary if good working relationships are to develop and a stream of innovations is to be maintained.

Providing Adequate Resources

Innovation also suffers when executives fail to provide adequate financial and human resources to ensure that programs and projects are implemented effectively. For example, R & D often lacks an engineering capability to deliver operational technologies to the business. In addition, technical personnel may be simultaneously involved in too many projects.

Consequently, major cost-reducing innovations often suffer from a loss of continuity because of periodic cutbacks in funding stemming either from budget pressures or a lack of interest on the part of top management. Given the difficulty of quantitatively evaluating the potential future value of technological improvements, uncommitted executives prefer to invest instead in tangible assets such as corporate acquisitions and hardware purchases. The result is a failure to deliver cost-reducing innovations in an appropriate time frame.

This problem can best be overcome by effective project selection techniques combined with vigorous portfolio pruning from time to time to ensure that stalled and irrelevant projects are weeded out. In addition, some corporations meet variable project loads by maintaining a relatively lean core staff and employing engineering and technical consultants when work loads are high. This approach minimizes the overhead costs associated with maintaining high staff levels and avoids the need for substantial employment cuts during periods of low activity.

Facilitating Transfer to Operations

There are probably thousands of processes and pieces of equipment standing idle that were once expected to revolutionize business through improved productivity and lower costs. What went wrong? More often than not, the concepts were probably valid and the technical work sound, but the process most likely never worked in practice. Very often, what was delivered to manufacturing worked in the laboratory, but could not be made to operate satisfactorily under factory conditions. Sometimes what was delivered to operations was not what was originally specified. In other cases, operations may have given up waiting and purchased what they required, or business conditions had changed, making the development irrelevant.

These problems can be avoided in several ways. Technical groups can be made aware of operating needs by transferring staff from R & D and other technical groups into operations and vice versa. Including operating personnel on development task forces is also effective. Some corporations have a requirement for a client representative on all large technical projects and programs. Periodic reviews, as part of a strong project-management methodology can prevent technical groups working on developments that are no longer relevant.

Some corporations have adopted the notion of a technology package for internally transferring technology. The creation of this package explicitly recognize that hardware, software, and liveware (people) are all important elements in the successful commercialization of cost-reducing projects.

At the prototyping or piloting stage, a comprehensive package is prepared that, in addition to technical specifications, spells out operating practices, maintenance requirements, and training needs, as shown in Table 9.6. This comprehensive description is then provided to operations adopting the new technology, together with appropriate technical assistance. This package can eliminate much of the concern that new developments have to be re-engineered by operations to make them usable. If multiple installations are anticipated, the package can be updated with improvements and enhancements derived from the first commercial application.

Creating a Climate of Acceptance

A variety of cost-reduction barriers are created at the operational level in most corporations. Plant managers often exhibit conservative tendencies when they are being pushed to meet tough production and profit goals. At such times they are unwilling to give up equipment or personnel to work on developments that have a payback longer than their personal economic time horizon. Consequently, pilots and trials of new processes and methods are continually deferred. In addition, when operating groups

Table 9.6.   The Technology Package

---

1. Process description and equipment detail
   Total system specification
   Flow sheet
   Layout
   Material and energy balances
   Drawings of proprietary equipment

2. Internal and external environmental standards

3. Process control logic

4. Performance specifications, targets, and limits

5. Installation and commissioning practices

6. Operating data
   Typical operating organization
   Operating practices
   Maintenance practices
   Trouble-shooting practices
   Training requirements specific to the technology

7. Range of Capital and Operating Costs

SOURCE: Gian F. Frontini and Peter R. Richardson, "Design and Demonstration: Critical Functions in Industrial Innovation," *The Sloan Management Review,* Summer 1984, p. 46. Copyright © 1984 by The Sloan Management Review Association. All rights reserved.

have spent considerable efforts in optimizing a process, they are usually extremely unwilling to let R & D personnel experiment for fear of upsetting the system, even if there may be potentially large cost savings as a result.

In large, multiplant corporations, a specific production unit can be dedicated to pilot work. Mead Corporation chose this route for piloting computer process control in its paper-making operations. Some R & D organizations have their own pilot plant facilities which can enable them to minimize technical risks and maximize operationality before having to take new developments into the operating environment. An alternative solution that sometimes works is to ensure that lost production due to technical experimentation is not charged against operating budgets.

When all is said and done, however, the major barrier to obtaining the full cost savings from technical change is the lack of acceptance by supervisors and the work force. In most Canadian and U.S. corporations, technical innovation is perceived as threatening to jobs and employment of the blue-collar workers.

Supervisors, who usually have to develop a mode of coexisting with these employees in order to survive and get their job done, often adopt similar views. Consequently, the full benefit of labor-saving or productivity-improving innovations is often never realized, or takes far too long.

Post-audits of labor-saving projects often reveal that either the equipment never performed to a level where the savings were possible or that new work was found for displaced employees, and labor costs were actually never reduced.

If a climate of acceptance can be created through cost management, employees can then be involved at an early stage in the development of an innovation. This involvement creates a sense of ownership which reinforces acceptance. Operating employees included in project teams can provide important advice on the selection, design, and operation of new processes. When the innovation becomes "their baby," they can be expected to go to great lengths to make it work well.

10.

Rewarding Cost-Reduction Successes

Recognition and Reward

To ensure the continuity of cost-reduction efforts, an appropriate scheme of recognition and rewards is required. A wide spectrum of options exist which should be an integral part of cost-management strategies. In some cases, finding ways to publicly acknowledge cost-reduction efforts is sufficient, especially if employees believe that the corporation is facing difficult times and that their activities help ensure continued competitiveness. Alternatively, a variety of individual and group financial rewards can be implemented which share the financial benefits of cost reduction throughout the corporation.

A variety of problems and issues that create feelings of envy, inequity, and frustration can offset the benefits of financial awards if they are not carefully developed and implemented. Avoiding financial reward systems because of these risks is not the right course of action. There is little doubt that money is a motivator for most employees and that the possibility of a significant cash award for developing and implementing an idea can be a powerful incentive for employees to get involved in cost reduction. In Falconbridge Limited, there was typically an upsurge of interest and suggestions following each major award to an employee. The notion of payment for implementation provides an additional incentive for employees to persevere with their ideas and to take an active role in the development and evaluation process.

The best approach is one that matches recognition and rewards to the cost-reduction strategy and the culture of the organization. In some corporations, individual monetary incentives are likely to fit in well, especially if the strategy emphasizes broad involvement. In other corporations, where there is no such tradition and cost-reduction emphasizes teamwork, either group rewards or no financial rewards at all may be more successful.

In multidivision or multiplant corporations, executives often wrestle with whether to establish corporate policies for recognition and reward or whether to allow individual operations to establish their own. If operations are very similar and executives are trying to establish a shared culture, a corporate policy may be appropriate. In some cases these may also be established to avoid a sense of inequity across the corporation which could develop if each unit set its own policies. This problem is frequently overestimated, however, especially in geographically dispersed corporations. In these cases, setting broad corporate guidelines within which each operation or division can establish its own approach may be more appropriate.

Recognition as a Reward

Some executives and many employees believe that recognition is the most powerful reward for most types of corporate achievement, and yet the most underutilized. There are a variety of ways to recognize outstanding cost-management performance, both formal and informal, ranging from the pat on the back to photographs and articles on outstanding individual and group efforts in company and community newspapers, as well as other media.

Some corporations fail to adopt these approaches because their executives feel that employee recognition and token awards are merely gimmicks. "It's not part of our culture," they say. Yet many of these same executives are to be found handing out similar give aways to visiting customers and executives from other corporations. There seems to be an unspoken sentiment among these people that employees should be satisfied to receive their paycheck once or twice a month. Of course, people will work for this reason, but recognition provides a stimulus to go further.

Typically, however, recognition activities are limited more by lack of management imagination and interest than any other single factor.

Correspondingly, a little thought and effort applied to this area can produce a well-integrated set of nonfinancial recognition signals that can be used to make employees feel pride in a wide variety of cost-reducing achievements. Some of the most common of these are described below.

Pats on the Back

As noted above, a pat on the back for good performance is all that many employees crave. In too many companies, employees complain that the only time they get noticed is when they make a mistake. As one supervisor once remarked: "There are plenty of pats on the back around here, the trouble is that they're a little too low." In lean corporations, supervisors and managers complain that they are too busy for such pleasantries, but it is interesting to note that they always complain when their superiors fail to recognize their own personal efforts.

Employees are frequently so starved for positive reinforcement and recognition that a little can go a long way. Finding different ways of saying thanks for a job well done can be extremely important in building commitment to cost reduction. As part of its cost-management strategy, one corporation which paid no financial rewards ensured that every employee who submitted a successful cost-reduction idea was personally thanked at their workplace by the vice-president of the operation. In addition, when the chairman of the corporation made one of his infrequent visits to the operations, he was always introduced to employees who had been responsible for major cost reductions. These two forms of recognition, carried out routinely, were enough to create significant employee interest in submitting ideas.

Public Recognition

At the Sikorski Division of United Technologies, all employee suggestions are acknowledged by being placed on bulletin boards, which provides visibility throughout the division. Other corporations routinely acknowledge specific employee suggestions in their company newsletters and magazines.

As noted in Chapter 9, Brunswick Mining and Smelting ensured that all employees who participated in its PLUS program were recognized by having their photographs taken shaking hands with the vice-president of the operation. The subsequent publication of these pictures in the local newspaper created a great deal of good feeling between management and employees. Brunswick also ensured that record-setting performances by particular crews and departments were acknowledged in a similar manner.

The Horne copper smelter in Quebec found a novel way to recognize the efforts of its employees to reduce costs. Photographs of many of them were included in its annual company calendar, which was sent out to suppliers, customers, local businesses, and employees' families. There were pictures of employees with their inventions, groups of employees in cost-reduction meetings, and portraits of the cost-management coordinators. In a similar manner, Falconbridge Limited filled the cover of its 1984 annual report with photographs of a number of employees from each of its operations around the world who had submitted cost-saving ideas. Inside the cover was a picture of the CEO awarding a check to an hourly paid employee for a major cost-reduction idea.

Token Awards

When employees complain that their small cost-reduction efforts are not recognized, corporations sometimes find that supervisors are providing this recognition, but that employees quickly forget the positive comments and remember the negative ones. In such cases, it has been found useful to have a set of small token awards, similar to those routinely handed out to customers. These include presentation coins, packs of playing cards with the company emblem, or company pens. Managers and supervisors can take these with them on visits to the workplace to leave with employees they find doing an outstanding job as a tangible reminder of their comments and appreciation.

A similar form of recognition can also be provided for outstanding team efforts that reduce costs. Falconbridge Limited always tries to award employees at its Sudbury operations with a small gift (value $5 to $10.00) for all major projects that they are involved in that come in on time and under budget. The supervisors of these activities are also encouraged to take their crews and their spouses out for a recognition dinner after such achievements. A specific budget was established to fund these activities. At Fahramet, a small Canadian foundry, each employee who submits an idea or suggestion to the cost management activity is awarded a provincial lottery ticket. Management has hopes that an employee will some day hit the jackpot with one of these awards.

Providing recognition for employee cost-reduction efforts cannot always be easily structured into corporate activities. Executives cannot simply tell managers and supervisors they should do more of this kind of thing and expect it to happen. They must provide leadership and set an example by doing more themselves to recognize cost-reduction efforts. They can also approve the minor expense necessary to obtain token awards. The existence of a cost-management coordinator or director also facilitates the process, because this individual is usually seeking ways to promote and reinforce the approach. In the end, recognition has to become an accepted part of organization culture which takes place without a great deal of conscious effort being necessary to make it happen.

Status Rewards

Recognition for cost-reduction performance can go beyond the levels described in the previous section if it confers some degree of status on the individuals or groups involved. McDonalds Corporation and Holiday Inns are among the organizations that have effectively used employee-of-the-month awards in recognizing individual performance and at the same time promoting role models for other employees. Although these two corporations make these awards largely on the basis of customer service performance, which is a key element in their strategy, there is no reason why corporations emphasizing cost reduction should not adopt a similar approach.

The conferring of some degree of status on high performers can be important in creating role models for the organization in respect to cost management. Employees who make outstanding contributions can be singled out for special recognition, and their achievements can be communicated to the rest of the organization. Other individuals or groups of employees may then be encouraged to match or emulate the standards and values reflected in the accomplishments of these individuals (or groups). This process can be particularly important when corporations are seeking to develop broad involvement in cost management among supervisors and operating employees.

Organizations have traditionally used promotion within the formal hierarchy as the single major way of conferring status on employees. Indeed, when cost reduction is one of the central threads of corporate strategy, it would be expected that an executive with a successful track record in this activity would be selected to lead the corporation. This appointment would be seen as symbolic of the company's commitment to its strategy, and also as recognition of achievement.

Promotion purely on the basis of being good at cost reduction, however, takes a very limited view of the corporate world, even in the leanest and meanest of corporations. Many other factors have to be taken into account when promoting employees. Additionally, in many lean corporations, promotion opportunities can be relatively few, and there will be a continuing need to recognize outstanding cost-reduction achievements on their own merits. If status is to be used as an element of recognition and reward, alternatives to promotion have to be developed.

One corporation that has had considerable success with a different approach has created a special club for individual employees who made contributions that saved the corporation over $100,000 in a single year. Senior executives are excluded because they are expected to save the company in excess of that amount each year as part of their job. About six employees are enrolled annually out of a work force of approximately 2,000.

Membership in this gold club, as it is known, entitles an individual to receive 200 shares of the company's stock and a special gold lapel pin in the shape of the company crest. There is also a banquet to which club members are invited each year at which the awards are presented. New members are announced in the company magazine, together with a brief description of their specific contribution.

Gandalf, a small Canadian manufacturer of modems and computer peripherals, created a Golden Carrot award to help attack a specific cost problem. This award is made to engineers who bring in development projects on time and under budget. The award was instituted by the company's vice-chairman Colin Patterson when he became concerned about the cost to the company of projects that were coming in late and over budget. The carrot symbolizes a notion he communicated to his employees about the cause of these overruns. Recipients of the award receive a gold carrot on a blue ribbon which they are asked to wear on a specific day each month.

Other companies do not go so far in creating status for individuals who make significant contributions to cost reduction. Some corporations will periodically profile in their newsletters or magazines employees who generate significant savings, especially those individuals who do so on a continuing basis. Others will create an annual president's honor roll or equivalent of generally outstanding contributors. For example, each year Northern Telecom, Canada's leading telecommunications manufacturer, spends approximately $100,000 on a president's banquet for recipients of cost-savings awards greater than $1,000. Recipients of these awards and their spouses are brought together from across the country at the corporation's expense for this event.

This approach is not without its risks and its critics. As with all "star" systems, it is open to the potential problem of personality cults. In unionized plants, employees who are selected for special management recognition may find themselves the target of ridicule and possibly abuse from their more militant co-workers. On the other hand, there is little doubt that in most organizations, there are employees everyone admires for their efforts, and where formal recognition is widely acclaimed.

Special status can also be accorded to work groups who achieve outstanding cost performances, in a similar way to recognition that is routinely provided in most corporations when production or safety records are established. One crew with a tremendous record of achievement in cost reduction at Falconbridge's Lockerby mine in Sudbury were reported to be extremely proud to have their photograph featured on the inside cover of the company's annual report with the CEO standing in their midst. Some companies in small communities often try to feature the picture of a crew or department team with outstanding performance on a monthly basis. People like to see their pictures in the paper.

There are risks with this approach as well, especially if the rewards are perceived to result in a lack of cooperation between work groups. For example, competition between shift crews in multishift operations could result in overall performance being suboptimized because each crew makes it as difficult as possible for the next shift to perform outstandingly well.

No approach to using status as an element in recognizing employee contribution to cost reduction is without its drawbacks. Some executives will find fault with all organized systems, preferring no status ("We're all equal here") or relying on an ad hoc, informal style. The drawback with these approaches is that they leave things to chance and they ignore the fact that for many individuals status obtained from contributions in their workplace is a powerful motivator.

Individual and Group Financial Rewards

There are a variety of ways individuals and groups can be rewarded financially for cost savings. In some companies, particularly those faced with basic survival issues, employees consider that keeping their job is sufficient reward. In other corporations and businesses, all employees ultimately benefit financially through profit or gain-sharing plans. In many corporations, however, individuals and groups of employees are rewarded directly for their cost-reduction efforts.

A substantial proportion of corporations certainly believe that rewards of some form should be paid, although how this is done varies greatly. A recent survey carried out by the New York Stock Exchange found that 53 percent of all corporations listed on the exchange had some form of human resource productivity programs, many tied to financial incentives.[1] The comparable figure for a representative sample of all U.S. corporations was 14 percent.

Of the larger firms covered by the study (more than 500 employees), 58 percent reported that cost reduction was a major reason for initiating their program. Of these corporations 13 percent had some form of suggestion system, and 8 percent engaged in profit sharing. Cost improvements were reported by 56 percent of the firms, and more than half the companies rated their approach as either successful or highly successful.

A 1986 survey by the National Association of Suggestion Systems, representing more than 1,100 organizations, estimated that employee ideas saved its reporting members $1.82 billion and that rewards amounting to $136 million were paid to employees for these suggestions.

In this section, only financial incentives paid to individuals or groups for direct cost-saving actions are discussed. Physical productivity incentives such as piece-rate pay can indirectly produce unit-cost decreases by motivating employees to work harder and increase output. These pay systems are described in detail by Freund and Epstein in *People and Productivity*.[2] Although these systems help increase human productivity and probably reduce costs in labor-intensive processes, they may have the reverse effect in other situations. In processes in which capital and material productivity are important cost factors, piece-rate incentives may actually result in higher costs if employees abuse equipment and waste materials in their drive for physical units of production. Production at any cost has been one of the first problems that many companies adopting a strategic approach to cost management have had to deal with.

To Pay or Not?

The payment of individual financial awards is the cause of considerable debate. Some corporate executives feel that employees should propose and implement cost savings as part of their normal job and should not be paid extra (many of these same executives do, however, award themselves substantial bonuses when they complete a successful takeover). Others agree with the idea in principal, but feel that the many issues and conflicts surrounding payment are not worth the effort.

There is no doubt that many problems do surround the awarding of substantial cash payments for cost reductions. Feelings of envy can arise if only the idea originator is rewarded and employees who make substantial contributions to implementation are ignored. Occasionally, employees will accuse their colleagues of 'stealing' ideas. In such cases, the integrity of the awards scheme depends on the corporation being seen to be scrupulously fair and honest in responding to complaints, but on the other hand, not being a pushover.

The problem usually seems to arise out of deciding what is being rewarded, the idea for the saving or implementation. If it is the latter, should the award be split in some way between the person originating the idea and the employees who implemented it? The experience of corporations with such plans is clear on the first issue: payment is best made for an implemented idea. In those few cases in which a good estimate of the value of a suggestion cannot be made for some time, a reasonable interim award is usually made. The second issue is harder to resolve. As noted, some corporations have tried to split the award between the idea originator and the group responsible for implementation. In other cases, managers attempt to develop broad ownership in the suggestion.

Who should be eligible to receive such awards is another problematic issue in corporations in which pay differentials between supervisory and professional staff are small. Engineers become quite upset when they have to work on a suggestion proposed by an operator or supervisor who they know will receive an award of several thousand dollars, while they receive nothing other than their salary.

Corporations have attempted to solve this problem in several ways. In some corporations, such as IBM, professional employees can receive awards for ideas made in areas that are not included in their areas of job responsibility. Other firms make middle managers and supervisory staff who make outstanding contributions to cost reduction eligible for membership in elite groups, such as the previously mentioned gold club, which usually have significant financial awards associated with them.

A majority of corporations, however, try to use some form of merit pay that rewards these salaried employees for a broad spectrum of outstanding performance, among which is contribution to cost reduction. These awards, usually made on an annual basis, can amount to between 10 and 30 percent of annual salary. In corporations that place a high degree of emphasis on cost reduction, the criteria for these awards can be skewed to reflect this priority. Naturally, these employees should be made aware that this bias is being deliberately adopted.

Executives might also be included in individual incentive schemes focused on cost reduction. An increasing number of corporations are tailoring executive compensation and bonuses to specific objectives, one of which may well be cost reduction. This situation is becoming quite common in multibusiness corporations, where the compensation of division executives is being tailored to match their business unit's mission and strategy. This approach runs the risk that executives will cut costs that affect long-run viability to make their bonus. Nevertheless, incentives of this type, sometimes amounting to 30 or 40 percent of annual income, are one way of ensuring cost reduction stays on each executive's personal agenda.

How Much to Pay?

In some corporations, employees can earn large sums of money by proposing cost-reducing ideas, usually within the scope of a suggestion plan. Individual awards are paid to employees by many of the most successful companies, including IBM, Hewlett Packard and Northern-Telecom. Awards vary in size, but typically range from 5 percent of annual savings to as high as 30 percent. The average for members of the National Association of Suggestion Systems in 1986 worked out to 7.5 percent. Because these benefits are usually taxable, some corporations also add an allowance to cover some proportion of this payment for the employee. Most corporations have a cap for the awards program. At IBM, the highest award that can be paid is $100,000. At Air Canada, the top award is $10,000.

Most of these awards are made on the net savings from the first full year of implementing an idea. For those that require capital investment, corporations usually subtract a proportion of this investment, say one-fifth, from the first year's savings to generate the base on which the award is calculated. Of course for savings that have a one-time effect (such as inventory-reducing ideas), the total amount of any capital investment has to be deducted.

In many corporations, rewards can be split among groups of employees who share ownership in an idea. In fact, some executives trying to encourage greater teamwork actively encourage employees to spread their ideas around. They try to point out that shared ownership generally makes implementation easier and also that over time, employees will benefit as their colleagues return the favor and share their own ideas.

Variations on the basic reward format can be made to try to obtain the best of both worlds. Fahramet developed a suggestion program in which 10 percent of the first year's savings from an idea is awarded to the originator and a further 5 percent is accrued in a pool for the originator's work group. Each work group decides when it wants to receive a payout. This reward split is intended to provide all employees with an incentive to implement suggestions.

So Where Do the Dice Fall?

During discussion of the creation of a cost-management strategy among senior managers at a refinery in northern Europe, the issue of rewards for suggestions arose. The managers were quite definite in their views that their work force would not respond to individual monetary incentives and that recognition was much more important to them. They decided, however, that 5 percent of the savings from employee suggestions would be accrued in a fund that would eventually be paid to the company union which could decide on how this money should be spent to benefit the work force. It was expected that the money would be used to build cottages for the employees at their mountain camp or some similar purpose.

The response to the suggestion plan was positive, but lukewarm. Some time later, a number of the hourly paid employees were asked about their views of the overall strategy and the suggestion plan. Generally they were enthusiastic about the approach the company had adopted, but they were quite scathing in their comments on the monetary awards. "There is nothing in it for us," they said. When told of the views of the managers on the subject of awards, they retorted, "Ah! but those are their views, ours are a little different."

The operation subsequently changed its reward structure to reflect work-force views. In the revised structure, idea originators received 7.5 percent of the first year's saving from their suggestions, and the employee fund was credited with a similar amount. The new scheme was received with much greater enthusiasm than the original.

In contrast, a successful cost-management strategy implemented at Noranda Inc.'s Horne copper smelter in northwestern Quebec has never paid financial rewards, and yet it has received many valuable ideas for cost reduction from its employees. In this case, management did a superb job in communicating the competitive reality to all employees, and a genuine belief was created that by cutting costs, the operation and the almost 1,000 jobs it provided, would survive.

So which route should organizations take? Proponents of both sides of the argument can bring forward examples to prove their case, together with others that discredit the opposite view. The resolution of this issue demonstrates the need for a sound cost-management strategy. Executives have to decide what form of reward fits within their overall approach and matches the culture of their work force. During the formulation of any cost-management strategy it is appropriate to create a small task force to make recommendations on whether or not individual or group financial rewards should be made available.

Organization-wide Incentive Programs

Organization-wide rewards can be either an alternative or a complement to individual and group incentives. Instead of providing rewards to individuals and work groups for specific results, these schemes reward everyone in the organization for overall gains in profits and costs. Gain-sharing plans are considered a better fit than profit-sharing ones with corporate strategies emphasizing cost reduction, because rewards can be more directly linked to these activities.

The New York Stock Exchange survey of financial incentives estimated that of 7,000 companies in the United States with 500 or more employees, 15 percent have some kind of gain-sharing plan.[3] As with individual incentives, some of these plans provide rewards related to measures of physical productivity improvement, whereas others stress economic results.

Profit- and gain-sharing plans are most appropriate in corporations approaching the pinnacle of employee involvement, as was shown schematically in Figure 7.1. Prior to this point in time, the motivational impact of this type of scheme is likely to be limited. The receipt of a bonus means very little if individual employees cannot find some link between the payment and their own efforts and those of their co-workers. In addition, the level of management-union-work force cooperation necessary for such a system to work effectively is not likely to have emerged. The stresses and conflict which are an integral part of developing these systems are not likely to be of great assistance in this respect.

In an authoritative study of worker democracy, Donald Nightingale identified five basic principles on which effective profit- and gain-sharing plans are based:[4]

The coverage of the plan is as broad as possible; all nonprobationary employees should be eligible to participate.

The profit-sharing plan should be combined with some form of employee involvement in decision making.

An effective means of communicating with employees must be in place.

Management and the work force should have confidence and trust in each other.

The plan should not be a substitute for wages and benefits.

These elements fit well with the type of culture and processes that exist in organizations when a broadly based cost-management strategy has been in place for several years.

A simple test of organization readiness can be applied by managers thinking of implementing such a scheme. This test simply involves determining whether a task force or steering committee of managers, staff, and hourly-paid employees and union representatives would be able to work cooperatively together to devise and successfully implement such a plan.

Profit Sharing

Profit-sharing plans differ from gain-sharing ones primarily on how rewards are earned. In profit sharing, corporations usually have to reach a certain minimum level of profitability before any payout is made. Rewards can be either paid out directly, deferred until a later date, or, increasingly commonly, distributed according to some combination of the two approaches.

Although this kind of incentive ties employee compensation directly into the economic success of the firm and may be highly appropriate for senior executives, there are a number of drawbacks in applying the approach to cost management.

In corporations having little control over prices or with a major cyclical factor to business conditions, profit levels are substantially beyond the control of employees. Thus bonuses may be determined more by market conditions than employee effort. In periods of strong demand and high prices, employees may earn high bonuses, even if their performance is poor. Conversely, they can perform magnificently in tough times by reducing costs, but there will be little or no reward for their effort. This feature of profit-sharing plans limits their application as a specific part of the rewards structure in cost-reduction strategies.

Some organizations in traditionally high-paying industries such as steel and mining are introducing profit sharing as a topping-up mechanism, negotiated into union contracts. At Whittaker Steel in Columbus, for example, employees are paid a base wage rate until corporate profits reach a certain level, after which payments increase proportionately to profits. This scheme has the effect of introducing a variable component into labor costs.

The elements of risk and variability in income associated with profit sharing are in conflict with the basic labor union principle of income security. They believe that the income of their members should not be vulnerable to the adverse effects, say, of poor management decision making. In addition, unions are concerned about profit sharing becoming a substitute for equitable wage and benefit levels.

Gain-Sharing Plans

Many corporations prefer to see bonuses more directly tied to factors employees can influence, such as output, quality, efficiency, and costs. As a result, gain-sharing plans have been developed in which employees share not in profits, but in the economic gains to the corporation arising from areas within their control.

Although some corporations devise their own gain-sharing plans, three systems have been widely adopted. These are the Scanlon Plan, the Rucker Plan, and Improshare. These systems are successful partly because they incorporate organization processes and incentives that permit employees to become involved in improving productivity which should result in lower costs. The major features of each of these plans are shown in Table 10.1. A considerable amount of descriptive material has been written on each of these approaches, and readers are referred to the works cited for additional detail.[5]

The Rucker and Scanlon plans both aim at providing incentives for employees to work more intelligently. Improved teamwork can result from implementation of these plans, as well as increased productivity, if there is mutual trust between employees and management. Both Rucker and Scanlon plans appear to work best in organizations with fewer than 500 employees. Improshare provides incentives for employees to work harder, but it lacks mechanisms to promote employee involvement, such as suggestion committees.

These approaches have worked effectively when senior management has been prepared to invest a tremendous amount of effort to make them successful. For example, in unionized organizations, it is a virtual requirement that the union be supportive of this type of initiative. Developing this support may take months and even years of management activity. In addition, implementation is not simple, as quite elaborate organizational

Table 10.1. Comparison of Gain-Sharing Plans

CHARACTERISTICS	SCANLON	RUCKER	IMPROSHARE
Involvement mechanisms	Production and steering committees	Optional suggestion committees	Suggestion committees increasingly important
Management role	Chair and sit on steering committee	Coordination and sitting on suggestion committees	Sustain interest in the plan
Focus	Reduce labor input per unit of sales	Increase value added; reduce labor costs	Improve productivity indicators
Bonus participation	Usually work force and supervision	Production personnel	Varies, usually everyone
Key ratio in calculating bonus formula	$\dfrac{\text{Sales}^a}{\text{Payroll}}$	$\dfrac{\text{Payroll}}{\text{Product value}}$	$\dfrac{\text{Engineering standard X base productivity factor}}{\text{Hours worked}}$

[a] Adjusted for inventory changes.

processes and administration systems are necessary to ensure that significant value is obtained for the corporation. For example, both the Rucker and Scanlon plans involve an elaborate network of suggestion committees.

Limitations of the Approach

All the standard gain-sharing programs have limitations, which various derivatives and hybrids have tried to overcome. For example, all three standard plans focus on reducing the labor component of either sales dollars or some measure of added value. Therefore, there is little incentive for employees to try to manage costs other than labor. In this sense, they are not truly comprehensive. Neither the Rucker nor the Scanlon works well in either capital-intensive operations or corporations that sell into markets with volatile demand.

Under these conditions, and in an attempt to broaden the type of costs included within gain sharing, corporations have developed their own gain-sharing plans, either as variants on these models or based on their own unique situation. For example, a few corporations in the mining industry, where prices are extremely volatile, have attempted to introduce plans based on increasing pretax operating profit contributions calculated at some normalized price for their product.

These schemes are intended to provide employees with an incentive to increase metal production volume, but at the same time reduce material, energy, and labor costs. Improvements in contribution are calculated over either one- or three-month periods, with bonuses paid at the same intervals. Similar committee structures to the Scanlon plan have been adopted to facilitate employee involvement.

Another approach, developed at the East Greenville, Pennsylvania, division of Knoll International, is described by Freund and Epstein.[6] Knoll pays a monthly gain-sharing bonus determined by a number of quantitative and qualitative factors. The basic quantitative determinants are measures of output per worker hour, shipment performance, on-time delivery, and inventory turnover, all of which directly influence unit costs. Among the qualitative determinants are quality, the number of employee suggestions made and implemented, and the number of suggestion meetings held. In addition, special themes may be introduced from time to time, depending on the division's priorities.

The Rucker and Scanlon plans, as well as most of the variants on them, require continuing improvements in productivity for bonuses to continue being paid, because the base level is continually recalculated on the basis of improvements achieved. Adjustments in the base are also made to reflect productivity improvements due to new capital investment. Although employees do not get rewarded for these improvements, new equipment and methods renew opportunities for subsequent cost improvements because of learning curve effects. Without continuing technological change, gains become harder to obtain, and bonus payments diminish. In this eventuality, employee enthusiasm in the plan may well decline, leading to its demise.

As with individual rewards, organization-wide gain-sharing plans may also lead to feelings of inequity. Typically, these plans are made successful by the enthusiasm and direct involvement of something less than the total work force. Employees who put substantial additional efforts into making the program a success can feel upset when other individuals who have not involved themselves, or who might even have opposed the activity, receive the same monthly bonus.

The adoption of gain-sharing virtually precludes the use of layoffs by management. Any subsequent work-force reductions will inevitably be attributed to productivity gains resulting from the program and, unless achieved through acceptable methods such as early retirement or attrition, will inevitably cause a withdrawal of support for the plan. In fact, the adoption of gain-sharing programs is usually accompanied by some form of management assurances on employment (as opposed to job) security.

In spite of these limitations, gain-sharing plans can be extremely effective in promoting broad work-force participation in the management of costs. In particular, they can complement other forms of recognition as well as individual rewards in making up the intergrated and comprehensive package of incentives necessary to sustain an effective cost-management strategy.

11.

The Future Challenge

The Power of Effective Cost Management

The cost-management challenge will not vanish. In fact, it is likely to intensify in the future as increasing competition is experienced from low-cost producers in newly developing countries. As living standards increase in maturing economies such as those of Japan and Korea, causing their costs to rise, other low-cost producers such as Brazil, India, and China will take their place. Nations who have joined the ranks of the world's developed nations such as Japan will increasingly produce the more advanced products such as computers, pharmaceuticals, and process equipment, making these markets even more cost competitive for Canadian and U.S. producers.

Markets traditionally characterized by domestic competition will not be immune to this process. Deregulation has already intensified cost competition in trucking, financial services, and the airline industry. Foreign firms with new approaches are starting to enter the Canadian and U.S. marketplace both directly and through acquisition in industries as diverse as banking, automobiles, and retailing. Finally, there will be continuing challenges from new firms with low-cost approaches, such as Magna, Apple, and People Express. Not all of these will be successful, but they will put a lot of pressure on the established firms to cut costs.

Looking to low costs as a primary competitive weapon does not mean less focus on other issues such as quality and differentiation. As Jan Carlzen, the president of SAS noted, low unit costs are no advantage if people do not want to buy your product.

Cost management should complement these other forms of competition by making them more powerful. Differentiated products will sell in far greater quantities if they are priced competitively. Employees can be convinced more readily of the importance of quality if they appreciate what the costs of falling short in this critical area are to their corporation and themselves. High-performing products will not be burdened with excessive overheads allocated from those that are marginal.

In this kind of business environment, the corporations that will do best will be those like Herman Miller and Sikorski that can develop and maintain a differentiated product, but which buttress that position by being lean and keen. In industries in which differentiation is harder to establish and maintain, the survivors will be firms such as Falconbridge and Crown Cork and Seal that are initially prepared to adopt a tough, uncompromising approach to costs, but then manage to imbue their employees with a fighting spirit.

The Executive Imperative

In spite of the obvious outcome of a failure to face this challenge, one of the first questions executives ask about cost management is ''What's in it for us?'' The successful implementation of an effective cost-reduction strategy requires major time commitments from executives and managers which they are unlikely to make unless they can perceive some personal rewards. In the short run, of course, they are more likely to face personal inconvenience, although the total organization may benefit.

Accordingly, one of the first things the senior executive group should determine is the value to them of adopting a strategic approach to cost reduction. The framework provided in Figure 1.2 and developed in subsequent chapters gives the general areas in which executives should seek the answers to this question.

Most important, for the corporation there should be improved long-run viability and competitiveness leading to increased profitability. Lower costs and improved profitability lead to additional investment opportunities, an interesting environment for executives and managers. From there it should not be difficult to make the connection to improved executive rewards, in terms of both financial renumeration and personal satisfaction. In addition, if broad employee involvement in cost reduction can be obtained, executives are more likely to be able to focus their attention on the major decisions involved with running the business.

Ultimately, the social and organizational tasks that accompany a successful cost-reduction strategy become increasingly pleasant for most managers. Fundamentally, the majority of executives dislike layoffs or being perceived as 'cheap.' As a cost-reduction strategy takes effect, there are more and more opportunities for managers to be seen in a positive role by the work force in general. Providing pats on the back, encouraging employee initiatives, and hosting awards ceremonies for successful cost-reduction contributors become more common. Many executives and managers obtain a lot of enjoyment and satisfaction from these types of activities.

Implementation Guidelines

Successful implementation of a cost-management strategy requires that executives bear in mind a number of important principles which have been highlighted throughout the book. These are:

Be tough when you have to.
Be strategic in making cost decisions.
Take an objective cost audit at the outset.
Obtain appropriate cost information.
Make cost management challenging and exciting.
Communicate effectively on costs.
Involve employees.
Be persistent.

Be Tough When You Have To

Effective cost management requires a tough mental attitude from executives at the outset. Not only must decisions be made affecting employees' lives and careers, but many familiar and comfortable practices and habits have to be abandoned. Most important, executives have to be prepared to set a personal example for their employees if they wish to be credible in managing costs.

Initiating a cost-reduction strategy without adopting this mental set is likely to lead to failure. If excessive staffing levels are not dealt with at the outset, work-force reductions at a later date are likely to result in continuing negative attitudes to cost management that effectively eliminate any hope of broad employee involvement.

This tough approach should not translate into an obsession with labor reductions and an approach to cost management that can be characterized as 'nickel and dime.' Obtaining and creating value should not be confused with being cheap. Tough attitudes toward cost management are characterized by a determination to eliminate redundant frills, a willingness to address awkward but critical strategic anomolies, and a refusal to tolerate poor performance from well-paid employees at any level in the firm.

Be Strategic in Making Cost Decisions

Adopting a strategic approach to cost management implies adopting a comprehensive view of costs within the corporation and not being limited to direct, measurable costs, as is the case with most of the traditional routes. This approach adopts a total cost perspective that includes a broad range of strategic and operating costs, both tangible and intangible, as shown in Figure 2.2. All corporate costs, including market-related and supplier-derived ones and not just those incurred for operations, come under the microscope. Management of these costs at appropriate levels in the firm is required.

Cost-management strategy has to fit with corporate and business strategies aimed at ensuring long-run competitiveness and profitability. By integrating cost management into these broader concerns, the activity is more likely to focus on the major cost elements of the corporation, which although difficult to affect, are central to future success.

The strategic approach also enables both short- and long-run needs to be accommodated. Any quick-hit has to be implemented within the context of maintaining future viability, which offsets the tendency to eliminate apparently discretionary expenditures, such as R & D and market development. In addition, once on the strategic agenda, cost management is more likely to be maintained in times of high profits than in the past, when it was generally ignored.

Take an Objective Cost Audit at the Outset

A cost audit is an essential element in the formulation of a cost-management strategy. The audit provides an assessment of the firm's cost position, compares it with those of competitors, and evaluates it in terms of the requirements for future profitability. If information is available, data should be obtained by major business units and product lines.

The audit also provides management with an opportunity to examine the effectiveness of the corporation's existing cost-management processes. The level of awareness and understanding and the adequacy of communications, information systems, mechanisms to involve employees, and rewards for cost-management efforts can all be assessed.

The whole senior executive group should participate in this process. Outside advice and assistance may be useful for this exercise to provide management with objective input.

Obtain Appropriate Cost Information

An effective cost-information system is essential to a successful cost-management strategy. Accountants and MIS personnel have to be convinced that management is just as important a client as the financial department and that their information needs have to be met.

Some accounting personnel may have much to learn about management information needs. A first priority is to define what reports are relevant to particular employees. Employees need to be supported in their cost-management efforts by data that are focused, rather than be overwhelmed by masses of data in which key numbers are buried. Report formats have to be clear and simple. Accuracy and timeliness are much more important than precision. Allocations have to be meaningful.

Management accountants can lead in this task and are likely to become central figures in cost management in the future because of their ability to match accounting's capabilities with the needs of its corporate clients.

Make Cost Management Challenging and Exciting

Employees will only become committed to cost management and involved in the process if management creates a culture in which it is viewed as challenging and exciting. In most organizations, the first task for executives is to change the image of cost reduction in their own minds and those of their managers and supervisors from that of a negative exercise to a creative, engaging way of running the business.

A strategic approach permits this reorientation to take place in an integrated fashion. Opportunities can be created for a broad cross section of employees to provide input to the way costs are managed. Creativity and innovation can become driving forces of cost reduction. With a little imagination, a variety of novel activities can be instituted that, at the same time as lowering costs, provide employees with job satisfaction. Recognition and rewards can be provided that make employees want to be associated with these activities. Ultimately, it is entirely conceivable that cost management might become fun.

Communicate Effectively on Costs

Employee awareness and understanding of the need to manage costs will only be created through effective management communication. Even when management is undertaking a tough, quick-hit program, employee resistance and uncertainty can be reduced if executives spend time in the operations making short presentations on why the actions are necessary and what employees can do to help.

Implementation of a cost-management strategy must start with a communications blitz informing employees of the financial position of the corporation (and of their own division and department if appropriate) and an outline of the proposed strategy. Every employee should be involved in these sessions, at which an opportunity for questions and discussion should be provided.

Once underway, a broad variety of communications vehicles should be used to inform employees about costs and related activities. Customers and suppliers should be included in these activities if appropriate. Seminars and other education vehicles can be used to impart the understanding necessary to use the information provided through these channels.

Involve Employees

Great leverage can be brought to bear on reducing costs if more employees can be involved in the task. As has been illustrated many times in previous chapters, employees at all levels in the corporation can make significant contributions to reducing costs if they are appropriately motivated. Learning, innovation, and simplification are all sources of cost reduction that arise through employee involvement.

An appropriate plan that reflects the unique situation of each corporation should be developed to gain employee commitment and participation. Usually, gaining effective management and supervisory involvement is an initial goal. The process requires careful management of employee expectations and motivation, because unrealistic interpretations of what involvement means can cause intense frustration and disappointment.

A variety of tools and techniques can be used to facilitate implementation. These ought not to be used en masse, but carefully selected to fit the situation and task at hand. They should also reflect and incorporate a balance of the five principal sources of cost reduction: economies of scale, capital investment, innovation, learning, and simplification. Management has to be prepared to spend in order to cut costs, even in some areas where initial financial returns appear to be intangible.

Implementation of cost-reducing activities has to be through mechanisms and organization processes such as task forces, suggestion plans, and project methodologies. When employees gain a shared understanding of these approaches, they become part of the corporate culture.

Employee involvement has to be recognized and successes rewarded. These can take a variety of different forms, ranging from simple recognition through to fairly complex gain-sharing plans. To ensure the best performance within cost management, a comprehensive set of these rewards should be developed that complement each other in ways that promote individual initiative as well as teamwork. This array of incentives need not all be developed and implemented simultaneously at the outset of an explicit cost-management strategy. Instead, they can be implemented gradually and thus parallel changes in management-employee relationships and attitudes.

Be Persistent

Although initial savings may be obtained quickly, full implementation of an effective cost-management strategy can take up to five years, and so persistence is definitely required. If cost management is treated as just another fad by executives and managers, employees will rapidly become disillusioned and cynical about the process. Canadian and U.S. corporations have flirted with so many fads and programs in recent years that when nonexecutive employees hear of the latest, they turn a deaf ear.

Persistence is one of the hallmarks of executives who are good cost cutters. They continually go back to their employees month after month, each and every year to remind them of the importance of cost reduction and tell them of their successes. They keep pursuing accounting and MIS to provide better information, and they continually use this information to identify areas of potential cost reduction. They keep insisting that their managers and supervisors implement the cost-saving ideas proposed by their people (until they do it naturally, of their own volition). They continually find new ideas to keep cost management challenging and exciting.

Successful corporations tend to be those that have found something they do better than anyone else in their field or industry and then keep doing it, sometimes for decades. To become a lean and keen corporation that is outstanding at cost reduction takes considerable time.

Executives are not being promised a rose garden in this book. Even happy, enduring marriages takes a lot of effort, encounter problems, and have to survive numerous challenges over the years. Similarly, management must be prepared to work hard at convincing their employees that embracing cost management is not just another romantic flirtation, but a long-run commitment necessary to meet the ultimate competitive challenge posed by cost reduction.

Notes

Chapter 1. The Cost Challenge

1. "Cutting Costs Without Killing the Business," *Fortune*, October 13, 1986, p. 74.
2. Quoted in "Management Layoffs Won't Quit," *Fortune*, October 28, 1985.
3. Walter Kiechel III, "Managing a Downsized Operation," *Fortune*, July 22, 1985.
4. "How Bob Price Is Reprogramming Control Data," *Business Week*, February 16, 1987, pp. 102–104.
5. "Fighting Back: It Can Work," *Business Week*, August 26, 1985, pp. 62–68.
6. See, for example, Robert H. Hayes and Steven C. Wheelwright, *Restoring Our Competitive Edge*, New York: John Wiley and Sons, 1984, and Richard J. Schonberger, *Japanese Manufacturing Techniques*, New York: The Free Press, 1982.
7. "Fighting Back: It Can Work," *Business Week*, op. cit.
8. See "Can United Afford Texas Air's Low Fares?" *Business Week*, February 16, 1987.
9. "General Motors: What Went Wrong," *Business Week*, March 16, 1987, p 107.
10. C.J. van der Klugt quoted in "Fighting Back: It Can Work," *Business Week*, op. cit.
11. See Thomas J. Peters and Robert H. Waterman Jr., *In Search of Excellence*, New York: Harper and Row, 1982.
12. James Henderson, President, Cummins Engine Corporation, in a speech at the Harvard Graduate School of Business, December 3, 1979.
13. "Why Gulfstream's Rivals Are Gazing Up in Envy," *Business Week*, February 16, 1987, pp. 66–68.

14. "After the Frying Pan, What?", *Forbes,* March 9, 1987, pp. 60–61.
15. See, for example, "Note on the Motorcycle Industry—1975," *HBS Case Services,* Harvard Business School, Boston, Mass., 1978.
16. See, for example, "The Meanest and Leanest Sit Down to Just Deserts," *Business Week,* February 9, 1987.

CHAPTER 2. The Strategic Approach

1. See, for example, Bruce D. Henderson, *Henderson on Corporate Strategy,* Cambridge, Mass.: Abt Associates, 1979.
2. See, for example, Wickham Skinner, *Manufacturing: The Formidable Competitive Weapon,* New York: John Wiley and Sons, 1985; and Derek F. Abell and John S. Hammond, *Strategic Market Planning,* Englewood Cliffs, N.J.: Prentice-Hall, 1979
3. See Wickham Skinner, op. cit.; William J. Abernathy, *The Productivity Dilemma: Roadblock to Innovation in the Automobile Industry,* Baltimore: The John Hopkins Press, 1978; and Robert H. Hayes and Steven C. Wheelwright, *Restoring Our Competitive Edge,* John Wiley and Sons, 1984.
4. See, for example, George S. Odiorne, *Strategic Management of Human Resources: A Portfolio Approach,* San Francisco: Jossey Bass, 1984.
5. For a discussion of the strategic implications of economies of scope see Michael E. Porter, *Competitive Advantage,* New York: The Free Press, 1985, pp. 323–363.
6. Peter F. Drucker, "Managing for Business Effectiveness," *Harvard Business Review,* May–June, 1963, pp. 56–63.
7. See Michael Porter, *Competitive Advantage,* New York: The Free Press, 1985, p. 62.
8. See Thomas J. Peters and Robert H. Waterman, Jr., *In Search of Excellence,* New York: Harper and Row, 1982.
9. William J. Abernathy, *The Productivity Dilemma: Roadblock to Innovation in the Automobile Industry,* Baltimore: The John Hopkins Press, 1978.

CHAPTER 3. Sources of Cost Reduction

1. See Wickham Skinner, *Manufacturing: The Formidable Competitive Weapon,* New York: John Wiley and Sons, 1985, pp. 71–82.
2. "How TI Beat the Clock on Its Twenty Dollar Digital Watch," *Business Week,* May 31, 1976, pp. 32–63.
3. See, for example, Mariann Jelinek and Joel D. Goldhar, "The Strategic Implications of the Factory of the Future," *Sloan Management Review,* Summer 1984, pp. 29–37.
4. "General Motors: What Went Wrong," *Business Week,* March 16, 1987, pp. 102–110.
5. A comprehensive discussion of economies of scale in manufacturing is given in Robert H. Hayes and Steven C. Wheelwright, *Restoring Our Competitive Edge,* New York: John Wiley and Sons, 1984, pp. 54–69.
6. Michael Porter, *Competitive Advantage,* New York: The Free Press, 1985, pp. 70–72.
7. Pankaj Ghemawat, "Building Strategy on the Experience Curve," *Harvard Business Review,* March-April, 1985, pp. 143–149.
8. See for example, Robert H. Hayes and Steven C. Wheelwright, *Restoring Our Competitive Edge,* New York: John Wiley and Sons, 1984, pp. 229–275; and Bruce

D. Henderson, "The Experience Curve Revisited," Boston: The Boston Consulting Group Perspective No. 229, 1980.

9. "Management Layoffs Won't Quit," *Fortune,* October 28, 1985, pp. 46–49.

10. See Rensis Likert and Stanley E. Seashore, "Making Cost Control Work," *Harvard Business Review,* March-April, 1963, pp. 96–108.

11. See for example, Harry Levinson, "When Employees Burn Out," *Harvard Business Review,* May-June, 1981, pp. 73–81.

12. See Wickham Skinner, "The Focused Factory," *Harvard Business Review,* May-June, 1974, pp. 113–124.

13. Dean M. Ruwe and Wickham Skinner, "Reviving a Rust Belt Factory," *Harvard Business Review,* May-June, 1987, pp. 70–76.

14. Much of the information in this section is drawn from Steven Prokesch, "Capitalism of the Cooperative Kind," *New York Times,* June, 1986.

CHAPTER 4. Obtaining the Right Information

1. See H. Thomas Johnson and Robert S. Kaplan, *Relevance Lost: The Rise and Fall of Management Accounting,* Boston, Mass.: Harvard Business School Press, 1987.

2. Patrick McGinty, "Cost Accounting Revisited: A Manufacturing Survey," *Journal of Cost Management for the Manufacturing Industry,* Vol. 1, No. 1, Spring 1987, pp. 35–44.

3. See Peter Drucker, "Managing for Business Effectiveness," Harvard Business Review, May-June, 1963, pp. 54–65.

4. See Jeffrey G. Miller and Thomas E. Vollman, "The Hidden Factory," *Harvard Business Review,* September-October, 1985, pp. 142–151.

5. See H. Thomas Johnson and Robert S. Kaplan, *Relevance Lost: The Rise and Fall of Management Accounting,* Boston, Mass.: Harvard Business School Press, 1987. p. 228.

6. Ibid., pp. 250–251.

7. See, for example, Ray H. Garrison, *Managerial Accounting: Concepts for Planning, Control, Decision Making,* Plano, Texas: Business Publications, 1982.

CHAPTER 5. The Lean and Keen Corporation

1. Tom Peters and Robert H. Waterman Junior, *In Search of Excellence,* New York: Random House, 1982.

2. "Restructuring Really Works," *Fortune,* March 2, 1987, pp. 38–46.

3. T.W. Lippman, "Nevin Plans Drive to Top for Firestone," *Washington Post,* September 13, 1981, pp. F1 and F7.

4. Dis-integration in basic industries is discussed in "The Smokestacks Won't Tumble," *Fortune,* February 2, 1987, pp. 30–32.

5. "Synergy Works at American Express," *Fortune,* February 16, 1987.

6. Michael Porter, *Competitive Advantage,* New York: The Free Press, 1985.

7. "What It's Like to Work for Frank Lorenzo," *Business Week,* May 18, 1987, pp. 76–77.

CHAPTER 6. Creating a Cost Conscious Organization

1. Jan Carlzon, president and CEO the SAS group, quoted in the SAS Group Annual Report, 1986, p. 3.

2. "What It's Like to Work for Frank Lorenzo," *Business Week,* May 18, 1987, pp. 76–77.
3. Christine Harris and Joseph L. Bowes, "Marks and Spencer Limited (A)," The President and Fellows of Harvard College, Cambridge, Mass., 1975, pp. 4–5.
4. "Cutting Cost Without Killing the Business," *Fortune,* October 13, 1986, pp. 70–74.

CHAPTER 7. Obtaining Employee Involvement

1. See Kenichi Ohmae, *The Mind of the Strategist,* New York: McGraw-Hill, 1982, p. 207.
2. See C.E. Frost, J.L. Wakeley, and R.A. Ruh, *The Scanlon Plan for Organization Development: Identity, Participation and Equity,* East Lansing Mich.: Michigan State University Press, 1974; also J. Ramquist, "Labor-Management Cooperation —The Scanlon Plan at Work," *The Sloan Management Review,* Spring, 1982, pp. 49–55.
3. See M. Fein, *Improshare: An Alternative to Traditional Managing,* Hillsdale, N.J.: Mitchell Fein, 1980.
4. This framework and many of the ideas in this chapter originally appeared in my article "Courting Greater Employee Involvement through Participative Management," *Sloan Management Review,* Vol. 26, No. 2, Winter 1985, pp. 33–44, by permission of the publisher. Copyright © 1985 by the Sloan Management Review Association. All rights reserved.
5. See, for example, Brian E. Moore and Timothy L. Ross, *The Scanlon Way to Improved Productivity,* New York: John Wiley and Sons, 1978.
6. See Ernesto J. Poza, "Twelve Actions to Build Strong U.S. Factories," *Sloan Management Review,* Fall, 1983, pp. 27–38.
7. See J. A. Klein, "Why Supervisors Resist Employee Involvement," *Harvard Business Review,* September-October, 1984, pp. 87–95.
8. "Stonewalling Plant Democracy," *Business Week,* March 28, 1977, pp. 78–80.
9. See W.E. Sasser and F.S. Leonard, "Let First Level Supervisors Do the Job," *Harvard Business Review,* March-April 1980, pp. 113–121.
10. See J.F. Bolt, "Job Security: Its Time Has Come," *Harvard Business Review,* November-December, 1983 pp. 115–123.
11. See Ernesto J. Poza, "Twelve Actions to Build Strong U.S. Factories," *Sloan Management Review,* Fall 1983, pp. 27–38.
12. See P. Goodman, "Why Productivity Programs Fail," *National Productivity Review,* Autumn 1982, pp. 369–380.

CHAPTER 8. Cost-Reducing Programs and Techniques

1. See "Heinz Pushes to be the Low-Cost Producer," *Fortune,* June 24, 1985, pp. 44, 46, 50.
2. See A.J. Magrath and Kenneth G. Hardy, "Cost Containment in Marketing," *The Journal of Business Strategy,* Vol. 7, No. 2, Fall 1986, pp. 14–20.
3. *Chain Store Age,* June, 1985, pp. 59–62.
4. See M. Porter and V. Millar, "How Information Gives You Competitive Advantage," *Harvard Business Review,* July-August, 1985, pp. 149–160.
5. See, for example, R.J. Schonberger, *Japanese Manufacturing Techniques,* New York: The Free Press, 1982; and Lee J. Krajewski and Larry P Ritzman, *Operations Management,* Reading, Mass.: Addison-Wesley Publishing Company, 1987.

6. See Wickham Skinner, "The Focused Factory," *Harvard Business Review,* May–June, 1974, pp. 113–124.
7. Material for this example was largely drawn from Robert F. Huber, "Sikorski Surrounds Its Cost Problems," *Production,* June 1985, pp. 67–71.

Chapter 9. The Lean and Keen Corporation in Action

1. More information can be obtained from the National Association of Suggestion Systems, 230 North Michigan Avenue, Chicago, Ill. 60601.
2. See Edwards B. Roberts and Alan R. Fusfeld, "Staffing the Innovative Technology-Based Organization," *Sloan Management Review,* Spring, 1981, pp. 19–34.

Chapter 10. Rewarding Cost-Reduction Successes

1. See William C. Freund and Eugene Epstein, *People and Productivity,* Homewood, Ill.: Dow Jones Irwin, 1984.
2. Ibid.
3. Ibid.
4. See Donald V. Nightingale, *Workplace Democracy: An Inquiry into Employee Participation in Canadian Organizations,* Toronto: The University of Toronto Press, 1982.
5. See, for example, ibid.; David P. Swinehart, "A Guide to More Productive Team Incentive Programs," *Personnel Journal,* July 1986, pp. 112–117.; Brian E. Moore and Timothy L. Ross, *The Scanlon Way to Improved Productivity,* New York: John Wiley and Sons, 1978.; William C. Freund and Eugene Epstein, *People and Productivity,* Homewood, Ill., Dow Jones-Irwin, 1984.
6. See William C. Freund and Eugene Epstein, op. cit., pp. 36–42.

Index